'*Accelerating Excellence* provides exclusive access into what it takes for both individuals and groups to excel. It's entertaining, uses real life examples, and is highly practical. It's about time this book was written.'

Per Lundstam
Director of Athlete Performance
Red Bull

'Greatness is not achieved accidentally; from developing athletes to coaching to managing employees, James King's *Accelerating Excellence* presents a deliberate and accessible roadmap for optimizing human behavior to maximise elite performance.'

Mark Shapiro, President & CEO
Toronto Blue Jays

'*Accelerating Excellence* is an important resource that provides valuable and unique insight on the topic of elite performance.'

RC Buford
CEO San Antonio Spurs

'An inspirational book where each and every chapter reveals unique insight into how to cultivate elite performance. A true route map to excellence.'

Senior Member
MI5 - The Security Service

'James transformed the selection and training process at Mandara and an exponential increase in revenue followed immediately. James is relentless in his pursuit of improved performance. If I were to start my company from scratch he would be my very first hire ahead of any other person I have ever worked with.'

Muwaffaq Salti
Founder and Chairman
Mandara Capital

'This book is a must read for anyone who wants to understand how to accelerate their own performance. Its bursting with highly practical insights, it debunks the myths around performance using science and storytelling, and leaves you armed with the knowledge, methods and motivation to help you get better at the things you want to get better at, every day of your life.'

James Worrall
Founder and Chairman
Leaders in Sport

'How do you accelerate excellence? The first step is to read this ground-breaking book, which is not so much a book as a detailed map of the newly revealed landscape of human performance. *Accelerating Excellence* will be on the desk of every coach in elite sport.'

Roy Hodgson
Former England and current Crystal Palace manager

'An incredibly detailed, yet easy to understand guide for anyone interested in achieving elite performance. King challenges your thought process and then prepares you for problem solving the puzzle that is elite performance. A must read for anyone seeking to become the best version of themselves- that means all of us.'

Ted Rath
Vice President of Player Performance
Philadelphia Eagles

'I've watched and admired how James designs and build sustainable human performance programmes that deliver results. *Accelerating Excellence*, is a long overdue manifesto for elite performance and James King is the ideal ambassador'

Command Sergeant Major
United Kingdom Special Mission Units

'This book is a veritable blueprint for building a high performance environment. James provides insights that span the gamut of development. From culture and communication, to building leadership, skills and routines. This is a highly educational read that will certainly become a go to reference for me in the ongoing quest for excellence.'

Jerry Dipoto
Executive VP & General Manager,
Seattle Mariner Baseball Club

'I love this book. An excellent read packed with information and clear steps on how to accelerate your pursuit of excellence. Read it at least once, if not two or three times.'

Keith Breslauer
Founder and Managing Partner
Patron Capital

'James King is the tip of the spear when it comes to motivation, confidence and resilience. His innovative and unique understanding of the mechanics of human performance make him the definitive coach of the future. He has cracked the algorithm for excellence.'

GQ

'This book is packed full of strategies, tactics and approaches you can use to identify, develop and engage people to systematically cultivate success. Its staggeringly simple in its application, whilst jaw droppingly insightful prompting deep reflection. With James' breadth of experience and insight expect to be simultaneously challenged and equipped to unlock the best version of yourself and your peers.'

Duncan Truswell
Strategic Lead Talent and Performance
Sport England

'If you want to maximize your impact personally and professionally, you cannot leave it up to chance. James King has now given every person and high performing team a comprehensive plan for optimal performance. This book should be in every locker room, team room and corporate boardroom.'

Trent Greener
Special Operations Human Performance Advisor

I owe James an insurmountable debt for what he has instilled in me. From day one his approach transitioned me from a young man with a naïve general desire to achieve, into a focused, aligned individual with a burning sense of mission. The principles in this book gave me a set of logical actions that enabled me to relentlessly advance my career beyond what I thought was possible- at lightning speed. Now, you have no excuse not to go out there and do the same.

Greg Newman
Chief Executive
Onyx Capital Group

'James King knows what it takes to make people excel! You can't afford not to know what he's teaching. How to progress will become very clear, very fast, and very exciting. James shows you the tools, they hit your brain, it clicks, you transform, and results follow.'

Mens Health

'I have seen first hand how James King builds elite performance individuals and organisations. *Accelerating Excellence* will show you how. The strategies contained are unique, innovative and proven. I unreservedly recommend this book to anyone involved in high performance.'

Jason Henderson,
Master Chief
Navy SEAL NSWDG (Retired)

ACCELERATING EXCELLENCE

ACCELERATING EXCELLENCE

THE PRINCIPLES THAT DRIVE ELITE PERFORMANCE

JAMES A. KING

First published in 2021

Design by Rebecca Wright
Printed and bound by KDP

A CIP catalogue record for this book is available from the British Library

Paperback ISBN: 9781838334918

For those who strive to make things better for themselves,
and those they care for, manage and lead.

This book is for you.

ABOUT THE AUTHOR

James King is a trusted advisor to elite and exclusive organisations around the world. Within the world of business he has advised CEOs, private equity (PE) firms, and hedge fund (HF) managers.

James has counselled government agencies and specialist military units. He also provides guidance to coaches, managers and athletes within the English Premier League (EPL), Team GB, and the National Basketball Association (NBA).

He has presented case studies on his work for the MBA programmes at the University of Oxford, Harvard University and Massachusetts Institute of Technology (MIT). James holds a first-class degree in Applied Sports Science, and an MSc in Performance Psychology, both from the University of Edinburgh.

CONTENTS

Preface: Ambition is not the Problem xiii

Part One: Introduction 1
1: The Tip of the Iceberg 3
2: Performance is Never a Coincidence 17

Part Two: Self-Concordance 33
3: Finding your Sweet Spot 35
4: The Best get Better 53
5: Disguising Repetition 77
6: Sacrifice, Fight and Belonging 95
7: Zero onto Target 109
8: Talent Identification 117
9: How to Predict a Superstar 133

Part Three: Skill Acquisition 157
10: Why it Looks Like Magic 159
11: Perceive, Decide and Execute 175
12: Principles of Three-Dimensional Training 189
13: The Power of Constraints 209
14: Coaching, Feedback and the Environment 223
15: Individual Development Plans 245
16: The F word 261

Part Four: Emotional Control 283
17: It's a Head Game 285
18: Flicking the Switch 299
19: Emotional Control Routines 315
20: Building Performance Routines 335

Part Five: Continuous Improvement 369
21: Post Summit Peril 371
22: Win the Day 383
23: Automating Excellence 419
24: The Unrelenting Pursuit of Excellence 437

Conclusion: The End of the Beginning 461

References 467

Bibliography 479

Index 515

PREFACE

AMBITION IS NOT THE PROBLEM

Accelerating: Increasing in rate, amount, or extent

Excellence: The quality of being outstanding

It was a disaster. A national embarrassment. Despite enormous ambition, effort and talent Britain's 300 athletes secured only one gold medal at the 1996 Atlanta Olympic Games. It left them in 36th place below Algeria and Kazakhstan in the medals table. Sometimes we need the humiliation that Great Britain experienced that summer to face the truth, look the monster in the eye and spark the change we need to achieve world-class performance.

Flash-forward to the Rio Olympics in 2016 and the British athletes, with the same ambition, talent and effort, won a total of 27 gold medals. Twenty years after a stinging Olympic failure, Team GB rose like a phoenix from the flames to become a sporting superpower, finishing second in the medals table, behind only the United States.

Why did Britain gain 35 places in that period? The British athletes had not obtained better results due to superior genetics, working harder, or elevated ambition. Instead, they had better understood how to channel their ambition, talent, and effort more effectively. This enabled them to accelerate their pursuit of excellence.

Humans have been striving to get better faster since the beginning of time; be it hunting and gathering, lighting fires or escaping sabre-tooth tigers. Tens of thousands of years ago, this could be the difference between life and death and we haven't stopped working to accelerate excellence ever since. We are hard-wired to pursue excellence, drawn by a vision of our future selves. Ambition is a defining element of our nature and the You 2.0 is always on the cards in some area of life or another.

People who buy books with titles like Accelerating Excellence possess particularly high doses of the desire to excel. We want it all and we want it yesterday. But the most crucial question facing those aspiring to excel is how to go out there and get it all. Very few of us know how to channel our talent and effort in order to fulfil our ambition. While we are born with this incredible and adaptable machine, the human brain and body, we aren't born with the software to run that machine optimally. That must be acquired.

Most of us follow a formula that has been taught to us with positive intentions by our parents, schools, and the organisations we work for. We're told that if we're ambitious enough, if we work hard enough, if we really put our minds to it, we can excel. If we don't make it then we just don't have what it takes, and the story of genius prevails. Yes, ambition matters. Yes, it's hard work. But the truth is that having ambition, working hard, and possessing talent is not the problem.

'While we are born with this incredible and adaptable machine, the human brain and body, we aren't born with the software to run that machine optimally'

In this book I set the record straight: performance is never a coincidence. Those who seem to have it all are often the people who have a system that allows them to go out and get it. Elite performers align with a specific set of principles - whether they realise it or not. These principles enable them to get better faster and capitalise on their ambition, talent and effort. In this book, I'm going to tell you what they are, why they are so powerful and how you can achieve alignment too.

'Performance is never a coincidence. Those who seem to have it all are often the people who have a system that allows them to go out and get it'

Aligning with these principles provides us with a psychological and biological edge that will unleash an inner motivation, resilience and confidence, accelerating our pursuit of excellence in our chosen endeavour.

When it comes to pursuing excellence, it's not a question of whether change is possible, but rather how much change is possible. We need to shift our perception from reaching potential to expanding potential. The great news is that under the right conditions, and not limited to genetic code, we all have the potential to develop exceptional abilities, which can lead to incredible achievements. This book is about what it takes to do so.

'It's not a question of whether change is possible, but rather how much change is possible'

My journey in human performance all started with a personal obsession. I have always been fascinated with those who excel at the highest levels - the statistical anomalies known as outliers - who raise the bar and shift the baseline by which excellence is perceived and measured.

I spent five years at the University of Edinburgh studying the science of human performance. The good news is there is so much ground-breaking information available. We know how excellence emerges, why certain individuals and organisations excel, and the science that drives the mechanics of this process. We know how to break the process into parts and align individuals and organisations with the mechanisms and principles. All of this has been confirmed by thousands of scientific studies.

I have spent the last fifteen years hitting all this theory hard with the biggest metaphorical hammer I could find, to see what breaks in practice. The hedge funds, specialist military units and sports teams I have been privileged to work with aren't content with inspirational speeches or optimistic theories about performance. They care about one thing - measurable and enduring results. For them this means mission success, profit, and gold medals. Their performers care about making the right call when enemy fire is raining down, hitting the buy button before the trade is gone forever, and scoring the winning penalty. Anything else is just talk. My work with them was judged on results. If I didn't deliver results for these organisations, I was out.

Change is constant. We know that the demands of human performance evolve across time, culture and generations. This book, and the human performance model within it, is about the fundamental principles of performance. The principles I hit with the hammer and which didn't break that can be built upon year after year to accelerate excellence.

My aim is to democratise access to this information so that the principles in this book are practised not just by an elite few, but by the majority. The better we understand how to accelerate excellence, the better we can collectively work to shift the baseline and make the things that matter to us all get better, faster. In my opinion nothing is more virtuous than striving to accelerate our pursuit of excellence in whatever it is we do. It requires us to enhance our ability to contribute, to solve problems, eliminate barriers and expand the way those around us perceive what is possible.

This book will raise your awareness, provoke insight, and shift the way you perceive potential, crushing some of the most entrenched assumptions on the way. Here the spotlight is set on expanding potential, bringing excitement, and chasing down excellence. My ambition is that the principles outlined in this book motivate, excite and inspire confidence, the way they did for me. You will emerge inspired about the possibility that exists before you, along with purpose, structure and direction.

Structure of this book

At its core, this book examines the scientific forces that can rapidly accelerate our pursuit of excellence. We'll explore some of the most pioneering organisations in the world, as well as exceptional individuals. The focus will always be on examining the controllable principles behind the action, so that you can immediately put the science to work and accelerate your pursuit of excellence.

I have divided the book into five parts. Each one will give you a precise set of instructions that will enable you to get better, faster. As we advance through each section you will see how one mechanism reinforces the next.

- **Part One** is the ground zero of human performance. It introduces a system that works to achieve any goal and from wherever you currently find yourself. In Parts Two through to Five we will shift the perspective to focus on each of the four mechanisms that make up our framework
- In **Part Two** you will learn the one principle that all elite performers have in common more than anything else. This mechanism is what enables us to activate the psychological fire-power required to generate the confidence, resilience and motivation we all know drive success.
- In **Part Three** you will be introduced to a set of principles that act as multipliers for the rate at which you acquire and retain the skills that will power you to the top.
- In **Part Four** you will learn how to psychologically prepare for peak performance, how to master the art of not panicking, and how to switch off and enjoy true rest.
- In **Part Five** you will learn how to operationalise the unrelenting pursuit of excellence so that you can avoid being the one-hit wonder. It will teach you to structure continuous improvement, as well as generate breakthrough disruptive solutions, which enable you to stay at the top and accelerate ahead of the rest.

Ideally, you should read this book straight through, like you would a novel. However, this is meant to be an active reference—a book to flick through to find useful guidance on specific topics when you need some perspective. If you do have a pressing interest in skill acquisition, emotional control or innovation please feel free to go directly to those sections. However, all these areas are interrelated and you may find answers to your questions in the other sections.

I know you're busy. The aim is to make you better faster, not prepare for a Ph.D. in human performance. The focus is not on scientific perfection, but accelerating your pursuit of excellence therefore, I simplify things so we can extract value fast. The mechanisms and techniques are not punishing, and small changes are all it takes. While changes may be small in isolation, they can produce enormous changes when used in combination, leading to explosive career trajectories and performance breakthroughs.

> ***Note:*** The definitions and illustrations used in this book are specific to the subject of human performance, the goal of accelerating excellence and the context of this book.

PART 1

INTRODUCTION

1

THE TIP OF THE ICEBERG

Never let the truth get in the way of a good story

Mark Twain

On 28th February 2016, at the Dolby Theatre in Hollywood, Leonardo DiCaprio donned his tux, black bow-tie and gleaming leather shoes and walked the iconic red carpet looking picture perfect. Owning the moment.

> Julianne Moore [Host]: 'And the Oscar goes to [pause as she looks down and opens the famous golden envelope]... Leonardo DiCaprio'[1]

The audience erupted with extended applause. Leo had emerged victorious winning his first Oscar for best actor. He went on to give gracious thanks to his fellow nominees, the cast, crew, past collaborators, and of course, a passionate message about the environment.

On the 28th January 2017 at Melbourne park, Australia, Serena Williams' powerful forehand drive was to much too handle for her sister Venus. Serena won the game, set and match in a straight sets victory. She dropped to her knees, before embracing her sister in the middle of the court she had dominated all week, claiming her 23rd career grand slam.[2]

On the 6th June 2018 we got to observe the ever-entertaining SpaceX and Tesla CEO Elon Musk launching his 27-engine Falcon Heavy rocket into space strapped to a cherry-red Tesla roadster.[3] The car along with its mannequin driver, Starman, have been exploring the final frontier ever since.

This is how we see elite performance; the actor receiving their Oscar, the athlete on the podium or the CEO at the product launch. They make it look so easy. The problem we all have with excellence is that we only ever see it in its final form, when the performer, expert or winner is finished.

The average person spends zero time around elite performers of any domain, be it business, sports, military, or art. Much like an iceberg, the part of excellence that is visible to us is much smaller and less significant than the part that isn't. The depth and breadth of human performance is lost on us all. Ultimately what we see, hear or know about why some people excel is only a fraction of what really drives excellence.

When we see these exceptional performers blast away the rest of the competition, we emerge inspired, we go out into the world and pursue our ambitions with vigour and might, at least for a while. But, more often than not, the grim reality is that we fail to deliver on our ambitions.

It is only natural to conclude that the likes of Leo, Serena and

Elon were winners of some genetic lottery. Did they just get lucky? Is there a repeatable methodology for elite performance? And is excellence even an option for us? 'Maybe I just don't have what it takes,' is a thought that will set in, when the reality is more like, 'Maybe you just don't have the right approach.' You aren't broken, the advice you have followed is wrong.

Whilst we're obsessed with excellence and are repeatedly bombarded with sciencey sounding stories about how to excel in an age where information about human performance is so readily available, why are blind spots still common? Why aren't we getting this right? And what can we do to fix this? It's a quality not quantity issue.

Any type of improvement begins with expanding what we know through seeking more knowledge. The natural way to do this is to source expertise from people who are in the know; maybe social media, YouTube, podcasts, books, lectures, or events.

The difficulty is that many of the people who are providing the information on human performance aren't the people working in elite performance. Those on the receiving end of their advice inevitably form a totally inaccurate perception of what reality entails.

> 'Many of the people who are providing the information on human performance aren't the people working in elite performance'

If our view of what excellence entails is wrong, then the actions we take based on that knowledge will be inferior. This means the results we produce won't reflect what we are truly capable of and will never be commensurate with the effort we put in.

The information on human performance can be filtered down to five sources; some are a blend of each. Each source has benefits, but also limitations, which can cause us problems. My intention in this chapter is to examine both, dispelling misconceptions as we go, so that we can leverage the benefits and mitigate the limitations. After all, the best way to solve a problem is to understand it so well that the solutions practically fall in our lap.

Source one- Single discipline specialists

My heart would pound and my eyes dilate each time I discovered the release of the latest and greatest tool or technique to engineer elite performance. There is so much new and exciting information out there. The personal development space can feel like a charged fire hose to the face.

We are presented with appealing strategies with bold promises of fast and easy change that lure us in. 'Seven days to a six pack,' 'three mind-sets that will transform your life', and 'more money than Bezos in less than a year.' They tell us what we want to hear when we want to hear it, which increases the probability we buy the book, follow the account and like the post.

The sexy and exciting technique has become the cornerstone of an entire performance improvement culture. Many of these specialists would like to have us believing that their technique, whether it be IQ boosting supplements, bulletproof coffee, or yogic breathing, will lead to some kind of elite performance. We want it to be that simple.

These promises appeal to our silver bullet bias, our very human obsession with the cure-all that will fix all our problems; the fountain of eternal youth, the six-pack supplement, or the winning lottery ticket.

Silver Bullet Bias: Our desire for a magical weapon that instantly solves a longstanding problem

The tools and techniques approach reduces elite performance to an awfully prescriptive to-do list. Here our problems have solutions, we just don't feel like doing any of them. Meditation, cold showers and hypnosis can be highly beneficial, if we do them. But more often than not we don't, at least not consistently. After the initial burst of excitement, the love is lost, the romance is dead and the willpower that was thrusting us through is spent.

Like any form of consumption, we buy ourselves new shoes; we care for them like they were the crown jewels, and then a few months later we just don't care anymore. Executing a to-do list of techniques is not the way outliers excel.

There is another challenge. Ever hear the one about the three blind men and an elephant? The first one feels the leg and concludes it's a tree. The second man feels the trunk and concludes it's a snake. The third man feels the tail and concludes it's a rope. All three leave thinking they know what an elephant is and create their own version of reality, which is limited in perspective. To the person with a hammer every problem is a nail. Single discipline specialists give us their solutions before they know our problem. 'Its all about mindfulness,' 'it's all about resilience,' 'its all about data'. The truth is excellence is never about one thing in isolation.

'Excellence is never about one thing in isolation'

These approaches can trivialise the real challenges of accelerating excellence. Too many of us become addicted to the aggressive consumption of marginal gain tools and techniques. We end up spending far too much time focused on the cherry to put on top of the cake we haven't even baked yet. There is a serious downside to this that needs to be acknowledged.

'We end up spending far too much time focused on the cherry to put on top of the cake we haven't even baked yet'

Accelerating excellence is a mighty challenge, and as a cost-benefit exercise, focusing on the latest tools and techniques is unlikely to be where we optimise our return on investment. Excellence in anything flows not from cosmetic adjustments but from mastering the foundational principles that drive excellence.

'Excellence in anything flows not from cosmetic adjustments but from mastering the basics'

For the record I use of all the techniques mentioned. From bulletproof coffee to ice baths, they are all potentially great habits to form, just never at the detriment of optimising the essential and fundamental drivers of excellence outlined in Parts Two to Five of this book.

Source two - Expert performers

The next source comes straight from the elite performers themselves. Hollywood superstars, political giants, and business titans including former US President Barack Obama, Facebook CEO Mark Zuckerberg, and the former Mr Olympia, movie star and politician Arnold Schwarzenegger, are inspirational, impressive and entertaining. Their incredible stories of adversity and triumph fuel our ambition, sparking us into action, which is precisely the role they should play.

The danger is that many expert performers might insinuate (knowingly or not) that the secret to our success lies in what they attribute their own success to. We call this outcome bias. For Obama it's 'stay focused'; for Zuckerberg, 'take more risk'; and for Schwarzenegger, 'No pain, no gain.'

Outcome Bias: When we evaluate the quality of an action after we know the outcome and the end justifies the means

So, there we are, setting the alarm for 04:00, channeling our inner Navy SEAL. We down three raw egg yolks from a glass, and off we go to run five miles in the dark. Back at home before sunrise, we proceed to do 100 press ups, 200 sit ups, take an ice bath, and replenish with a kale smoothie. We use positive thinking to keep us from projectile vomiting across the room, followed by sitting cross-legged for thirty minutes, chanting along with the sounds of Tibetan monks. This ensures we're in the zone when we start work at 07:00, one step ahead of the rest. All because our idol told us, this is what it takes to win.

The truth is that these individuals often succeed for reasons even they don't really understand. Expert performers aren't necessarily performance experts. We focus on the winners and mistakenly assume that traits like taking risks was the key to their success. What about all the other people who took risks but didn't succeed?

Yes, our experts worked hard, took risks and set ambitious goals, but what about the chance events, favourable market conditions, or being at the right place at the right time that gave them a 50% tailwind? False beliefs about success and luck are dangerous because they can lead to us forming inaccurate perceptions of what really drives excellence.

'Expert performers aren't necessarily performance experts'

When we conclude that modelling the behaviours of our heroes will lead to the same destination, our success protocol then becomes one of simplified cause and effect: If I want to be successful, I'll be more confident, positive, motivated and [fill in the blank]. Whilst we might admire those who exhibit that behaviour, it's never that clear how we can. Plus, for me, I don't care how positive I try to be or how hard I work; I am not going to play number nine for Chelsea.

Advice like 'never quit,' 'be positive' and 'believe in yourself' are about as practical as being told to 'be taller'. They are the white bread of psychological nutrition. It tastes nice, but there is no substance to it. This adopt a mind-set advice all sits at the tip of the iceberg. The mechanisms that generate these behaviours are something much deeper below the surface.

Obama, Zuckerberg and Schwarzenegger are right: we do need to stay focused, take more risks, and adopt the no pain, no gain attitude at times. But the question we really need to answer is: How do we summon the confidence, resilience and motivation to do so? We still don't know what we can do today so that we can generate these characteristics as our default mindset tomorrow.

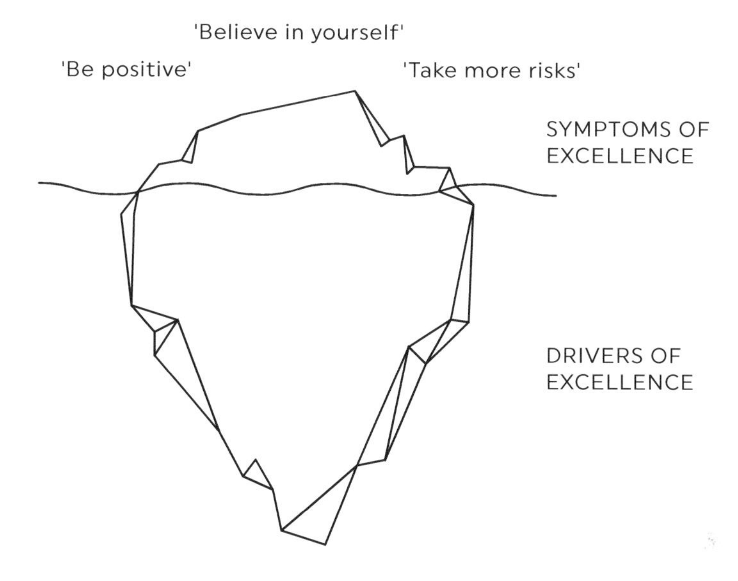

Source three- Expert writers

Their books have us leaning in, slack-mouthed, nodding slowly as we read; they are entertaining, fascinating, and addictive. They are well written, full of compelling headline titles, and bold claims that get us hooked. The authors are journalists who specialise in translating the science to the masses in a palatable, commercial way. Their words broaden our awareness, expand our thinking and fan our interest in human performance, which is exactly the role that they should play in our development.

The challenge for us is that some accomplish readability by cherry-picking research findings and singling out gripping headline titles as the answer, at the expense of all the other crucial components. The product they offer inevitably lacks substance and fails to provide us with the full picture.

The danger arises when the media then pronounces them 'performance experts' and their inaccurate advice spreads through the aspiring masses like wildfire.Perhaps the most famous example of this is the 10,000-hour myth, which actually stems from one study on one set of pre-screened performers in one domain of human performance. The average time to excellence was actually closer to 11,000 hours. Half achieved expert status in under 10,000 hours; one person did it in less than 3,000 and another in 25,000. Some research participants needed eight times the practice of others to reach the same level. Deducing that the key to excellence is 10,000 hours of practice is therefore inaccurate and misleading.

If it takes us 10,000 hours to excel then there is something seriously wrong with our methodology. On average, it takes a lot less. It is possible to become an Olympian, Special Forces operator, hedge fund manager or professional athlete in less than four years. The number of hours we need to put in is relative to the other people we're competing with. In a new or emerging field, we can become an expert in 200 hours. In a complex established discipline like chess, we're probably looking at 30,000 hours to reach expert status.

'If it takes us 10,000 hours to excel then there is something seriously wrong with our methodology'

A primary focus on clocking thousands of hours will injure or burn anyone out and is certainly not a recipe for elite performance. Plus, investing 10,000 hours is simply not an option for everyone, which can lead to many not even bothering to try. Finally, what about the hundreds of thousands of people who have invested more than 10,000 hours in a specific area who remain painstakingly average at best?

As entertaining as these books are, people like us, who want to expand our potential and chase down excellence, need substance we can act on with conviction.

Source four - Academic experts

Academics think hard, set aside their biases, evaluate the quality and meaning of their evidence, and stay objective. Other scientists hit them with a stick to make sure they don't let their biases interfere with their results. Their breadth of knowledge, cerebral dexterity and empirical validation brings enormous substance. This means that committing to act on what they say becomes a lot easier.

The challenge is that academic information is not user-friendly. The truth is it can be painful to read and excruciating to extract the application. It took me approximately four years to learn to translate, structure, and communicate the learnings that lie deeply encrypted within academic journals and textbooks.

The challenge for many academics is that they don't know how to explain things at a level that untrained people can understand. Communication seems a universal problem with science across the board. Scientists, whether the subject is global warming, economics, or human performance can struggle when it comes to teaching the public about important issues.

Often these academics only speak, write, and talk to each other in their own language with little or no contact with the people the science serves. They use terms such as 'dynamic systems,' 'self-determination,' and 'self-efficacy' that just don't mean anything to normal people. This means it's difficult to connect all that theory to the real world and put it to work.

If we are to leverage great scientific work then its paramount we translate the information from this source into digestible, actionable chunks we can apply in a meaningful way so that we can put the science to work.

Source five- Performance experts

Individuals such as INEOS Grenadiers' General Manager Sir Dave Brailsford, Manchester City's Simon Timson and former UK athletics performance director Professor Dave Collins are performance experts.

These individuals and myself included have multi-disciplinary scientific backgrounds; they have tested ideas themselves, in the real world, using their own hands; they have seen the results of those interventions, using their own eyes, and they have thought hard about what those results mean with their own brains. The product of which is that they really know their stuff. Their work is empirical, credible, and highly actionable. They are working where we need to, below the surface of the iceberg, and they deliver elite performance programmes in the exclusive environments that have the budget to fund them.

The role of the Performance Director is to ensure that an individual or organisation is applying the right tool at the right time and in the right dose. At certain times any individual or organisation is highly responsive to certain types of performance intervention. We maximise our development when we pick the intervention that stimulates a maximal response. Otherwise we leak progress.

Performance experts are methodology people. Most of us are drowning in techniques but starving for a methodology. A methodology is a systematic way of doing something, telling us what steps we need to take, the order we need take them and how to execute those steps. Most importantly, it explains the why those steps should be taken, in that particular way.

'Most of us are drowning in techniques but starving for a methodology'

In this category, although the substance is profound, the content is scarce. Due to the edge their expertise provides to the organisations and individuals they are hired to work for, performance experts' knowledge tends to remain private and confidential. Of course they can't share their trade secrets with the competition. These experts are usually reserved for work with government organisations, and the world's most elite sports teams. This means that information from this source is few and far between. Until now.

The knowledge upgrade

In Chapter Two we begin the knowledge upgrade that will uncover a methodology that will channel our ambition, talent and effort on the right interventions, at the right times, so that we can maximise our development trajectory and start accelerating our pursuit of excellence. The methodology I introduce in the next chapter works smarter not harder to develop a 'you' that is driven by an internal desire to be more confident, resilient and motivated so that believing in yourself, taking risks, and staying focused becomes your default action. We will start with defining the thing we want to improve: human performance.

CHAPTER SUMMARY

- While we are born with this incredible and adaptable machine, the human brain and body, we aren't born with the software to run that machine optimally.
- Performance is never a coincidence. Those who seem to have it all are often those who have a system that allows them to go out and get it.
- Elite performers have, consciously or not, aligned with a set of principles that enables them to get better faster and capitalise on their ambition, talent and effort.
- It's not a question of whether change is possible, but rather how much change is possible. We need to shift our perception from reaching potential to expanding potential.
- The people who are providing the information on human performance aren't the people working in elite performance.
- Excellence in anything flows not from cosmetic adjustments but from mastering the fundamentals that drive it.
- If it takes us 10,000 hours to excel then there is something seriously wrong with our methodology. On average, it takes a lot less.
- We are drowning in techniques and starving for a methodology.
- A methodology tells us what steps to take, in what order and how to perform them. Most importantly, it explains the reasons why those steps should be taken, in that particular order.

2

PERFORMANCE IS NEVER A COINCIDENCE

Slow is smooth and smooth is fast
Anon. Navy Seal

In gambling there is one certainty never left to chance. The house always wins. Casinos enjoy this position because they have built-in advantages known as the house edge. The casino leverages the laws of probability to obtain a certain gain in an uncertain situation. The design of the games and minimum bets all result in a steady accretion of advantages that end up as overwhelming odds. The game is rigged and the gamblers know it.

Gambling: Betting an asset (time, money, effort, risk) on the occurrence of an uncertain event (success)

Casinos have gone to desperate measures to keep us in the game. They are designed to make sure we lose track of time (and the money we're losing). That means no windows. The lack of clocks, bright lighting, cool air, free food and drinks, all have the same purpose. As far as the house is concerned, the longer you play, the greater their odds. Battles will be lost. Even the casino can't guarantee success. No one can. When losses do arise the casino doesn't feel sad, angry or fearful because they know that, over time, the house always wins.

Battles will be lost. Even the casino can't guarantee success. No one can.

We are all to some extent playing a game of chance and the point here is: be the casino. Just like the casino Accelerating excellence is not a single game, but rather a series of games. People can get lucky and win a game, and we can do everything right and lose. But through aligning with the principles of human performance, we can build overwhelming advantages that stack the probability of success so high in our favour, they enable us to win the series.

'We are all to some extent playing a game of chance and the point here is: be the casino'

This chapter will introduce the concept of exponential thinking, deconstruct human performance into its component parts, and outline a methodology that will enable us to leverage the same power of edge building as the casino.

The Exponential Breakthrough

> Compound interest is the eighth wonder
> of the world. He who understands it earns it,
> he who doesn't pays it
>
> Albert Einstein

Mark Zuckerberg and his signature hoodie came from nowhere, up- ending the way we communicate with his start-up Facebook. French footballer Kylian Mbappé rose to stardom signing for Paris Saint-Germain for €180 million aged just 17 and winning the World Cup a year later aged 18, scoring in the final. Whichever way we look a few exceptional performers burst onto the scene. The question is how? These exponential, explosive breakthroughs often appear unexplainable. One of the reasons is because we are programmed to think in a linear way.

With linear thinking we expect things to be constant and consistent. To visualise this, if we take 30 steps linearly, one, two, three, and so on... we will advance 30 steps forward.[4] This is our brain's default setting.

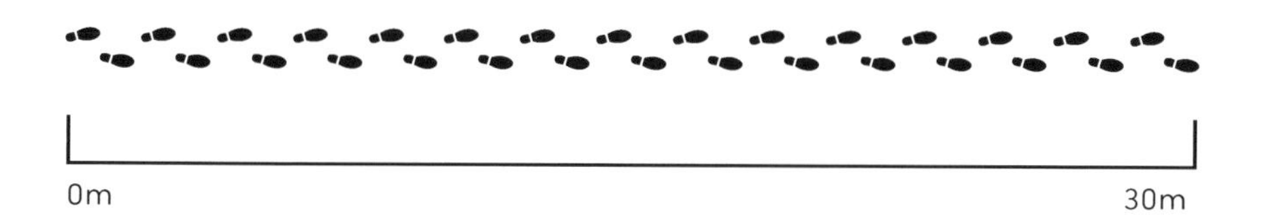

30 X 1 METRE LINEAR STEPS TAKES US 30 METRES

Linear thinking is why, if we were able to build a time machine, travel back in time and tell the technicians who built the first computer at MIT that the smart phone in your pocket is

Illustration adapted from: Singularity hub by Alison E Berman, Jason Dorrier and David J. Hill.[4]

several billion times more powerful and a thousand times smaller, they would think we were crazy.

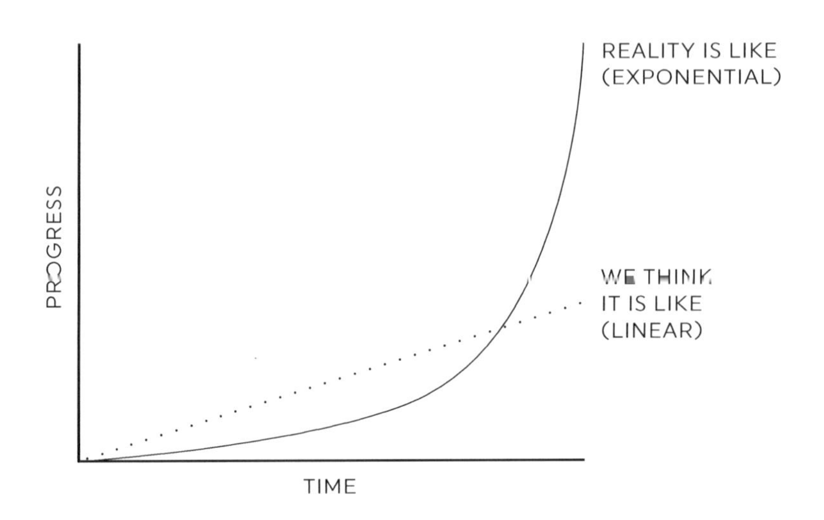

There are two problems with linear thinking:

Problem one- The fact that it takes one breakthrough to enable us to perceive the possibility of the next, means that so many of us stay blind to the enormous amount of latent potential that exists within us. Due to the fact our nature is to want to blow everyone out of the water and go straight from A to Z, if we can't see a straight line to the top as a realistic option some of us don't even bother to try.

'It takes one breakthrough to enable us to perceive the possibility of the next, means that so many of us stay blind to the enormous amount of latent potential that exists within'

Problem two- When we expect our results to be relatively constant, and it turns out they aren't, unsurprisingly we experience frustration and disappointment at how ineffective our efforts seem to be. Progress feels slow, the up and downs feel volatile and excellence can feel like a distant dream. Inevitably many of us decide to give up.

The good news is that our pursuit of excellence follows a very predictable and exponential trajectory. Here each step we take is increasingly bigger than the last. When we take 30 steps exponentially, one, two, four, eight, and so on.... we will get to a billion steps.[4] This takes us around the world twenty-six times due to the compounding effect.

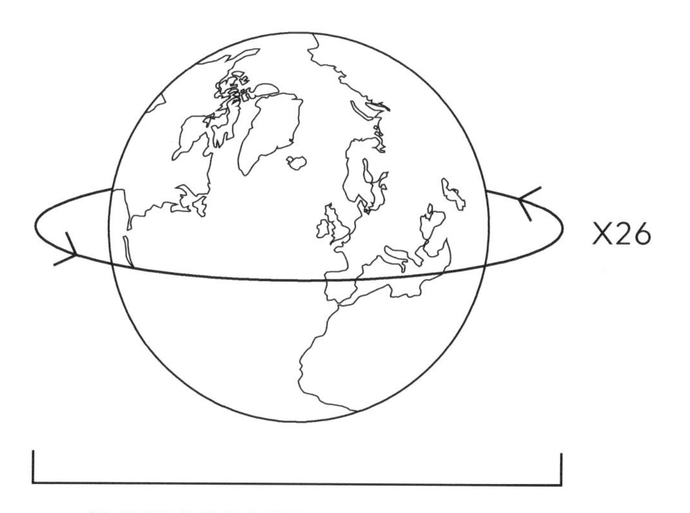

30 STEPS EXPONENTIALLY TAKES US AROUND THE WORLD 26 TIMES

Here, each burst of improvement we make stands on the shoulders of its predecessors. So, as we become better at one skill, it becomes relatively easier to acquire subsequent skills, and so on and so forth. This is how we begin to accelerate excellence.

Illustration adapted from: Singularity hub by Alison E Berman, Jason Dorrier and David J. Hill.[4]

'As we become better at one skill, it becomes relatively easier to acquire subsequent skills, and so on and so forth'

The principle benefit of upgrading to exponential thinking is that it shifts our perceptions of potential. Understanding that the changes that seem small, mundane and unimportant, like reading this book, repetitive development work, and asking what might feel like stupid questions, will eventually compound increases the likelihood we engage in them. Those small steps become bigger steps, and all of a sudden we reach a tipping point where rapid and dramatic change occurs. Then congratulations, we're an overnight success.

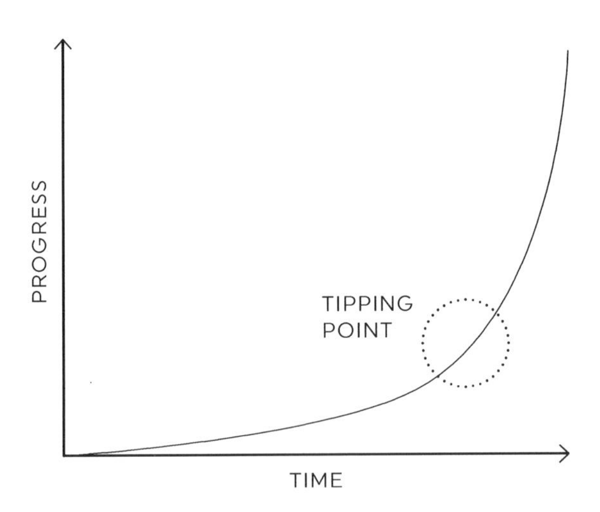

Tipping Point- the point at which previous actions unlock the potential for explosive growth

When it comes to accelerating excellence, slow is smooth and smooth is fast. The message is that if we can just get a little bit better, a little bit faster, then over time we will develop a giant gap from the rest. The process of exceptional improvement always hinges on that one small next step that has the potential to lead to incredible leaps that might feel impossible to imagine, let alone believe.

'If we can just get a little bit better, a little bit faster, then over time we will develop a giant gap from the rest'

Compounding is the mechanism behind every exponential, explosive and seemingly unexplainable performance breakthrough and it will be the mechanism behind yours.

Defining human performance

We're so eager to get started, plus defining the problem is hard, so we often skip the definition phase and jump straight to the action bit. Its no wonder we want to dive straight in. The inability to define what human performance is and isn't leaves us with an "all talk no walk" body of knowledge that is hard to implement.

Human: Relating to a person

The word human is important. Performance can technically encapsulate tools, such as technology, equipment, and weapons, whereby each has a function to fulfill. But ultimately, human beings are the decisive factor. The human gives birth to technology; we code the software, programme the AI and fire the weapons. The human is always the lead domino or detriment in any performance enhancement programme, so that is where we will focus.

Human performance interventions as defined in this book are not about the artificial or technological aspects that have the potential to impact performance; the computer chips, limitless pills, and Iron-man suits that are proposed to unlock all of humanity's potential. Nor is it about the medical and biosynthetic technology that currently focuses on repairing, but not yet enhancing, performance.

This book is about the human factors, the biological and psychological factors that are accessible to anyone and everyone, and which can be enacted by you today. That is why this is a book about human performance and not just performance.

Performance: The accomplishment of a given task measured against completeness, cost, and speed

Next we come to the word performance, meaning the accomplishment of a given task. This is where context comes in; the task might range from a student sitting exams to a team of scientists curing cancer, and everything in between. The point here is we all have human performance demands imposed on us.

There are three constructs that make up performance: completeness, cost and speed.

1. Completeness: The state or condition of having all the necessary or appropriate parts

Completeness is where we traditionally tend to focus. This makes sense seeing as we are usually measured by the outcomes we produce. For example, a perfect 10 in an Olympic gymnastics final is more complete than a score of 9. An A grade is more complete that a C grade. And £10 million profit is more complete than £3 million profit. Whenever we increase completeness we increase performance.

2. Cost: The required payment in resource (time/money/effort/loss/sacrifice) necessary to obtain the completeness achieved.

Cost can manifest in the form of hours spent by executives who toil away all day, into evenings and through weekends. Or it could be intensity, as some literally work themselves into physical and mental exhaustion. Or in the hard currency of capital, the $10 billion spent in the US each year on personal development books, workshops and coaching services. There is also the risk taking, as people wholeheartedly launch themselves into challenges where the overwhelming odds are that they will fail.

The key point when it comes to cost is that, if we can get person A to the same standard as person B but with half the cost (time, money, resources, risk or effort), then we have increased performance. If our gymnast achieves the perfect 10, the student receives the A grade and the business generates the £10million in profit, all with 5,000 versus 10,000 hours of coaching we have enhanced performance.

Cost must always be considered in relation to performance. The objective is to maximise the return (completeness) on investment (in terms of amount of risk, time, effort, financial, and health) the same way we might measure the return we make on a financial investment.

3. Speed: The rate at which something happens or is completed

Last but not least is speed, the total amount of elapsed time taken to accomplish the given task from initiation to completion. If we can get the gymnast to score that perfect 10 in three years versus five years, we increase performance. Likewise if we can achieve the A grade without having to re-sit the year, we also improve performance. If our business can generate the £10million in profit in five years of trading versus ten, then performance increases. The objective here from a performance standpoint is to reduce the latency between the initiations, considered against completeness and cost.

When we positively impact any of these components – completeness, cost, and speed – we improve performance.

> ***Note:*** There is one critical stipulation to improving performance. Improvements must be accomplished with quality of health (and life) alongside and after achievement. This stipulation rules out employing techniques that are unsustainable short-cuts like working harder for longer, cheating through violating rules and regulations, taking performance enhancing substances or study drugs, or just plain short-sightedness, like copying others.

The outliers: Modelling excellence

The process through which we break human performance down into its constituent parts is through modelling excellence using the scientific method.

The little black dot highlighted in the top left-hand corner is what the traditional scientist would describe as an outlier. One of the first things an aspiring scientist learns on their degree programme is to disregard outliers because they risk messing up

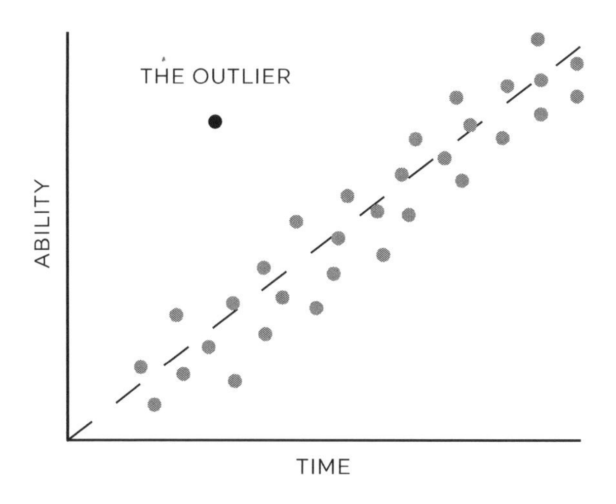

the rest of their data and could prevent it being published. This is fine if the objective of the scientist is to work out something like, how long it takes the average child to learn to read. With this new knowledge the scientist can then seek to identify children who fall below the average and subsequently design interventions that aim to bring that child back to the average reading range.

If our aim is to excel, then there is a problem with this approach. The negation of low performance doesn't result in high performance. Not being depressed doesn't make us happy, and not being obese doesn't mean washboard abdominals are imminent. Studying the average means we only learn about the average. Average and excellent are two distinct pictures. If we want to learn about excellence, we need to study excellence. Instead of deleting the outlier, we must study the outlier. Whether it's learning to read, musical ability, athletic ability, or intellectual ability, the question the performance scientist poses is: why is this person so far above the curve?

'Instead of deleting the outlier, we must study the outlier'

The aim in the human performance sciences is to identify these outlier individuals and organisations that consistently sustain elite performance at the upper limits of current human capacity. Once we have identified these outliers, we can break down the causal principles that drive such exceptional performance. Armed with the knowledge of what drives elite performance, we then seek to bring the individuals and organisations we work with into alignment with these principles. When it comes to elite performance, the aim is not to bring everyone to average, it's to move the average up. This is known as shifting the baseline

'When it comes to elite performance, the aim is not to bring everyone to average, it's to move the average up'

If human performance is Z, then our aim is to understand how A+B+C+D= Z. The counterintuitive thing about performance is that the results (Z) are never the problem. Results are merely the symptoms of our process for achievement (A+B+C+D).

'If human performance is Z, then our aim is to understand how A+B+C+D= Z'

Studying the outlier has enabled us to expose the constituent parts that comprise excellence (A+B+C+D). Understanding the principles that produce the results and the relationships between them is what allows us to prioritise the most important areas to focus. Multiple disciplines contribute to produce elite performance, and to excel, understanding how those pieces work together is critical. With understanding comes clarity in terms of what to prioritise and where to focus, innovate, combine; when, and in what order.

'Multiple disciplines contribute to produce elite performance, and to excel, understanding how those pieces work together is critical'

When we understand the process improving results becomes algebraic. We can simply work towards optimising the letters through systematic measurement. This is fundamentally how science works. It moves us from mindless or wishy-washy problem solving to mindful, quantifiable and objective problem solving because now we understand the principles (A+B+C+D…) that produce elite performance (Z). This formula provides us with a methodology for accelerating excellence.

The Methodology

Progress isn't linear. There are no straight lines to the top and there are no exceptions to this rule. Two steps forward, five steps back; six steps forward and one more back, before a fifteen-step breakthrough. In order to persist through this volatility, we need a methodology to help us navigate through the inevitable doubt, fear and uncertainty.

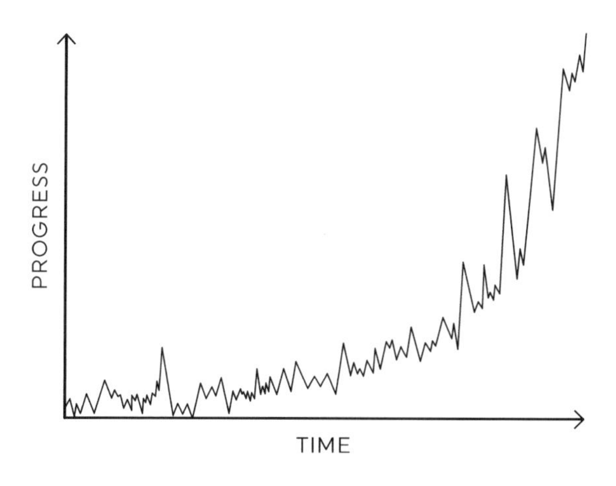

'Progress isn't linear'

A principle-based methodology means that committing to achieving excellence becomes a set of logical actions rather than a dream-chasing exercise. It allows the brain to rest because there is a formula for how to proceed. We might not be there yet, but we now have a formula to get there, and this means we can stop worrying.

'A principle-based methodology means that committing to achieving excellence becomes a series of logical steps rather than a dream-chasing exercise'

This methodology can be applied in any human enterprise; to win world championships, build the next silicon valley unicorn, or to end global warming. The methodology does not tell us how to do something, but it identifies how to proceed, and what steps to take. Although the content may vary between the Olympic athlete and the CEO, the approach remains the same.

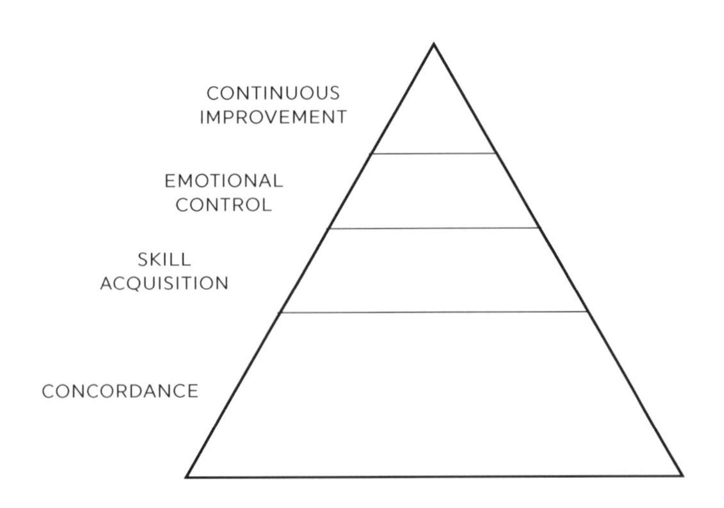

The methodology comprises four mechanisms that operate as part of an interconnecting whole to which the rest of this book is dedicated. Imagine excellence as a pyramid representing a hierarchy of needs, with those at the bottom taking precedence over those higher up.

If we haven't optimised the goals we pursue to begin with, the benefits of quality practice lessen. *Part Two shows you how to do this.* Once we're pursuing the right goals, we may begin to worry about maximising the rate at which we acquire skill. *Part Three shows you how to do this.* Once your practice is optimised, we can begin to focus on delivering those skills on demand and under pressure. *Part Four shows you how to do this.* At the top of the pyramid the focus is innovation, the desire to capitalise on your expandable potential and stay ahead of the rest. We had better make sure we retain our success once we finally have it. *Part Five shows you how to do this.*

Each mechanism contains sets of principles, and every principle we align ourselves with has a multiplier effect on our rate of progress. The more principles we align ourselves with the higher the probability of producing winning results and generating exponential breakthroughs.

'The more principles we align ourselves with the higher the probability of producing winning results'

The methodology within the following pages is the basic blueprint for stacking the odds and generating exponential breakthroughs in any pursuit: align with these principles as closely as you can. The returns are indeed enormous.

CHAPTER SUMMARY

- We are all to some extent playing a game of chance and the point here is: be the casino.
- This book is about the biological and psychological factors that are accessible to anyone and everyone, and which can be enacted by us today.
- Performance can be defined as the accomplishment of a given task measured against completeness, cost, and speed.
- Improvements must be accomplished with quality of health (and life) alongside and after achievement.
- We break human performance down into its constituent parts through modelling excellence. Instead of deleting the outlier, we must study the outlier.
- It takes one breakthrough to enable us to perceive the possibility of the next, which means that so many of us stay blind to the enormous amount of latent potential that exists within us.
- To accelerate excellence we have to upgrade to exponential thinking. The good news is that our pursuit of excellence follows a very predictable and exponential trajectory.
- As we become better at one skill, it becomes relatively easier to acquire subsequent skills, and so on and so forth.
- Excellence is volatile and there are no straight lines to the top and there are no exceptions to this rule.
- A principle-based methodology means that committing to achieving excellence becomes a series of logical steps rather than a dream-chasing exercise.

PART 2

CONCORDANCE

3

FINDING YOUR SWEET SPOT

Know thyself and to thine own self be true
Polonius in Shakespeare's *Hamlet*

Concordance: When a person's nature, the qualities that make one unique, are in agreement/harmony

Professional footballer Gareth Bale, who is referred to as a superstar (which he certainly is), was also once ridiculed and insulted, described by Tottenham Hotspur fans as a jinx. This was around the time Bale was his former self: a left-back with no defensive awareness, who leaked goals from his flank on a regular basis. The so-called gung-ho, risk-prone and unreliable defender was singled out as the sole reason for Tottenham's horrific start to the 2013 English Premier League season.[5]

Despite Bale's terrible performances, his manager, Harry Redknapp, continued to laud his technical and physical abilities.

These weren't the problem. Bale's defensive role was suffocating his greatest psychological strength. To attack! He was playing in the wrong position. This made Gareth a low-performing left-back despite his incredible physical and technical capabilities.

It wasn't until he aligned his intrinsic desire to attack by switching roles that he had nuclear effects on the opposition defence as an attacking winger. No longer a liability, by mid-season of the same year, Bale had transformed into 'an inspiration,' 'world class' and 'player of the year,' breezing past defenders, scoring goals for fun.' A season later, the jinx had become the most expensive player in the world. He signed a record £85.3m transfer to Real Madrid where he went on to win a record three back-to-back Champions League finals, scoring one of the best goals in history, which was an overhead kick to beat Liverpool in the 2018 final. No longer fighting resistance, he was performing in harmony with the qualities that make him unique, smack bang in his sweet spot.

Sweet spot. We have all experienced moments where everything just clicks and the task at hand felt like pushing on an open door or listening to a perfect symphony. On the flipside, we have also felt the repercussions of not being in our sweet spots. Nothing clicks, the door feels barricaded shut, and the sounds of the perfect symphony are replaced with fingernails against a chalkboard.

We each have a sweet spot and, only when we pursue goals that lie within it, do we allow ourselves the opportunity to excel. In the field of human performance, this state of performing within our sweet spot, where the qualities that make us unique are congruent with the goals we pursue, is called concordance.

'We each have a sweet spot and, only when we pursue goals that lie within it, do we allow ourselves the opportunity to excel'

Our sweet spot is as unique to us as our fingerprints, our DNA, and retina pattern. No one gets to adopt our fingerprints, DNA or alter the pattern of our retinas. Nor can we just choose or copy theirs. Pursuing goals which align with the qualities that make us unique is the first critical step for anyone who intends to excel. Nothing comes before this.

'Pursuing goals which align with the qualities that make us unique is the first critical step for anyone who intends to excel. Nothing comes before this'

Imagine if today's elite performers had pursued different goals. What would have happened if Warren Buffet, one of the most successful investors of all time, had opted for a career as a lawyer? Would Lebron James who is considered one of the greatest ever basketball players have excelled as a soccer player? And would superstar musician, singer and songwriter Ed Sheeran have excelled in comedy? Just like these icons, we need to make sure we're chasing the right goals in the first place.

There is a potential everything we could be, and we start to realise and expand upon it when we pursue concordant goals. In fact, self-concordance[7] is the essential foundation that all excellence is built from, which is why we're going to dedicate this section to helping you find your concordant goals.Elite performers have aligned more closely with this principle than any other.

'There is a potential everything you could be, and you start to realise and expand upon it when you pursue self-concordant goals'

Behold the truth: We cannot be anything we want to be, and when we try to be, we squander our ambition, talent and effort, which keeps us from achieving our goals. The theory that anyone can do anything largely derives from the positive-thinking mob, who preach that excellence is a matter of hard work and determination. This assumes that we are all clones, possessing the same default set of strengths, interests and values. It is absurd. And it sets us up to fail. Yes, anyone can get better at anything, but not anyone can excel at anything.

'Anyone can get better at anything, but not anyone can excel at anything'

The work hard, get what we want, mind-set is the antithesis of concordance, and buying into it leaves us swimming against the tide, eviscerating our potential to excel. More importantly, pursuing goals that fail to align with our natures wastes time that could have been spent honing the skills required to excel in a goals that are tailored to match our unique strengths, interests and values.

Concordance relies on us shifting from 'we can be anything we want to be' to the more accurate 'we can be a hell of a lot more of who we already are.' Whether it is God-given, or a gift of millions of years of evolution, we have a unique nature, and to get the most out of ourselves we need to align the goals we pursue and how we pursue them with it.

'Self-concordance relies on shifting from "we can be anything we want to be" to the more accurate "we can be a hell of a lot more of who we already are'

When we pursue concordant goals, we perform from our sweet spot. Just like a golf club or tennis racquet has a point at which the ball absorbs the maximum amount of the available forward momentum and rebounds away with greater velocity than if struck by any other point, so do you. Our sweet spot optimises our performance in the very same manner.

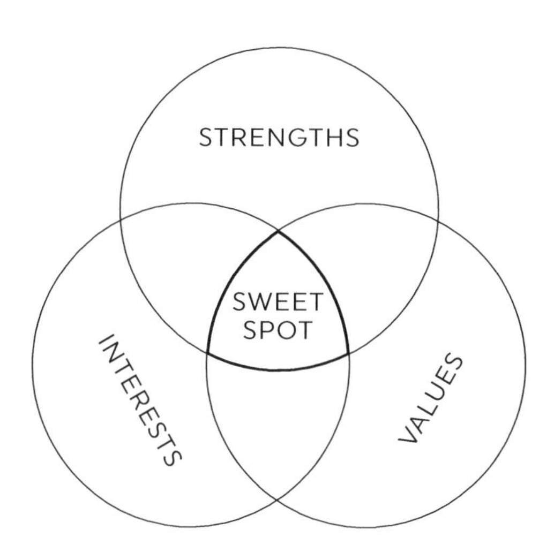

Concordant goals exist at the intersection of three things: our strengths, interests and values. This intersection is our sweet spot.

Strengths: A pre-disposed high baseline or responsiveness to training

Illustration adapted from: Tal Ben-Shahar's groundbreaking Positive Psychology course at Harvard University. The most popular in the University's history.[8]

Interests: The feeling of wanting to know or learn more about an area

Values: What is most important to you

Each element is advantageous on its own but it is the convergence of all three that results in a maximum response for a given amount of effort, and this is the key to accelerating excellence. Remove one element and the process slows exponentially.

'The evolutionary role of our sweet spot is to guide us along our path of maximal development'

Operating outside our sweet spot, by living in a state of misalignment, dooms us to mediocrity. Why? Because we can't re-write our evolutionary programming or re-deal the sets of cards we have been dealt by Mother Nature, God, science or whatever we choose to call it.

The greatest poker player isn't the one with the best hand; but the one who can leverage the hand they have been dealt best. The message is: we must play to win with the cards we have, not the ones we wish we had.

'We must play to win with the cards we have, not the ones we wish we had'

The fact is that elite performers make it look easy, and that's because to them, it kind of is. Warren Buffet dominates the markets, Lebron James dominates the NBA, and Ed Sheeran dominates the charts. Elite performance is easy once you know how. The challenge is getting to the knowing how, and that takes blood, sweat and tears.

You want to be an athlete? Hedge fund manager? Or YouTube sensation? No wonder. No-one struggles with the idea of being excellent in a culturally elite discipline. We know that ambition is not the problem. We all want to shine like a diamond; it's the getting cut bit we struggle with. Doing excellence is the problem; the non-negotiable experience that requires blood, sweat and tears.

'We all want to shine like a diamond; it's the getting cut bit we struggle with'

The big reveal for me over the last fifteen years of working in high-performance was the fact that elite performers are differentiated from their less successful counterparts by an ability to activate the psychological fire-power that enables them to endure the grunt, graft, and grind required to excel. In fact, when elite performers do this, a lot of the time they don't feel they are enduring anything. What we might naturally perceive as hard work doesn't feel like work at all to elite performers because, when pursuing concordant goals, the spot from which they are performing is … well, sweet.

The tough conversations, awkward silences, hurt feelings, psychodrama, risky moves, sacrifices, delayed gratification, uncertainty, repeated failures, late nights, unfair decisions, being told we won't make it, all in the face of the overwhelming odds that we will fail, might drive us crazy at times, but, when our goals are concordant, it doesn't deter us.

'The overwhelming odds that we will fail, might drive us crazy at times, but, when our goals are concordant, it doesn't deter us'

We had better have concordant goals if we want to generate the psychological activation necessary to deliver what is required to excel. Our level of concordance has a direct impact on our ability to out-struggle the rest. So, this is where we must start.

> Psychological Fire-power: Characteristics including: confidence, motivation, creativity, and resilience (amongst others). These are all interrelated having a direct and indirect impact upon one another. They all flow from the same source, the predatory circuitry of the brain located in the left pre-frontal cortex.

The substance concordance brings provides us with a scientific and practical way to activate the psychological fire-power that exists within us all, and moves us from empty statements such as 'follow your passions,' 'be yourself' and 'find your purpose', to actionable biochemical edge over the competition.

The two yous

> Everybody is a genius. But if you judge a fish by its ability to climb a tree, it will live its whole life believing that it is stupid
>
> Albert Einstein

Like many things, concordance exists on a continuum; meaning that we can have more or less of it. More is better. Our ambitions, aspirations, and goals are the same at each end, we all possess the same desire to achieve and to compete, but the mind-set we exhibit is very different. Only the high-concordance end of the continuum is optimal. We're not always at one end or the other,

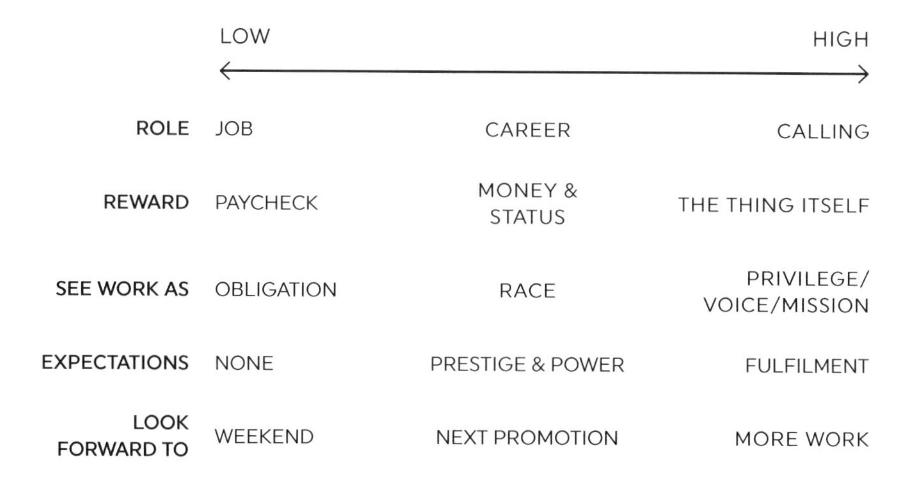

and because it's a continuum we can move up and down. By being aware of the impact of concordance on our mind-set, we can start to think about where we are now, and where we want to be, before moving on to explore what actions will take us there.

Finding Your Sweet Spot
LOW
HIGH
ROLE
JOB
CAREER
CALLING
REWARD
PAYCHECK
MONEY & STATUS
THE THING ITSELF
SEE WORK AS
OBLIGATION
RACE
PRIVILEGE/ VOICE/MISSION
EXPECTATIONS
NONE
PRESTIGE & POWER
FULFILMENT
LOOK FORWARD TO
WEEKEND
NEXT PROMOTION
MORE WORK

Non-concordant goals are the enemy. To conquer it, first we need to understand it, which is why we're going to explore what happens when we opt for the wrong goals. I'll then illustrate why pursuing non-concordant goals is the biggest threat to performance. Most importantly, we'll see what happens when we get this right. We'll spend some time reflecting on where we are today, where we might want to be tomorrow and how to get there.

> ***Note:*** Once I realised the significance of this concept I couldn't sleep. The first reason was relief and the second, excitement. I couldn't stop thinking about how the vast majority of challenges I had experienced personally and professionally were due to low concordance. This made everything so much harder than it needed to be.

Continuum adapted from: Tal Ben-Shahar's Work Orientation model in Harvard University's Positive Psychology course.[8]

Low concordance

Low concordance means low activation. At this end of the continuum our psychological fire-power is like an elusive and sporadic trickle. Life is terrible and relentless; at least that's what we think. We are our own worst enemies when pursuing goals outside our sweet spots. We just can't summon the energy or enthusiasm to act on that ambition the way others seem to be able to. When eventually coerced into taking some kind of action, we go through the motions, and do the minimum required to get by.

We lose focus and attention fast. All of us have problems sustaining attention and no doubt a lot of this is down to constant stimulation from the chaotic modern world we live in. But that's not the only reason. We will always have some degree of attention deficit for the stuff we just don't really care about. The truth is that our lack of motivation stems from the fact that deep down we're just not concordant with our goals. When we lack concordance it's just not possible for us to activate the psychological fire-power required to commit, pursue and achieve them.

'We will always have some degree of attention deficit for the stuff we just don't really care about'

When it comes to learning we memorise, regurgitate, and call it a day. When we're not invested in our goals, our brains are less engaged. If the information doesn't relate fast (and at this end of the continuum, it usually doesn't) the information is forgotten faster. This apathetic state of mind leaves our brain making fewer internal connections. There is also less of the firing and wiring needed to make new connections and upgrade our brains to better suit the task at hand. From each bout of training in this mode, less progress results. Eventually our brains degenerate and regress.

At the heart of the low concordance state is the question, 'why bother?' What makes the sacrifice, effort, and risks required to progress, let alone excel, worthwhile? Apathetic, whining and riddled with excuses, we end up full of self-contempt, doubting whether we're even cut out for it; whatever 'it' is for us. We're like a bird with no wings riddled with existential angst. We know that things aren't quite right, but we're not quite sure how to fix them.

We are not built to be whiny and apathetic which is precisely why we are so attuned to feeling the grunt, graft and grind. When we pursue goals that aren't really our own, fear is triggered, which is why we literally fight, take flight or freeze at the thought of work. The emotional brain, or amygdala, activates the famous stress response with the aim that the adrenaline released will prompt us into doing something about the fact we're pursuing goals that fail to expand that potential everything we could be.

> 'We are not built to be whiny and apathetic which is precisely why we are so attuned to feeling the grunt, graft and grind'

When we're pursuing the wrong goals to begin with, following advice from expert performers who tell us to be positive, and willing our way through a to-do list of techniques from the single-discipline specialists leaves us fighting an uphill battle destined for failure.

We might feel like we can never hold onto those elusive moments where we feel that trace of confidence, rush of motivation, or trickle of resilience kick in. But this is wrong. We can seize control, through our ability to identify, set and pursue concordant goals, which activate the psychological fire-power that exists within us.

Understanding this fact should feel liberating. This isn't an excuse for our negative attitude, it's the opposite. Once we're aware this attitude is the product of our lack of concordance, we no longer have excuses. This awareness puts the ball firmly in our own court.

High concordance

When we perform from this part of the continuum, we are in our sweet spot. It's like having a new brain that knows how to do all the stuff the old one didn't. Performing from our sweet spot transforms our brain into a more complex organ that functions at a higher level. Unleashing our best selves though the activation of psychological fire-power, we ignite the confidence, motivation and resilience that drive success. The amount of activation is proportionate to the level of concordance.

This might sound mystical but it's very much a biological mechanism. The secret behind concordant goals is that they tie in our incentive reward system, which is the evolutionary mechanism that compels us to move forward confidently and consistently in the face of adversity. Put simply, when our goals align with our nature, our brain gives us all the good chemicals.

'The secret behind concordant goals is that they tie in our incentive reward system, which is the evolutionary mechanism that compels us to move forward confidently and consistently in the face of adversity'

The state of concordance initiates a cascade of neurochemical changes, such as releasing the super six: norepinephrine, dopamine, serotonin, oxytocin, anandamide and endorphins. These hormones amplify our psychological and biological capacities, as well as delivering an analgesic effect that shuts off pain and suppresses anxiety.

In a state of concordance, it's not just the amount of psychological fire-power that changes, it's the quality. When it comes to learning we still acquire facts, but our focus is on how the facts fit together and relate to the bigger picture. We look for themes that are emerging, addressing challenges in a conceptual way.

Consequently we are significantly more responsive to training. Each bout of progress stands on the shoulders of its predecessors. The compounding process begins, and our ability to improve expands, remoulding our brain as we go. As the challenge increases, the complexity of the brain aggressively follows suit adapting to a superior level each time.

Goals feel easier to achieve even though they remain objectively difficult. The perceived ease of the challenge is influenced by the confidence, motivation, and resilience to conquer it. This is the reason outliers are able to take on and conquer what others perceive as insurmountable tasks such as winning a gold medal, becoming CEO, or writing a bestseller.

The fact that pursuing concordant goals is the reward itself means work no longer feels hard in the traditional sense. Feeling clear about what we're pursuing, and why, makes it easier to stop sweating the small stuff. Obstacles are now opportunities for improvement. This is why the concordant performer chases down every opportunity, arrives early, stays late, brings questions, trains hard, and plays to the last whistle.

'The fact that pursuing concordant goals is the reward itself means work no longer feels hard in the traditional sense'

Performance itself becomes addictive; the luxury of existing within the moment, making breakthroughs, and competing provide enormous pleasure to concordant performers. Sticking to the plan, digging deep, and pulling all-nighters feels natural and enjoyable because of the internal compulsion to perform and compete. Just thinking about doing the work can make us feel good.

The perception that commitment to performance limits other aspects of life is nonsense. It is entirely possible to be happy with a lifestyle that others might perceive as unconventional and extreme. When the work is enjoyable and takes us where we want to go, there is no sacrifice. It is liberating to enjoy the here and now and know that it's driving us forward. Training demands and commitment that might appear superhuman to others can feel perfectly balanced and well adjusted for us.

'When the work is enjoyable and takes you where you want to go, there is no sacrifice'

We appear healthier and in higher spirits because that's exactly what we are. Besides the performance-enhancing aspects, the neurochemicals mentioned earlier are also mood-enhancing chemicals. Plus, observing that our day-to-day efforts are moving us towards our concordant goals makes us feel good. This is energising and works like an alternator in a car engine, recharging the battery as the engine operates; recharging us as we go, creating a virtuous cycle. This doesn't mean we never need to rest, our energy will deplete eventually, just like a car battery will. But it goes a lot further before it does.

Concordance is not a panacea. This isn't about unrelenting highs of confidence, motivation and resilience, it's about being at our best now and entering a state where all our capacities become expandable. The pursuit of excellence is still anxiety provoking and threatening, but when it comes to the 'why bother?' question, the response is: 'why would anyone ask such a stupid question.'

Concordant performers know that consistent daily happiness is idealistic and detached from reality, but they don't care because the unrelenting fulfilment from their concordant goals is very real. Here, actualisation becomes part of the journey instead of some elusive far-off state achieved after thirty years sitting on a mountaintop in Tibet. We can achieve these states moment-to-moment, day-to-day, right now, when pursuing concordant goals.

How to become concordant

We achieve a state of concordance through pursuing concordant goals. The aim is to identify where we are concordant so we can start to shape the goals we pursue and how we pursue them. Our job is not to shape ourselves into an idea we think we ought to be, but to find out who we are and be that. Until the vision inside our own heads of who we are and what we're about becomes clear, we will fail to optimise our performance.

> 'Until the vision inside our own heads of who we are and what we're about becomes clear, we will fail to optimise our performance'

Our sweet spots are hidden from the naked eye and this means it's tricky to identify where we truly align and fit in. Concordance is a perception, reflection, and blind-spot problem. We haven't been trained to figure it all out. Plus, it's an unconscious process, therefore the feedback is more subtle than the bucket of ice-cold water some of us need.

Getting concordant is about understanding what drives our behaviour. Yes, we have an enormous repertoire of potential behaviours and often find ourselves in situations characterised by complexity. But we are also consistent. Our choices are not random, and this means our potential to excel in certain areas can be accurately predicted if we take the right approach. Based on how we're wired, we will respond to certain situations in certain ways. This provides us with clues.

Whether you are a graduate, making a fresh start, or an established CEO, NFL or Hollywood sensation who is having a blip and can't work out why, the answers are available, already influencing what you feel, think, and do. Whenever we feel those bursts of motivation, confidence, and resilience, no matter how fleeting, in that moment we were thinking, feeling or doing something highly concordant. We just have to unpack it.

The following three chapters deconstruct why the components of our sweet spot- our strengths, interests and values - are such critical multipliers for progress. The second half of each chapter comprises a set of questions and tools that will allow us all to elicit our own sweet spot.

CHAPTER SUMMARY

- Pursuing goals that align with the qualities that make us unique is the first critical step for anyone who intends to excel. Nothing comes before this.
- There is a potential everything we could be, and we start to realise and expand upon it when we pursue concordant goals.
- Concordant goals exist at the intersection of three things: our strengths, interests and values. This is our sweet spot.
- Each element is advantageous on its own but it is the convergence that results in a maximum response for a given amount of effort, and this is the key to accelerating excellence.
- Concordance relies on us shifting from 'we can be anything we want to be' to the more accurate, 'we can be a hell of a lot more of who we already are.'
- The evolutionary role of our sweet spot is to guide us along our path of maximal development.
- The secret behind concordant goals is that they tie in our incentive reward system, which is the evolutionary mechanism that compels us to move forward confidently and consistently in the face of adversity.
- Performing from our sweet spot transforms our brain into a more complex organ that functions at a higher level. This unleashes our best selves through the activation of the psychological fire-power we all know drives excellence.

4

THE BEST GET BETTER

Do not try to teach a pig to sing - it wastes your time and annoys the pig

Robert Heinlein

Strengths: A pre-disposed high baseline or responsiveness to training

UFC 194: Aldo vs. McGregor was a mixed martial arts World Championship fight on the 12th December 2015, MGM Arena, Las Vegas, Nevada:[9]

Mike Goldberg [UFC commentator]: 'Jose Aldo, Conor McGregor.'

Joe Rogan [UFC commentator]: 'Conor looks extremely loose. Aldo looks [Silence]… Like he is feeling the pressure of this moment.'

Mike Goldberg: 'HERE WE GO! Green trunks for the southpaw, the notorious Conor McGregor, black trunks for the champion Jose Aldo Junior.'

Joe Rogan: 'Conor relaxed and smiling... OHHHHHHH [Joe Rogan's eyes pop out of his skull] just like that!'

Mike Goldberg: 'AND THE NEW UFC FEATHER WEIGHT CHAMPION OF THE WORLD!'

Joe Rogan: 'OHHHHH, UNBELIEVABLE, OH MY GOD' [Silence] 'Unbelievable, the first punch he threw, slept him.'[10]

Conor McGregor is an expert performer, a mixed martial artist who rose to super stardom after winning the Ultimate Fighting Championship (UFC) featherweight championship, defeating the former champion of ten years, Jose Aldo via knock-out after 13 seconds, the fastest in history. McGregor went on to become the first fighter in history to simultaneously hold two world titles in two weight divisions. During an interview this is what he said:

Conor McGregor:

'There's no talent here, this is hard work. This is an obsession. Talent does not exist, we are all equals as human beings. You could be anyone if you put in the time. You will reach the top, and that's that. I am not talented, I am obsessed.'[11]

The clip went viral on the internet, it was printed on t-shirts, mugs and trended on social media. As discussed in Chapter One, this is classic expert performer advice, inspirational, from the heart, and with progressive intentions. However, it's wrong. Yes, work-rate matters. There isn't a single sport scientist, psychologist, geneticist or physiologist who would argue with that. Conor McGregor is an incredible athlete but his advice is misleading. Everyone that excels does so using their strengths. Excellence is always a hardware and software story, elite performance does not happen without both. To be clear, our strengths don't eliminate hard work; they clarify what to work hard on.

'Our strengths don't eliminate hard work; they clarify what to work hard on'

So, if looking at this quote in isolation, McGregor is wrong. Talent (natural strengths) certainly exists. We don't all share equal strengths, and we can't be anyone, no matter how much time we put in, and by God, McGregor is insanely talented. But he is also right. Elite performance is hard work, it is an obsession, and we all have the opportunity to excel within our own sweet spot. To excel, we must pursue goals where our strengths give us an advantage and our weaknesses don't matter.

'To excel, we must pursue goals where our strengths give us an advantage and our weaknesses don't matter'

The hard work and determination myth

The idea that we can do and achieve anything we put our minds to is deeply alluring. Who wouldn't want to believe that their potential to pursue ambitious goals is limited by their imagination?

This is well intentioned, and it's meant to make us feel good. But it's incorrect. The insinuation that being able to do anything is a simple matter of putting our minds to it suggests that being unable to excel at a task is merely a product of not trying hard enough.

Even with the most determined spirit, no amount of extraordinary courage will allow me to fly. It is not because I'm not brave or haven't tried hard enough. It is because I'm a human being, born with arms and legs, and not wings. Neither do I possess the hand-eye coordination to be a Royal Air Force fast-jet fighter pilot nor the IQ required to become a Cambridge University mathematics professor. Even if I dig deep and really set my mind to it, the hardware issue with my brain and body won't change.

In any discipline there will be minimum thresholds our strengths must meet in order to be eligible for excellence. The likes of Usain Bolt, Jamie Dimon (Chairman and CEO of JP Morgan Chase), and best-selling author JK Rowling (Author of the best-selling book series in history, Harry Potter) all had the strengths required to be world class in their craft. However, possessing the hardware was not the decisive factor, but a necessary buy - in that qualified them for the success they went on to achieve.

'In any discipline there will be minimum thresholds our strengths must meet in order to be eligible for excellence'

There were many other individuals scattered around the planet with equivalent or superior genetic profiles that would have enabled them to emulate their achievements. The reasons these unknowns didn't excel like Bolt, Dimon and Rowling is due to a whole host of other factors that will all become clear as we progress through this book.

Strengths alone cannot predict who will reach the top, but they can predict who will never win a gold medal, run a bank, nor write a masterpiece. This is not the same as saying that we can't get really good if we don't meet the minimum requirements. We can. But to become the very best we must identify goals where we have the strengths required to excel.

'To become the very best we must identify goals where we have the strengths required to excel'

Responsiveness to training

The greater our strengths, the greater our responsiveness to training. When we're using our natural strengths, the pathways in the brain are already there. It's a lot easier for our brain to build on the wiring that already exists than to develop it from scratch. Therefore those who excel at the start of training improve faster as the training progresses - it's a case of the best get better.

'The greater our strengths, the greater our responsiveness to training'

Learning anything such as writing code, to throwing a left-hook, or derivatives trading, requires us to process the steps involved in our mind. Someone with less natural strength will have to stick with the steps for longer. They'll experience linear growth. They will get the activity just enough to be functional, just enough to hang on, but lack the hardware required to develop the trajectory required to truly excel. This shows the powerful compounding effect in action.

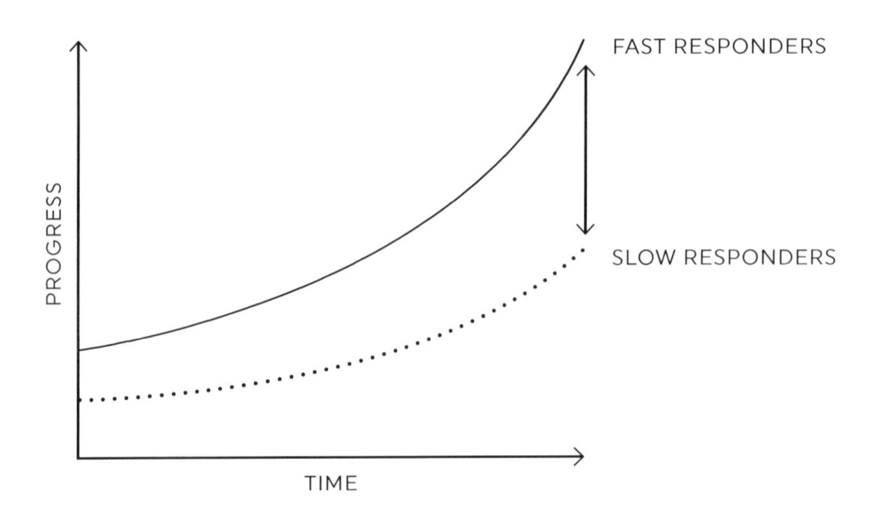

If Person A learns two units of progress in a session and Person B only acquires one unit of progress, those small differences amplify fast over time. Very quickly Person A will be so far ahead that Person B will never catch Person A up. The more complex the skill, the more amplified this effect is.

Stacking strengths

If you look at a standard bell curve, average people make up that big peak in the middle. We do not have to be in the 99th percentile, the majority of us will be average at most things. But, when it comes to strengths the further to the right they are the better.

If you're thinking, 'I don't have any off-the-charts strengths', you don't need to panic. You don't have to be exceptional in one area. David Beckham's right foot, Picasso's right hand, or Mozart's perfect pitch are not necessarily what we're looking to emulate. An insane level of strength in a single area is just one way to excel. Good

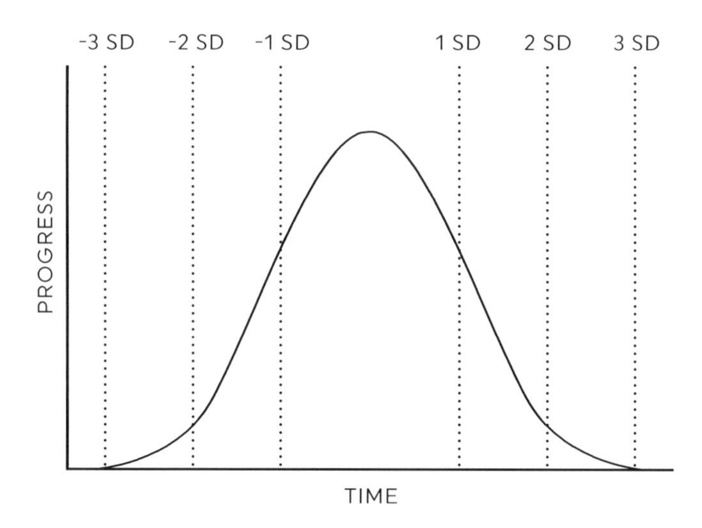

plus good can equal excellent. In many cases having a number of complementary strengths is better than being excellent at one.

'In many cases having a number of complementary strengths is better than being excellent at one'

The late former chairman, CEO and co-founder of Apple, Steve Jobs, was not world class at engineering, sales, or design. But he was good at all three and was able to weave engineering, sales and design into something far greater than the sum of the component parts. Another powerful demonstration of the compounding effect. The fusing of good strengths to create exceptional is how most excel.

When we understand that strengths have the potential to be layered, it is possible to understand the infinite variety of ways in which human beings have the potential to excel: something we can witness just by looking at the world around us.

'When we understand that strengths have the potential to be layered, it is possible to understand the infinite variety of ways in which human beings have the potential to excel'

Two types of strength

We have two types of strengths: technical strengths and personality strengths.

Technical strengths

Technical strengths are abilities that typically have a strong biological loading: perfect pitch in music, a specific athletic ability (speed, strength, endurance), or a specific type of intelligence (words, numbers, patterns). Traditionally we focus on technical strengths, just like Gareth Bale and his coaching team did.

Anything less than a rigorous assessment of athletic ability in sport would be absurd. Assessing these technical strengths gives us a crucial indicator of our potential to excel. It's not that one strength is better than another, but that one strength more readily fits one goal more than another. For example, size 15 feet are like a dolphin's tail fin when it comes to generating forward momentum in a swimming pool, but are not so useful when it comes to controlling a 22cm football.

'It's not that one strength is better than another, but that one strength more readily fits one goal more than another'

This is why physical test batteries are used to screen athletes for high potential. These include anthropometry (the measurements and proportion of the body) as well as tests for the various components of fitness; flexibility, power, strength, endurance, co-ordination, and cardio-vascular fitness. The score acts as a predictor for success that can accurately suggest whether you have a higher probability to excel in a given role. A height of 2.10 is one indication of potential to excel in basketball like Lebron James. A high VO2 max score (cardio-vascular fitness) is an indication of the potential to excel as a middle-distance runner like double Olympic champion Sir Mo Farah. Enough flexion in our ankles implies we have the potential to excel in ballet like Dame Darcey Bussell, former Principal Dancer at the Royal Ballet.

In the knowledge-working world, the same rigorous assessment on cognitive ability is conducted at many companies. Cognitive test batteries measure strengths like verbal fluency, abstract logical, and numerical abilities. These also act as predictors for success. High numerical reasoning implies high potential for working with numbers. Strong language and verbal skills might indicate potential excellence in a career that involves communication. A high score in abstract, logical reasoning is an indication of potential to excel in problem-solving roles.

Personality strengths

We each have a natural way of thinking and behaving. Gareth Bale's innate desire to attack meant he couldn't hold himself back when opportunities were presented to him. Personality strengths are another component of our pre-programmed hardware. These traits are often the missing part of the puzzle in elite performance, and by undermining their power, we create a blind spot that has the potential to significantly undermine performance.

> ***Note:*** Whenever we find ourselves scratching our heads trying to understand why someone delivers mediocre performance despite their enormous technical gifts like Gareth Bale did, it's probably because they have neglected to align their personality make-up with their role.

The important point here is that the conditions that allow one person to flow will cripple another. My personality strengths include the following: I'm outgoing, great at getting things started, optimistic, and enjoy being busy. I'm excited about imagining possibilities; I'm also high energy and like to have fun, which can have a motivating effect on others. I see problems as a big puzzle and like to read between the lines to find the deeper meaning of things and I learn best through conversation. I'm in my sweet spot when I have the freedom to drive things forward, be involved in creative projects, promoting ideas, motivating and leading others. I need discussion, debate, and ultimately action to get the best out of myself.

'The conditions that allow one person to flow will cripple another'

My weaknesses include the fact I am terrible at finishing things, prone to taking on too much, and sometimes can be too optimistic. I am poor at tasks that require detailed focus, and on too many occasions I run with the first idea, I can end up people-pleasing and in the process lose track of my own goals, and I can expect too much from others. I get pulled out of my sweet spot when I have to be involved in time keeping, looking after everyone, keeping views to myself, learning through textbooks, examining detail, patient listening, and project management.

Knowing this, my objective becomes pursuing goals where my strengths are an advantage, and my weaknesses don't matter.

Managing weaknesses

When it comes to the hard work and determination narrative Conor McGregor describes the things we perceive to be hard work are in fact usually weaknesses we must overcome in order to reach the minimum threshold required to advance.Of course it's possible to develop talent where little exists, but we have to work harder, for longer to compensate for our lack of strength in the area, and that is when we start to feel the grunt, graft and grind, which increases the odds of apathy setting in.

> 'It's possible to develop talent where little exists, but we have to work harder, for longer to compensate for our lack of strength in the area'

We need to avoid focusing too much on our deficiencies. Of course we need to manage our vulnerable areas, especially those that hold us back. But weaknesses need to be managed not mastered. Once we acknowledge that we are terrible at something, doors open for working around the issue at hand. Here are some options:

> 'Weaknesses need to be managed not mastered'

- Option one - Stop doing it

  In an ideal world if something is a weakness, stop doing it. Consider whether it is necessary to operate in this area in the first place. Perhaps assign the task to a person or organisation that possesses strengths in that area? Batman had Robin, Iron man had Pepper Potts and Superman had Jimmy Olsen. No person is an island. We need a team that is strong where individuals are weak. The art of combining strengths to achieve a goal that could not be achieved by either person alone is the essence of teamwork. In this case, one plus one equals three.

- Option two - Schedule more time

If the luxury to stop, or delegate doesn't exist, we must learn to manage the weakness, not overcome it. Another way forward when forced to perform in a weaker area is to schedule more time. Addressing things when we're well rested, and full of energy and willpower, is one sensible strategy.

- Option three - Minimum Effective Dose

When engaging in weaker areas is unavoidable, always do so with the concept of Minimum Effective Dose (MED) in mind.

Tim Ferriss:

(Best-selling author and productivity expert):

'To boil water, the minimum effective dose is 100 degrees Celsius at standard air pressure. Boiled is boiled. Higher temperatures will not make it more boiled. Higher temperatures just consume more resources that could be used for something else more productive.'[12]

For example, if we're terrible at public speaking, we can communicate with videos and interactive exercises that reduce the need for us to actually speak. When it comes to weaknesses the smallest effort required to produce a result is sufficient.

The Strengths Appraisal

We are about to examine your life, dissecting it so it informs you. You're going to be asked questions. Pay attention to subtleties. Be honest and as specific as possible. Although the focus in this chapter is to elicit your strengths, some of the answers to their respective questions will intersect and overlap with your interests and values, the same way they converge to form your sweet spot. That's fine.

Don't jump to making assumptions. The goal initially is to accurately identify where our sweet spot really is. Not to think about potential careers. We need to move beyond 'I'm good at math, so I should be an accountant,' or 'I like the gym, so I should be a personal trainer'. Until we are clear on what our strengths, interests and values really are, we simply won't be able to optimise the goals we decide to pursue and the way that we pursue them. The same strengths can be applied through an infinite combination of interests and values.

> ***Note:*** A strength is an inner ability that can be performed or actioned. Advantages are material. A degree from Oxford University, a million-dollar inheritance, or the fact you live in London are advantages, not strengths. Whilst they might provide knowledge, networks or opportunities a strength is required to capitalise on the advantage.

1. Where do you excel versus the rest?

Usain Bolt:

'I remember running the 400-metre finals in an inter-schools meet and for a while I was neck and neck with the fastest other kid in the lanes... He was sprinting alongside me, giving everything he had. The veins were popping in his neck, I swear his eyes were on stalks with all the effort [At this point in time Usain hadn't had a single hour of formal sprint training]... I hadn't even got into second gear. As I came off the corner I looked over and smiled, "Yo, later," I shouted and showed him a clear pair of heels.' [13]

Blowing the rest of the competition away is one of the most obvious signs of a strength. With this in mind, reflect back to the early stages of any skill endeavour, be it from school, sport, professional training, or even social situations, general reading and discussion.

Perhaps it is telling a story with a swelling arc and active dialogue. Maybe you are always the one who rises to a threat, thriving in conflict when others shrink? Or did you launch the javelin twice the distance of anyone else or dust people in the 1,500m?

- Where have you experienced that 'I just know how to do this' feeling?
- Where have you cruised like Usain Bolt where others were popping veins?
- Are there things you intuitively know how to do?

2. Where have you experienced rapid learning?

Elon Musk:

'It had four games you could play, and you would pick which of the four you wanted to play,' he said. 'That was it. And then it went from there to the Atari and Intellivision. And then one day I was in the store, and I saw a Commodore VIC-20. And I was like, 'Holy cow! You can actually have a computer and make your own games.' I thought this was just one of the most incredible things possible.'[14]

When Elon Musk, the man who built four multi-billion companies by his mid-forties in four separate fields (software, energy, transportation, and aerospace) bought his Commodore VIC-20 he stayed up for three days and learned the BASIC programming language course that was supposed to take six months.[15]

It's not always the people who start out the smartest who end up the smartest. Some people are like a set of explosives awaiting someone to light the fuse. What might appear as not that gifted could become a very different picture after some initial training.

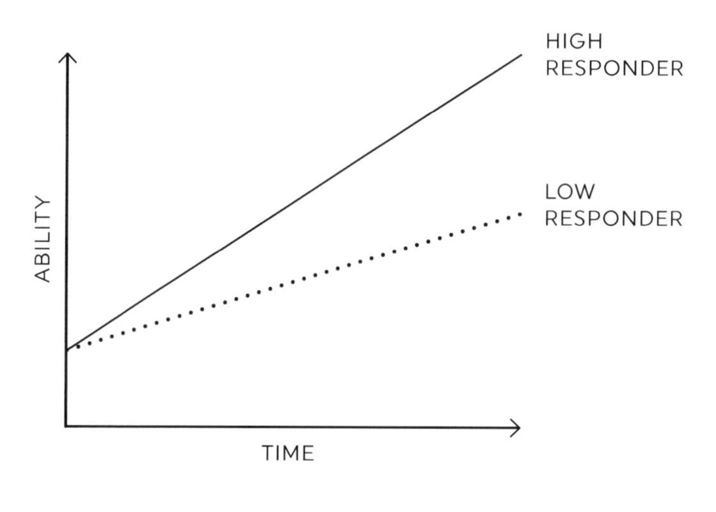

Instead of looking at snapshots of elite performance, which are great for identifying high baseline strengths, we can also look at the development trajectory of our ability over a series of performances.

Maybe your first essay at university ranks bottom half of the class, but the second was mid table, the third was in the top three, and the fourth obtains the number one spot. This means that you are a high responder to essay writing. Maybe your child just picked up how to play the piano, or you're someone who goes to Spain for a week and comes back fluent in Spanish.

- Where you have had rapid learning?
- What do you pick up quickly?
- In what areas are you a high responder?

3. Where have you had moments of excellence?

Milton Friedman:

'Son, I really appreciate you sending this to me. While I agree with some of your points, you're wrong about a, b, c and d, and there's some faulty logic here and there.'[16]

After writing an exceptional paper on Nobel Prize-winning economist Milton Friedman's capitalism and freedom during his economics degree, Jamie Dimon was encouraged by his professor to send the paper to Friedman himself. The famous economist was so impressed he took the time to respond with an eight-page letter critiquing Jamie Dimon's critique.[17]

A moment of excellence does not have to mean the extreme, like a stadium full of people chanting your name, a Nobel prize, or New York Times best-seller. Praise can be a lot subtler: a nod from the coach, a pat on the back from a teammate, or 'nice one' uttered by a colleague. Activities that invoke the respect and admiration of others are signs of a strength.

Activities that invoke the respect and admiration of others are signs of a strength.

Even infrequent and sporadic moments of excellence are valid demonstrations of natural strength breaking out from inside. If we can do it once, the strength is there, and this means we can do it a thousand times should we wish. Even if it was a two-minute cameo in a role, arena, or organisation you despise; even if it happens once a month, year, or decade, it is still a sign of a strength. That's all we're after for now, so capture it.

'If we can do it once, the strength is there, and this means we can do it a thousand times should we wish'

Maybe your enthusiasm injected people with energy. It could be that your detailed analysis saved the day. Perhaps your charisma and charm pushed the deal over the line.

- Looking back, where do you receive praise?
- What did you do well?
- When have there been eruptions of genius?

4. What frustrates you?

Jamie Dimon:

'College is a lot like camp without the counsellors. You have to wake yourself up in college. You have to make sure you do the homework yourself.'[16]

Jamie Dimon studied at Tufts University, where he majored in psychology and economics. He found his university experience frustrating; in his opinion, too many of the students didn't take it seriously enough and this made his blood boil. He went on to excel academically and graduate summa cum laude.

The next time someone or something frustrates you, draw breath and release with a heavy sigh, pause, and be grateful, because they have just indicated a strength you possess. Given that strengths are pre-existing capacities, they feel natural to us. We presume everyone else can do the same, or we expect they should. This results in frustration and impatience when they can't. The downside is that it's easy to fall into the trap of not recognising the strength as anything special. This is why so many of us take our strengths for granted.

If pessimistic people get on our nerves, it may be a sign that we have a strength for optimism, that we expect the best and work to achieve it. If people who constantly push boundaries annoy us, this could allude to a strength for making careful, considered choices, and not saying or doing things that might later be regretted. Or maybe we get frustrated working with a new team where all is haphazard and nothing happens on time; this could point us toward having order and organisation as a strength.

- What annoys you?
- When do you get frustrated?

- When are you most impatient?

5. What are your weaknesses?

JK ROWLING:

'(Reflecting on her role as a secretary) I am one of the most disorganised people in the world and, as I later proved, the worst secretary ever... I was never paying much attention in meetings because I was usually scribbling bits of my latest stories in the margins of the pad, or choosing excellent names for the characters.'[18]

Note: All JK Rowling ever liked about working in offices was being able to type up stories on the computer when no one was looking.

A weakness usually has a strength as a silver lining. There is duality between strengths and weaknesses, a connection we can use for clues. The opposite of a weakness generally points towards a strength. JK Rowling's lack of organisation points us to her creativity for building fascinating storylines.[19]

So what if we're pessimistic, that also makes us more realistic. If we are terrible with numbers maybe we're maestros with words. Or are we inept with technology, but fantastic with people?

- What are our biggest weaknesses?
- What's the opposite of each weakness?
- Where is the strength?

6. Where do you feel confident?

Anon Classmate[Jamie Dimon]:
'Imagine 80 or 90 people, most of them feeling insecure, that they were an admission mistake or some sort. And then Jamie raises his hand and says to the professor, 'You've made a mistake.' Everyone froze. We all thought he was committing suicide. But Jamie walked up to the board and changed a few things and the next thing you know the teacher said, "Oh my god, you're right." There was a confidence with no fear.'[16]

Note: Jamie was famous at Harvard Business School for his inclination to challenge his professors. Another day in class at Harvard, he challenged his lecturer on his suggestion that investing in a long-term zero coupon bond that had a 15% yield to maturity was a bad idea.

Jamie Dimon:
'If you don't see the merits of investing in our 15% coupon bond, Professor Light, then you probably shouldn't be teaching this class.'[16]

Dimon's powerful independent streak when it came to economics was another potential sign that it was a subject that came naturally to him.

When we are using our strengths we will usually feel high conviction in any activities that involve that strength. It makes us feel confidence in overcoming challenges, confidence in performing well, and pride in exerting effort and competing in that area.

- Where and when are you most confident?
- When is your conviction highest?
- Where are you prepared to confront others like Jamie Dimon did?

Tools

Tool one- Cognitive test batteries

A cognitive test battery exposes us to a variety of exercises that assess our cognitive abilities and determine which percentile of the population we fall into. Completing a set of cognitive test batteries will give an indication of where we excel naturally. Using our cognitive strengths gives us an enormous head start in succeeding in our fields. Or in contrast, reveals a hill to climb. The result is a report that suggests the types of cognitive tasks and activities that the science suggests we have the most potential to excel in.

- I recommend: https://www.cognifit.com/cognitive-assessment

Tool two- Psychometrics

There are a number of great psychometrics tests out there. Psychometric just means measuring psychological variables. They take the form of a series of questions which invite people to agree or disagree with a series of statements that are then combined in particular ways to establish our personality strengths to a greater or lesser degree. A detailed report is compiled that predicts how we can optimise which goals we pursue based on our psychological strengths, and how we can potentially shape the way we perform to leverage these strengths.

- I recommend: https://www.123test.com/personality-test/

CHAPTER SUMMARY

- Strengths refer to a pre-disposed high baseline or responsiveness to training.
- The greater our strengths, the greater our responsiveness to each bout of training. It's a case of the best get better.
- In any discipline there will be minimum strength thresholds we must meet in order to be eligible for excellence.
- Our strengths don't eliminate hard work; they clarify what to work hard on.
- The reality is that we can (and should) try anything we wish to try, but real excellence will elude us unless we determine early on the things we have pre-existing strengths for.
- It's not that one strength is better than another, but that one strength more readily fits one pursuit than another.
- Technical strengths are abilities that typically have a strong biological loading: perfect pitch in music, a specific athletic ability (speed, strength, endurance), or a specific type of intelligence (words, numbers, patterns).
- Personality strengths are another component of our pre-programmed hardware. We each have a natural way of thinking and behaving and the conditions that allow one person to flow will cripple another.
- An extreme strength in a single area is just one way to excel. In many cases having a number of complementary skills is better than being excellent at one.

- The things we perceive to be hard work are usually weaknesses we must overcome. Weaknesses need to be managed not mastered: Where possible stop doing it, where not possible schedule more time, or minimum effective dose it.

5

DISGUISING REPETITION

The most powerful weapon on earth is the
human soul on fire

Ferdinand Foch

Interests: The feeling of wanting to know or learn
about something

You don't need to motivate a child to play, and that's where interests always begin; with a sense of play. Like an internal magnet, our interests draw us towards certain things.

Elon Musk:

'It's remarkable how many things you can get to explode. Saltpeter, sulphur, and charcoal are the basic ingredients for gunpowder, and then if you combine a strong acid with a strong alkaline, that will generally release a lot of energy. Granulated chlorine with brake fluid- that's quite impressive,' he explains. 'When I was a kid, I built model airplanes, train sets, rockets, explosives, a radio, lots of software. Built a primitive MRI machine in college.'[20]

Note: As a child Elon Musk would engage in dangerous experiments involving explosives and rocket building. He admits his interests were a little on the dangerous side and how shocked he is to have kept all his fingers.

Outliers like Usain Bolt, Jamie Dimon and JK Rowling might exceed the minimum thresholds for strengths in their respective fields, but if they fail to possess sincere interest in the craft then those strengths count for nothing. JK Rowling had the strengths to excel in writing crime, Jamie Dimon could have excelled as a politics major, and Usain Bolt as a 400m runner. But when we pursue goals in areas in which we have limited interest, we exponentially reduce the psychological fire-power we bring to the party. Interests dictate where we decide to deploy our strengths. The question is what game do we elect to play?

'You don't need to motivate a child to play, and that's where interests always begin; with a sense of play'

Interests are instinctual, which means they are an ancient part of us. Humans have had interests as long as we've had thirst and hunger. Instincts lie deep in the hypothalamus, the unconscious part of the brain that is responsible for maintaining the body's internal balance and mood. This is why interests reveal themselves to us, just like the feelings for thirst or hunger.

We don't get to pick our interests, they pick us. There is an intrinsic desire that draws us to engage in a certain activity.

The instinctual attractiveness of the interest reveals an internal compulsion that sustains our continued involvement. We engage in our interests freely for no other reason than it feels enjoyable and natural.

'We don't get to pick our interests,
they pick us'

The reward of the interest is the interest itself, it disguises repetition, like an anaesthetic to the pain of unrelenting immersion in one single area. Engaging in the interest will feel like play to us; we just want to be close to it, in it, or around it. This enables us to become the gym rat; where we're first in, and last out. We feel at home when we're pursuing our interests. There is no clock watching, daydreaming nor going through the motions.

'The reward of the interest is the interest itself, it disguises repetition, like an anaesthetic to the pain of unrelenting immersion in one single area'

The roots of our interests are deep, stable and consistent. This results in energising emotions, such as excitement, enjoyment, and pride in our accomplishments. We become absorbed in the task without the constant need to reflect on its significance, costs, or rewards. This gives us staying power. Enabling us to exert consistent effort in a particular direction.

When we're interested in an area, we're not content with our current level of knowledge or ability. This is why interests fuel curiosity-based exploration. This manifests as an intense desire to understand our craft. We pursue information vigorously with the aim of forming an accurate knowledge base, testing what we know, and acquiring new information to expand our competencies in that area.

Trying things out and failing is an inescapable part of the learning process. For most it's a miserable grind. But not when we are truly interested. This is an example of how those who are interested can out-struggle the rest. We still get frustrated and impatient at times, but just as there are healthy and unhealthy bacteria, this type of frustration and impatience is psychologically nutritious. In fact, we may even find ourselves breaking things down, so we can build them back up in a better way.

'Those who are interested can out-struggle the rest'

We must be aware of passions. If passions are an affair, then interests are a marriage. To excel, we need a marriage. When the passions approach plays out over time, it doesn't work. Why? Because we can't compound passion over time; it's never around long enough. Passion is an expedient and transient emotional state. It sends us chasing idealistic bliss through the mindless impulses of our animal nature. This leads us astray, bouncing us from one thing to another as we lustfully seek the next high that inevitably fades. Sacrificing the future for the present we end up squandering our ambition, talent and effort on dead ends.

Interests Appraisal

Reflecting on, and evoking, our interests is the next part of the self-assessment. The good news is we already know our interests; we're just choosing to ignore them for one reason or another.

The problem is not always a lack of awareness for our interests.

The problem is sometimes perception. As you reflect on the following questions forget whether or not the interest appears practical or realistic. If something opaque comes up like fishing, salsa dancing, or Lego, just capture it.

1. What moments have gripped you?

Kevin Costner:

> 'As I approached my senior year, I had a real talk with myself about what I wanted to do and whether I just wanted to please other people,' he comments 'And it was at that moment that I actually said to myself, "I'm interested in storytelling."' He continued 'If you want to look at a high point in my life, it wasn't a movie,' he said 'It was that internal talk I had with myself, where I said I'm burning my ships like Cortes, and I am going to go where my heart wants to go… and I'm not going to be caught up in trends and what's popular.'[21]

Two-time Academy Award winner, three-time Golden Globe Award winner, and Emmy Award winning actor and film-maker Kevin Costner describes the moment his interest in film gripped him.

When we are exposed to a real interest our brain lets us know, 'yes, this feels right, let's do more of this.' Like a thirst we have to quench. Our hypothalamus is like an internal barometer, trying to guide us on to target, but we have to learn to listen to it.

'Our hypothalamus is like an internal barometer, trying to guide us on to target, but we have to learn to listen to it' '

When the brain triggers thirst or hunger we still have to take the action required to eat and drink. The instinctual purpose of the interest is to facilitate us becoming the potential everything we can be. Our interests guide us as we go, drawing us closer and closer to where we are optimised.

'The instinctual purpose of the interest is to facilitate us becoming the potential everything we can be'

- ▶ Reflect on what grips your attention?
- ▶ What has jumped out at you?
- ▶ What things do you notice?

2. What ideas just pop into your head?

JK Rowling:

'The idea came out of nowhere, and I could see Harry clearly, this scrawny little boy.' She stated that the idea of 'all the details bubbled up in my brain, this scrawny, black-haired, bespectacled boy who didn't know he was a wizard became more and more real to me.' Rowling went on to explain, 'I can't describe the excitement to someone that doesn't write books except to say, it was that incredibly elated feeling that you get when you meet someone you might fall in love with, that was the feeling I had.' [22,23]

This is how interests work, they reveal themselves when we least expect them. The excitement JK Rowling experienced to pursue an idea that seemingly came from nowhere is the evolutionary mechanism that prompts us to take action.

Sometimes interests announce themselves in the form of ideas that just pop into our heads. They ignite a spark that moves us into action. We might not be able to rationally explain why x, y, or z just popped into our heads, it just did. And that's all we need to know.

- What ideas announce themselves to you the way Harry announced himself to Rowling?
- What fills you with excitement?
- What ideas and possibilities pop into your head?

3. Where do you take action?

Kevin Costner:

'I remember thinking, "Well, there's got to be a prince in it. I'll just be the prince" I made that leap.' He didn't get the part, 'but that only increased my desire to find out about this profession' [24]

Sitting bored in his accounting class, flicking through the student newspaper, Costner switched off and turned his attention to the student newspaper, on the back of it there was some advertising to audition for a play called Rumpelstiltskin. Something about it excited Costner. Despite no prior acting experience, a near-death road traffic accident on the way and having to hitch-hike to the audition, Kevin Costner actually turned up and auditioned for the part.

When we're interested, we make it happen, we clamber over

the obstacles, and get it done. Like an internal magnet, interests have a pull or attraction that influences us to act, to go and build something; to take a class, write a blog, or start a business, despite the obstacles.

'Like an internal magnet, interests have a pull or attraction that influences us to act'

At some point we have all thought, I'd love to learn to dance, do wine tasting, or write a book. However, if we haven't taken specific action in the direction of the activity, chances are dancing, wine, and writing are not sincere interests for us.

It is worth noticing that whenever we hear ourselves say, 'I tried to do it,' understand that what we tried to do probably isn't that important to us. Every time we force ourselves to do something that just does not fit who we really are, we will always unconsciously rebel. What is truly important is what we actually do or have done. That's why we kept doing it.

'Every time we force ourselves to do something that just does not fit who we really are, we will always unconsciously rebel'

Maybe we say, 'We should throw a party,' and find ourselves at the helm of party-planning? Have you tried golf and found yourself at the driving range more than you expected? Maybe you have taken up fitness and are now spending your evenings educating yourself on exercise physiology?

- What do you talk about that you also make happen?

- What things have you gone the extra mile for to make happen?
- What always gets done?

4. What things have momentum?

Kevin Costner:

> 'I wasn't good at academics, but when I hit on acting, everything changed. I started to study. I was on fire. I had found my place. I wasn't guessing anymore at what it was.'[24]

Kevin switched from accounting to film studies at California State University. The first day of class he had already read the entire book. One night class a week turned into two nights a week, turned into three, turned into four. He didn't want to improve in accounting, but in acting he was determined to go to school, he found something he wanted to learn. This desire to move forward and expand knowledge is the classic sign of an interest.

Remember, interests disguise repetition, which is what allows us to clock repetitions for free in terms of willpower spent. This is why interests have such a compounding effect.

- Where have you turned up and already read the book?
- Where have you pulled all-nighters with a smile on your face?
- What would you be prepared to go to school for?

5. Where do you find outcomes don't matter?

Kevin Costner:

'We don't have to get to the ending, but if we think we're on the right trail, we're kind of ok. I wait for the big "No" to hit me, and when it doesn't, I keep going…' Costner adds 'I don't give up. I'm a plodder. People come and go, but I stay the course.' He continues 'Being engaged in what you do will sustain you.'[24]

Acting is a notoriously tricky profession in which to succeed. Costner was going up against up against Sean Penn, Nicholas Cage, Ken Wahl, Mel Gibson and Richard Gere who had twenty plus films behind them before he had even started. Maintaining sanity against these types of odds is only possible when we're sincerely interested. When it's only about the outcomes, the pressure eventually causes most sane people to implode.

We know that the interest is the reward itself. This means risks become less threatening and we care less about the odds we face. External motivators lose their grip, be it money, people pleasing or the threat of punishment.

- Where have you engaged in activities for no reward other than the enjoyment that activity brings you?
- Where have you applied yourself with no expectations of reward?
- What activity, to you, is the reward itself?

6. When do you feel free?

Ed Sheeran:

'My Uncle Jim told my dad that Eminem was the next Bob Dylan — it's pretty similar, it's all just storytelling — so my dad bought me 'The Marshall Mathers LP' when I was nine years old, not knowing what was on it," he told the crowd. "I learned every word of it, back to front, by the time I was ten. He raps very fast and melodically and percussively, and it helped me get rid of the stutter.' [25]

As a young boy Ed Sheeran had a surgery that went wrong and left him with a lazy eye and severe speech problems. He was bullied at school, mainly for his stutter and oversized NHS glasses, so he soon stopped participating in class. Surprisingly, that wasn't the case when it came to music. Sheeran enjoyed singing in the local church and has said that playing the guitar in his room was the only time he felt in control.

One day his father bought him Eminem's *Marshall Mathers* album. Amazed by how fast Eminem was rapping, Sheeran was inspired and he learned every word of that album by the age of ten. He began to write his own music, and suddenly his stutter faded away. Eventually it was gone for good.[26]

When we pursue our interests there is a feeling of contentment. They shift us to a place where we feel free, where the weight of the world comes off our shoulders, and everything becomes possible.

- What activities fill you with a sense of peace and solace?
- What feels comforting to you?
- Where have you experienced these feelings of freedom, even if only momentarily?

7. What have been consistent themes across your life so far?

Gary Vaynerchuk:

'I was making signs, for five to seven hours a day, as a seven year old, walking in the streets of New Jersey, sitting on corners, watching cars drive by and trying to legitimately figure out which tree or which sign, which bush, or what angle their eyes were looking at while they were driving, and where to put my sign. I did not learn that in college, I did not learn that by watching a keynote video on YouTube, I did not learn that by reading a Seth Godin book, I learned it because it was inherently in me.'[27]

Note: This quote from best-selling author, entrepreneur, and marketing icon Gary Vaynerchuk demonstrates how his interest in people's attention has been a consistent theme throughout his life that he continues to excel in today, albeit digitally, through his company VaynerMedia.

The ability to differentiate real interests from transient passions (which go in the hobby basket) is that they will have a sense of consistency. A key feature of our interests is the staying power they bring. It took Kevin Costner six years to get hired for his first film. JK Rowling also spent six years writing her first Harry Potter novel.

- What have you stuck with, that with a little more attention could spiral into something special?
- What activities have been permanent features across your life?
- Where were you plotting adventures, painting pictures, or losing yourself in strategic games?

8. Where have you engaged in people pleasing?

JK Rowling:

'Certainly the first story I ever wrote down (when I was five or six) was about a rabbit called Rabbit… He got the measles and was visited by his friends, including a giant bee called Miss Bee. And ever since Rabbit and Miss Bee, I have wanted to be a writer, though I rarely told anyone so.' She expands, 'I was convinced that the only thing I wanted to do, ever, was to write novels. However, my parents, both of whom came from impoverished backgrounds and neither of whom had been to college, took the view that my over-active imagination was an amusing personal quirk that would never pay a mortgage, or secure a pension.'[28]

Too many of us ignore our interests, to conform to what our families, friends, or society expect of us. Many children are heavily influenced by their parents' opinions. The problem is that professions change so rapidly. The booming careers ten years from now are not today's career day staples.

Children today dream of becoming a YouTube superstar or an Esports pro-gamer, the way my generation used to dream of becoming an athlete or Hollywood star. With the best intentions most parents will respond to this type of career aspiration the way Rowling's did, saying, 'that's not a real job,' or smile and say 'great honey, you go for it' secretly shaking their heads at the naiveté of youth.

It's not always others; sometimes we just decide that professional success has to look a certain way. That's exactly how someone born to teach philosophy ends up becoming a lawyer, or someone designed to be a movie critic ends up in investment banking, or the person who cannot go a day without scribbling away ends up as an executive assistant.

- What things you do you fight to suppress in order to please others?
- When you get distracted at work, what by?
- Where does your mind wander?

9. How do you spend your time?

> Douglas Costa:
> 'It's impossible to follow Cristiano Ronaldo at training. When we arrive, he's already training and when we leave he's still training. I've never seen a player like Ronaldo it's unbelievable. It borders on sickness because he always wants to be the best at his job. He competes in everything.'[29]

Note: Douglas Costa is a Brazilian footballer who plays with Cristiano Ronaldo at Italian side Juventus.

Maybe Cristiano is just more interested? There are 168 hours in a week. Where we have total control over how we spend our time we need to delve into what we do.

- We all have to work, so what do you do on your evenings, weekends, and holidays?
- Where do you arrive early?
- When do you stay late?

10. What conversations do you have?

> Christie Nicholson [Friend of Elon Musk]:
> '[The first time we met] I went to [Elon and his brother Kimbal's] apartment, north of the city of Toronto. It was small, there were about 12 people there maybe. I remember it vividly, possibly because I was walking into a room where I knew nobody. It was family and close friends. Literally, we said "Hi," and then two sentences in, he asks me "What do you think about electric cars?"'[30]

Don't just pay attention to the content of the conversation. When we talk about things that really interest us, we are positive, energetic, and engaging. Our body language will be more open and receptive to whomever is willing to engage in conversation, and we'll be more enthusiastic about that conversation, which in turn leads us to learn more through conversation.

We need to pay attention to the tone, flow, and energy of our conversations to see what indicators they may provide for the presence of particular interests. Perhaps we were super busy and then, all of a sudden, an opportunity to speak with someone came up and our schedule opened up.

- Who was that person?
- What was the conversation about?
- Are there topics that you find yourself asking questions about?

11. What books do you read?

Scott Haldeman [Uncle of Elon Musk]:
'Elon never went anywhere without a book in his hand. He was always reading, and it was often advanced books. That was one of the earliest things you started seeing. It was this intense reading, and they were books about the future and about success.'[30]

We seek knowledge in areas in which we are interested. The things we read grip us because they allow us to make contact with our interests. The material that has us hook, line and sinker, shifting the way we think. Or the book we've skimmed so much it's dog-eared with blotches of tea and jam over it. That book points us to an interest. Capture it.

- What books do you actually finish reading?
- On what subject could you read 100 books without getting bored?
- Maybe there are podcasts, non-fiction TV shows or film documentaries that you seek out?

12. What is your physical and digital footprint?

Jeff Heilman [Colleague of Elon Musk]:
'I went to his apartment one time. There was a mattress on the floor in one bedroom, and about 30 Chinese food to-go containers. That was it. Almost as if having an apartment was something you thought you should do because other

people do it, but functionally it had no purpose. It had no purpose because they lived at the office.'[30]

We can look around and notice our interests by the tangible proof of the items around us. It is uncanny how people are busily collecting material things, but don't notice how often one theme is so evident in their homes or offices.

If we searched our web browser history or followed our social media activity and feeds what would we learn about ourselves? Our digital footprint includes information we've deliberately collected and curated, including Facebook, Instagram and LinkedIn endorsements and recommendations, comments, photos, and videos posted. These all offer clues about our interests.

- Look around. What do you see?
- Does your basement house Lego masterpieces, model airplanes, or train sets?
- Who do you follow, like, comment on?

CHAPTER SUMMARY

- Every time we force ourselves to do something that just does not truly interest us, we will always unconsciously rebel.
- Our hypothalamus is like an internal barometer, trying to guide us on to target, but we have to learn to listen to it'.
- We don't get to pick our interests, they pick us. Like an internal magnet, our interests draw us towards certain things.
- We don't need to motivate a child to play. Interests always begin with a sense of play. The reward of the interest is the interest itself.
- If we fail to possess sincere interest in the craft then we exponentially reduce the psychological fire-power we bring to the party.
- Interests are like an anaesthetic to the pain of the unrelenting immersion required to excel that disguise repetition.
- We become absorbed in the task without the constant need to reflect on its significance, costs, or rewards. This gives us staying power.
- When we are exposed to a real interest our brain lets us know, 'yes, this feels right, let's do more of this.'
- We might not be able to rationally explain why x, y, or z interests us, it just does. And that's all we need to know.
- Our interests guide us as we go, drawing us closer and closer to where we are optimised.
- The instinctual purpose of the interest is to facilitate us becoming the potential everything we can be.

6

SACRIFICE, FIGHT AND BELONGING

He who has a why to live for can bear almost any how
Friedrich Nietzsche

Values: The things that are most important to you

Our values are what command, drive, and inspire us. Aligning with our values is what makes us almost impossible to compete with. We bring the blood, sweat, and tears to achieve our goals because doing so fulfils our values. They give us a reason to sacrifice, fight, and to belong to our goal.

Hugo Pina:

'He [Cristiano Ronaldo] would wake up in during the night and go to the gym without making a sound. Two or three times a week. He would go on his own or take a couple of friends. They would jump the fence where the gym was, go up on the roof and get inside it through a window.' Pina continues, 'He would then do weightlifts and run for around forty minutes on the treadmill. He would often get caught because he was not allowed to be there and yet he would go back. He was fourteen! Crazy! He was already playing for a team in the year above (U17) [actually two years above] he did not need to do more! They had to install locks to stop him getting into the gym.'[31]

Note: Hugo Pina was a teammate of Cristiano Ronaldo at Sporting Lisbon's youth academy.

Our values dictate the intensity with which we work, the sacrifices we're prepared to make, and the odds we're prepared to face. Values are way more powerful than logic. They enable us to grunt louder, graft harder and grind longer. We might think we want it easy, but our nature is to seek something to fight for - a cause bigger than ourselves.

'Our values dictate the intensity with which we work, the sacrifices we're prepared to make, and the odds we're prepared to face'

Values prompt us to capitalise on that potential everything we can be through influencing the worth we attach to specific activities. They comprise a set of internal needs we're unconsciously driven to satisfy. Our personal values are a central part of who we are and who we want to be. Values bring the intensity through the release of a formidable desire to act. This manifests in the form of psychological fire-power, the type that drove Cristiano Ronaldo to break into the gym in the dead of night.

The scarcity of time is what makes values so important. Once time has passed, it's gone, and it's gone forever. When we pursue goals that don't align with our values we meander half-heartedly and begin to drift off course. When we are aligned with our values we feel pleasure, when we are in conflict with them we feel anxiety. This is how they keep us on track.

Whether we realise it or not we are constantly deciding how to invest our time, effort and attention. Right now, you are choosing to read this book. There are countless activities you could be engaged in, but right now, you are choosing to be here. This is an example of a simple, values based decision. If your phone rings and it's someone special on the other end, your brain will make a calculation based on your values, and perhaps you'll choose to answer the phone.

Where does it all go wrong?

Too many subordinate who they really are in exchange for the lucrative pay deal, the job title, or to please others. Achievement is a gateway to numerous benefits including power, prestige, and popularity. The car we drive, the likes we receive on Instagram, and the size of our bonus are all symbolic indicators of success, but the danger arises when the benefits become the end in themselves. Many of us adopt goals without taking the time to reflect on what is really important to us beyond the veneer of success that provides us with superficial nourishment that fades fast.

'Too many of us adopt goals without taking the time to reflect on what is really important to us beyond the veneer of success that provides us with superficial nourishment that fades fast'

This works like a child in the school playground saying 'Well, I really love drawing; it's so fun and I'm really good at it, but Premiership footballers are cool and make more money, so I should force myself to play football every lunch time.' Then every day the child comes home and complains how much they hate play time.

When we pursue goals that fail to align with our values we trade out our incentive reward system that catalyses the psychological fire-power we need to excel. Instead our consummatory reward system kicks in. This works the same way as hunger; we get hungry, we eat, we're not hungry anymore, and our motivation shuts down. The product is best described as rat-racing behaviour. We end up in a competitive struggle, full of tension and anxiety, as we attempt to earn rewards, competing ruthlessly against those around us.

Rat-racers are in love with the summit but not the climb. They have no interest in the daily drudgery of practice, the administration required to compete, and the difficulty of finding breakthrough opportunities that constitutes the mile-high climb to the top. Taking the shortest path to achieve their desired outcomes, they cut corners and fail to engage in the deep foundational work from which excellence is built. Rat-racers fast-forward through everything in a sprint to a fictional finish line, and they burn out fast. Getting the promotion, delivering the project, and getting the big bonus, all make them happy. But then what? The happiness fades fast. No one is fist-pumping today about a goal they hit a year ago. Because of all this, they fail to excel.

'No one is fist-pumping today about a goal they hit a year ago'

Status, prestige, money, and praise all matter. They matter to me. But appreciation, compensation and admiration should be the side benefit to achieving what is important and meaningful to us, not the end itself.

The sexy myth

As a society so many of us are obsessed with reality TV, celebrity and other forms of vicarious fantasy. We become mesmerised, pumped high on glory and status by the prestige associated with pursuing culturally elite roles such as athlete, entrepreneur and CEO. The lives of these individuals are depicted as an effortless constant high; the power, money and admiration of it all. The sexy myth fuels a fantasy which we mistakenly confuse with reality. I've worked with the people you may have fantasised about, and I'm telling you they don't have the life you think they do.

'The sexy myth fuels a fantasy which we mistakenly confuse with reality. I've worked with the people you may have fantasised about, and I'm telling you they don't have the life you think they do'

Take, for instance, the Premier League footballer who is paid millions to play the sport they love in front of 50,000 spectators who cheer their name. Maybe it's the Special Forces operator, heroically eliminating the enemies of Her Majesty's Government, jumping out of planes from 30,000 feet to save the day. Don't forget the CEO, dressed in sharp suits, travelling the world in private jets, dining in Michelin star restaurants, with an entourage at their beck and call.

These clichés make up less than five percent of what reality entails. Even then, only those who reach the absolute pinnacle in these endeavours enjoy these benefits. The other 95% is completely different. For the footballer it is intensive training, strict diets, early nights, media scrutiny, and the constant fear that one injury, one tweet, one bad game will mean it's all over. For the Special Forces operator, it's packing kit, checking kit, cleaning weapons, planning ops, cancelled ops, and brutal training demands. The CEO doesn't have it easy either; bureaucracy, regulation, apologising for, and fixing, other people's mistakes, handling demanding board members, trying to retain key staff, media obligations, ceaseless conflict, and sleepless nights.

The sexy moments are few and far between, and they are over in a heartbeat. We spend the majority of our lives in the doing, which is precisely why we need to be doing things with which we are intrinsically aligned. When it comes to money, fame, or glory, we should enjoy them when they come our way, but never confuse these temporary highs with what's really important.

'We spend the majority of our lives in the doing, which is precisely why we need to be doing things with which we are intrinsically aligned'

Values Appraisal

Luckily we each have our own internal barometer, trying to keep us in our sweet spot. We must listen to it. Many of us haven't taken the time to reflect on what our values are. Or we have shoved it down like the child who loves to draw but plays football instead. Before we know it, we're way downstream doing something we didn't intend to sign up for in the first place.

The question we're trying to get to the bottom of here is why do we want to go into medicine, join a start-up or become a Navy SEAL? Is it something we feel obligated to do because it's a prestigious job, or is it something truly important to us?

> ***Note:*** The real values that inspire and motivate us are always much deeper than our first answer. This requires second-level thinking. If we are asked, 'Why do you work?' We might say, 'I work for money.' The second-level question would be 'What do you want the money for?' Freedom? Your family's future? A scorecard? In this example, money isn't the thing that drives you; instead freedom, our family, and competing are our real values.

1. What and who inspires you?

Usain Bolt:

> 'I caught my first glimpse of the Olympics when someone showed me some video footage of the 1996 Atlanta games. That clip blew my mind. It was one of the most amazing things I've ever seen. Man, I want to be somebody like Michael Johnson. I want to be an Olympic gold medallist.'[32]

Figuring out what inspires us most reveals what we value most. Some of the people I am inspired by include, amongst others, psychologist Professor Jordan Peterson, Hedge Fund Manager Ray Dalio, and entrepreneur Peter Diamandis, people who have challenged the status quo, are action-orientated, and contribute through democratising access to their expertise. This question helped me uncover that I value action over talking, putting the principles of my craft to work, and contributing to making things better.

'Figuring out what inspires you most reveals what you value most'

- Who are your heroes and what has inspired you in the past?
- Which peers, friends and family members do you admire?
- What do the people who inspire you have in common?

2. Where do you challenge the status quo?

Rose Marcario:

'The values I try to bring to work are about this belief that people and planet and meaningful work can all work together in a healthy, synergistic ecosystem. Those are the things that will move the world forward. Business could be the biggest positive agent for change - without compromising financial results.' She continues 'As many punches as I've taken about all kinds of stands I've taken publicly, I would do it again in a minute. It's the right thing to do.' [33]

Rose Marcario is the former CEO and President of outdoor clothing company Patagonia. Under her guidance Patagonia has become one of California's first Benefit Corporations (b-corp); donating millions of dollars to grassroots non-profits; hosting annual training for activists in the US and Europe; and building global supply chains around environmentally friendly ingredients. It funded the award-winning documentary film Damnation as part of its environmental advocacy. She even closed Patagonia's doors on Election Day in 2016 to raise awareness about the importance of voting.

For Rose, fixing capitalism, the environment and putting people first are her highest values. Due to the fact that her goal pursuits are so aligned with these values she brings ferocious intensity to challenge the status quo on these matters. Rose was frequently under fire from other CEOs, the media and President Trump due to the way she fought for change.

- When have you stood for something others haven't?
- When have you spoken up, pushed back, raised your voice?
- When have you taken a punch in order to stand by what's important?

3. What have you said no to?

Jamie Dimon:
'My goal in life was not to be an investment banker. I love the concept of helping build a company, the whole painting, something that was yours over a long period of time you can be really proud of.' [34]

Upon graduating from his MBA at Harvard, Goldman Sachs gave Jamie Dimon an opportunity to work at Wall Street's most prestigious and lucrative partnership. Very few people ever refuse this offer. Reflecting on what was more important to him; making the most money or continuing along the fastest learning curve, Dimon decided to go and work at American Express. He knew full well he wouldn't make half of what he'd be making at Goldman. But he would have a far more concentrated and high-pressure job and a real opportunity to build something.

He didn't let the glitter and glamour tempt him away from his true values. Jamie's ambition was to build, not broker deals. By choosing American Express over Goldman Sachs, he set himself apart from the crowd by turning down the status and financial reward most Harvard graduates would have killed for.

Decades later towards the peak of his career, Goldman would come calling again with a lucrative offer.

Jamie Dimon:

'I don't do what I do for compensation.' He commented, 'I'm sixty-one. This is my company. I bleed JPMorgan blood. I won't go anywhere else.'[34]

When anyone, anywhere says no to the highest bidder, like Jamie Dimon did, it is because they are compensated in some other way. Identifying moments where we have done the same points us to another clue to our values.

- Where have you conceded on financial rewards like Jamie Dimon did?
- What did you get in return?
- Where have you said no to opportunities that most others wouldn't or don't?

4. Where do you feel friction?

Rose Marcario:

'I achieved success by my immigrant grandparents' measure (values): a college degree and a professional job. I was CFO of a public company in Silicon Valley when I was in my 30s, and I thought I had arrived.' She adds, 'At the same time, I

> was studying Buddhism and having a whole spiritual life that felt disconnected from my work life… to feel this huge divide between how I was spending the majority of my time and what kind of an impact I wanted to be having in the world.' She continues 'When I left Silicon Valley, they were asking me to be the president of the company, but at the time I couldn't do it. I felt like I would be burying myself deeper into a model I wasn't totally bought into.' Marcario adds, 'It started to feel so disingenuous that I couldn't figure out what to do next. To be honest, I had kind of a mid-life crisis. I quit my job, which was crazy because I was at the height of my career.'[35]

These feelings of friction, guilt or frustration, are common signs that our values are in conflict with our actions. As we satisfy our values, new ones emerge. As Rose Marcario satisfied her value for money and security, her desire to make an impact on the world began to emerge. Remember, when we're off-track, our brains naturally release adrenaline which generates feelings of anxiety to prompt us into taking action. The purpose is to guide us back on course. Examining these moments is a great way to help elicit our values.

> 'When we're off-track, our brains naturally release adrenaline which generates feelings of anxiety to prompt us into taking action. The purpose is to guide us back on course'

- When have you felt off-track?
- Where have you felt friction?
- Where have you felt conflict?

5. When do you feel motivated, driven, and competitive?

Elon Musk:

'I've spent all my money and all of my friendships on this. It has to succeed. You need to do whatever is possible to make this happen - you need to use Special Forces methods to make this transmission happen.'[36]

Dave Lyons [Elon's colleague]:

'I watched in his eyes that night how incredibly invested this guy was. I have never seen anybody in my life who was willing to put everything on the table the way I saw him that night.'[36]

Elon Musk's total commitment characterises how our values generate the intensity required to deliver whatever it takes to maximise our chances of success. This affords outliers like Elon to enact what others might perceive as extreme behaviour.

We don't need probing to do the things we value. Deconstructing the activities, relationships, and goals in which we're disciplined, reliable, and focused will elicit what we value most.

- Where have you put your neck on the line and taken risks?
- In what moments have you forgotten to eat, skipped sleep, and stripped away everything else?
- Where are you most reliable, disciplined, and focused?

6. What do you spend money on?

Rose Marcario:

'Patagonia will owe less in taxes this year [Donald Trump's 2019 tax break]—$10 million less, in fact. Instead of putting the money back into our business, we're responding by putting $10 million back into the planet. Our home planet needs it more than we do.'[37]

As the saying goes, talk to me about what you think you value and I might believe you, show me your finances and I'll tell you. We don't part with money for things that aren't important to us.

'Talk to me about what you think you value and I might believe you. Show me your finances and I'll tell you'

- How would you spend a tax rebate on?
- What do you spend your money on now?
- And what do you always find more money for?

CHAPTER SUMMARY

- When we are aligned with our values we feel pleasure, when we are in conflict with them we feel anxiety. This is how they keep us on track.
- Our values are what command, drive, and inspire us. We bring the blood, sweat, and tears to achieve our goals because doing so fulfils our values. Deep down we all crave a cause to fight for.
- Values give us a reason to sacrifice, fight, and to belong to our goal. The intensity we bring is in direct proportion to how much the goal aligns with our values.
- The scarcity of time is what makes values so important. Every moment of every day, whether we realise it or not, we are deciding how to invest our effort. Our values influence what worth we attach to specific activities.
- Consistent daily happiness is idealistic and detached from reality, but when we pursue goals that fulfil our values, the unrelenting fulfilment they give us is very real.
- Too many subordinate their real values in exchange for the lucrative pay deal, the prestige associated with pursuing culturally elite roles, or to please others.
- Status, prestige, money, and praise all matter. They should be the side benefit to achieving what is important and meaningful to us, not the end itself.
- We spend the majority of our lives in the doing, which is precisely why we need to be doing things with which we are intrinsically aligned. The sexy moments are few and far between, and they are over in a heartbeat.

7

ZERO ONTO TARGET

> The two most important days in life are the day you were born and the day you discover the reason why
>
> Mark Twain

Through taking the time to ask questions, deconstruct and investigate what we do in Chapters Four, Five and Six, the vision inside our heads about who we are and where we fit in should have become clearer. Our sweet spot should no longer be completely hidden from our naked eyes. This understanding empowers us to make more intentional choices about the goals we opt in for and the methods by which we pursue them.

The total overhaul

For some, it might be time for a total overhaul. It's not easy to abandon goals that we had thought were our own. It took a 'mid-life' crisis in her thirties before Rose Marcario stepped out of her well-paid and culturally elite Silicon Valley CFO position. The status quo will have us thinking that we're crazy. The self-help gang will say we just weren't positive enough and recommend we do some affirmations. The performance experts will shout 'no pain, no gain' and tell us that we didn't get up early enough. The reality is that your performance is about you and you are the expert on you. Holding onto pride is the wrong thing to do. Admitting to being off course is the right thing to do. Especially after all the reflection we've just done.

'Your performance is about you and you are the expert on you'

Role shaping

If we're in a situation where we're not concordant with our goals, then we have to focus on what change is possible, because there is always a way to optimise. It goes without saying that we don't get to just quit our jobs or abandon existing commitments.

In the short-term the challenge becomes crafting our roles, and the responsibilities within them, so we can start to leverage our recently uncovered dormant strengths, latent interests and subordinated values. We can adapt a role to fit the person; we can't adapt the person to fit the role.

'We can adapt a role to fit the person; we can't adapt the person to fit the role'

The role we currently find ourselves in is probably not set in stone. Different people can deliver the same outcomes in different ways. Maybe we have to ask for the opportunity to perform our roles the way we think we are optimised or maybe we will have to earn that opportunity.

Better beats perfect

Concordance is a game of better, not a game of perfect. As soon as we have an idea of what concordance looks like for us, we need to try it on. Go and test it. We must start right now with something small, like, switching up our classes, conducting some online research on organisations that share our values, or communicating with management about how we want to craft our role.

> 'Concordance is a game of better, not a game of perfect'

It can be tempting just to sit back until we get this sweet spot thing perfect. Don't. While we sit still trying to get it perfect progress will be accelerating away from us. So, if you're squinting your eyes thinking, 'I'm not sure that's my sweet spot?' The truth is it might not be. The probability is low that we get this perfect the first time around. But we probably will make it better, and better is better.

> ***Note:*** The trickle effect- Pursuing concordant goals, even for a few hours in our evenings or weekends, initiates the trickle effect. Here, the residual confidence, motivation, and resilience can be deployed in other areas of our lives. The key is to just start, no matter how

small, control what we can control, and over time the small things will become big things.

We get sharper as we go

The process of finding our sweet spot is best described as a process of zeroing in on that potential everything we could be. Our precision enhances as we try things out over time. It's not until we try things on that we realise we weren't as interested as we thought we were, or we chance upon a hidden strength that takes us off in a new direction, or maybe the value we thought was really important turns out not to be. This will be frustrating. But recognising what to stop doing is progress.

'Recognising what to stop doing is progress'

As we progress, we start to zero in on the target. With every small step we earn interest on the next. We start to mobilise the compounding effect.

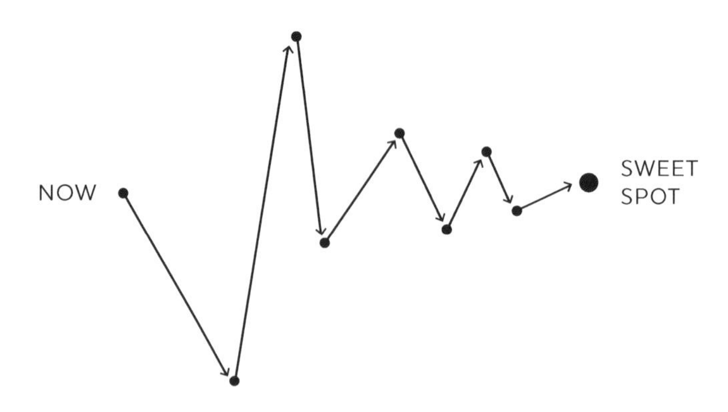

The closer we get, our intuition improves, we magnify our perception, and our psychological fire-power will transition from subtle spark to roaring blaze.

It's like cranking and cranking to get to the top of the rollercoaster, the summation of all those small steps and then WHAM. We step right into the slipstream of exponential progress. Suddenly we explode onto the scene like a tidal wave that seems to have come from nowhere. One day, we look up and there it is- we're an overnight success.

It's not a panacea

Concordance is not an indefinite route to ultimate virtue. There is no such thing. If you think you're supposed to be dealing with rejection, competing against the best, and risking it all like JK Rowling, Jamie Dimon and Elon Musk, and loving every minute of it, you've been scrolling through too many Instagram memes. We're not entitled to love every second of every goal we pursue. I am highly concordant with my goal pursuits and I still hate (on average) about 25% of the doing. Some days more, some less. But the meaning never leaves.

'We're not entitled to love every minute of every goal we pursue'

Keep a finger on the pulse

Concordance is not a permanent thing, it is likely to evolve, and we need to evolve with it, if we are to maximise our development. As we grow we will be pulled in different directions, so to stay concordant we must adapt accordingly. Elon Musk transitioned from software, to cars, to space rockets. Kevin Costner evolved from accountancy, to acting to directing and ultimately to production. We will adapt too.

'Concordance is not a permanent thing, it is likely to evolve, and we need to evolve with it'

Pursuing concordant goals isn't a luxury, it's what we are genetically hard-wired to do. We know that our sweet spots act as our internal barometers guiding us along our paths of maximal development. We must listen to our instincts like they were thirst or hunger signalling what and when to eat.

'Pursuing concordant goals isn't a luxury; it's what we are genetically hard-wired to do'

When we get that nagging feeling that things aren't going to plan, check in, and calibrate. Chances are that we will have slowly deviated away from our sweet spot. There are numerous reasons this can happen; the manager adapting our role, peers changing the culture, or the obligations that come with stardom, to name but a few. Checking in, and restoring alignment is always the antidote.

CHAPTER SUMMARY

- Your performance is about you and you are the expert on you.
- If we're in a situation where we're not concordant with our goals, then we have to focus on what change is possible, there is always a way to optimise.
- The challenge becomes crafting our roles, and the responsibilities within them, so we can start to leverage our dormant strengths, latent interests and subordinated values.
- Concordance is a game of better, not a game of perfect. As soon as we have an idea of what concordance looks like for us, we need to try it on. Go and test it.
- The process of finding our sweet spot is best described as a process of zeroing in on that potential everything we could be.
- The closer we get, our intuition improves, we magnify our perception, and our psychological fire-power will transition from subtle spark to roaring blaze.
- It's like cranking and cranking to get to the top of the rollercoaster, the summation of all those small steps and then WHAM. We step right into the slipstream of exponential progress. Suddenly we explode onto the scene.
- Concordance is not a permanent thing, it is likely to evolve and we need to evolve with it, if we are to maximise our development. To stay concordant we must adapt accordingly.
- Pursuing concordant goals isn't a luxury; it's what we are genetically hard-wired to do. This is not just for accelerating excellence; but also for the sake of maximising our quality of life.

8

TALENT IDENTIFICATION

> No man will work for your interests, unless they are his own
>
> David Seabury

In August 2012 founder and CEO of Mandara Capital, Muwaffaq Salti, studied the menu at Nobu in Mayfair, London, where we were having dinner. Mandara Capital is an oil derivatives trading house set up by the ambitious forward-thinking former Goldman Sachs oil trader.

His objective was to identify and develop a team of superstar oil derivatives traders with whom he could share his trading secrets. Alf's challenge was in identifying concordant performers. Up to this point Mandara had taken on over 15 candidates using traditional talent identification methods, which we'll shortly discuss. Despite great CVs and impressive interviews, however, the candidates just weren't demonstrating the confidence, resilience, and motivation required to excel.

The principles of trading are relatively simple. The crux of it is being able to abide by them at the high intensity and speed at which the market moves, and to keep a cool head in the face of enormous financial risks. The new hires were failing to make the mark. Most became prisoners of their own emotions. They froze when the intensity amplified. That's when I got a crack at the whip and was given an opportunity to build excellence.

Muwaffaq and I set out to maximise our chances of identifying concordant performers, those who would improvise, adapt and overcome the developmental obstacles the trading floor would throw at them. By the summer of 2013 we had hired our first cadre of super-traders. Inside three years, the class of 2013 had exceeded our wildest expectations and put Mandara on the map. The performance metrics of our superstar traders had not only matched the 25-year outlier super-trader, Alf, but in some cases exceeded him.

Mandara had transitioned from a company where 15 hires generated zero profit to having 10 hires who produced $42million in a year. Net. The class of 2013, and subsequent graduates of the Mandara talent programme, have gone on to dominate the oil derivatives space, generating billions in revenue and hundreds of millions in profit. The oil giants Glencore were paying twenty-four-year-old Mandara traders million-pound signing bonuses to switch allegiance and work for them, and guaranteeing bonuses well into the millions.

In 2020 the Mandara alumni continue to dominate the oil derivatives industry. It is estimated that graduates from the Mandara talent pipeline are responsible for over 50% of all the volume traded in the oil derivatives space. Their combined net profit since 2014 is estimated to be over $500million.

The talent identification principles we're about to discuss helped Mandara transition from a one-man show to the world's biggest oil derivatives trading house (by volume) in less than three years. Through leveraging the power of concordant performers, Mandara obliterated the competition in their industry - and you can too.

How to predict a superstar that isn't one yet

In sport, coaches are on the constant look-out for the next Cristiano Ronaldo, Lebron James and Tom Brady, to convert the team from aspirational contender into championship winner. In business, venture capitalists are constantly on the look-out for the entrepreneurs on the cusp of launching the next Facebook, Uber or Amazon.

'Coaches are on the constant look-out for the next Cristiano Ronaldo, Lebron James and Tom Brady, to convert the team from aspirational contender into championship winner'

All over the world in every field, from academia to music, thousands of hours are spent on identifying potential high performers. Many organisations spend millions attracting superstars, only to cough up enormous severance packages to pay off their failures.

It seems exceptionally difficult to spot superstars in any profession. Each domain has its own lingo, culture and heritage, but the talent question torments us all. Failures in talent identification are an ongoing source of angst for many organisations. Getting it wrong leads to job losses, bankruptcy, relegation, plummeting share prices, and hundreds of millions of pounds flushed down the toilet.

Whatever the domain, we all want to find the superstars before our rivals do. There is intense competition to identify and retain the best performers. If we don't unearth Ed Sheeran, Mark Zuckerberg, or JK Rowling, someone else will, or worse, these people may simply choose another path altogether. Ultimately we are looking for a competitive advantage. If we can identify talent more effectively than the competition, we increase the probability of producing winning results.

'If we don't unearth Ed Sheeran, Mark Zuckerberg, or JK Rowling someone else will'

Success is usually recognised at the organisational level; whether it be the inner workings of Google, SpaceX, or Goldman Sachs. But an organisation is just a group of people pursuing a common goal, which is why an organisation is only as extraordinary as its people. Because people are so critical, identifying and retaining talent (concordant performers) is possibly the biggest challenge any organisation faces. One of the best chances of ensuring our organisations excel is to make sure we have the right people pursuing the right goals.

'An organisation is only as extraordinary as its people'

A question I am bombarded with is: 'How can I motivate this person?' This is the wrong question to ask. The real question is: 'How do we create the conditions in which the person will motivate themselves?' How do we identify individuals that will thrive in the realistic conditions they will be exposed to; within the role we're asking them to perform, in the arena we're asking them to do it, and for this specific organisation? In other words, concordant performers.

'A question I am bombarded with is: "How can I motivate this person?" This is the wrong question to ask. The real question is: "How do we create the conditions in which the person will motivate themselves?"'

When we talk about talent we should do so in terms of concordance. The question is: 'How concordant are the performers in our organisation?' Despite our best efforts, do some seem apathetic, spiritless and limp? Or are they energetic, loyal and determined, bursting with creativity, motivation and confidence?

No doubt we all want our organisations to be teeming with concordant performers. But how do we predict future superstars? How can managers hire concordant performers? And do we even know what we're looking for?

Talent identification is basically venture capital. We're making an investment. It's about people, time and money. We all have limited resources (salary caps, effort, management, coaches, squad space). We must apply a filter to decide how to spend those resources on the performers we think will be successful.

'Talent identification is basically venture capital. We're making an investment'

At its root, the problem is prediction. The objective is to learn to predict who is going to become a gold-medal performer in their respective field. Outlier organisations already know this and expend infinitely more effort on screening for concordant performers.

Talent identification pipelines must be created organically, not discovered nor outsourced to a sales team. The problem in business is that we pay millions to recruitment consultants who, in reality, aren't talent identification specialists; most are salespeople.

'Talent identification pipelines must be created organically, not discovered or outsourced to a sales team'

The issue with hiring the wrong people is that we end up having to live with, fix, or fire them. It's only a matter of time before other team members suffer by compensating for their teammates' deficiencies. One weak member results in a devastating reduction in overall performance as teammates are forced to mop up errors, divert attention from their primary role, and re-do work. Most organisations spend a trivial amount of their time, effort and finances on talent identification and the vast majority managing their mistakes.

'The issue with hiring the wrong people is that we end up having to live with, fix, or fire them'

A team's momentum is derived from all the members performing from a place of concordance within their roles. The overarching idea behind teamwork is that the whole is worth more than the sum of its parts; concordant performers standing on the shoulders of each other creating a compounding effect.

'A team's momentum is derived from all the members performing from a place of concordance within their roles'

When we increase the concordance of the talent we bring into our organisations, we will receive back tenfold in terms of saved time, money, management, morale, leadership, sick days, innovation, and most importantly, the spoils of superior performance.

This chapter and the next present how any organisation can take concrete steps, like Mandara did, to improve their ability to identify and retain concordant talent. In almost every organisation I have consulted with, I immediately see the colossal mismatch between what science knows about talent identification and the traditional manner in which most organisations approach it.

To introduce a step-by-step approach to conducting world-class talent identification, we first need to understand the detriments of the traditional manner in which organisations identify their talent.

The traditional approach

There are some key limitations with the status quo when it comes to talent identification, starting with the belief that talent can be bought.

Limitation one - Sign 'er up!

We like to think we can just budget in a ready-made superstar who will blink all our problems away. This is possible only if:

(1) you're rich, and you don't mind sharing your riches,
(2) you stay rich, and
(3) no one else gets richer than you.

Even then, there are no guarantees the superstar will be concordant with your organisation. The research suggests organisations in sport and business are terrible at this game.

The reality is that it's not even an option for most organisations. Plus, constantly buying talent is not a real edge, it's a band-aid, magic pill, or a silver bullet. Inevitably, the price of the silver bullet is inflated thanks to bidding wars, and it becomes a race to the bottom. Most poaching attempts are leveraged by the recipient to bargain for higher pay from their existing employer. Then we are held to ransom by established superstars. Inevitably, organisations with bigger budgets will win this game. There will always be someone with deeper pockets ready to pounce.

'Constantly buying talent is not a real edge, it's a band-aid, magic pill, or a silver bullet'

We can't beat home-grown talent, whether it's the New York Yankees Core Four, Manchester United's class of '92, or Mandara's 2013 cadre. The ability to generate home-grown talent is a key predictor of an organisation's ability to excel.

Limitation two- The smart and competent trap

The smart and competent trap is one of the ways organisations fool themselves by hiring people with enormous, but not the right, talent. When not head-hunting for superstars to poach, the traditional approach to talent identification includes intense preoccupation with a person's qualifications. In particular, the belief that those with good grades from highly ranked universities make the best performers. Likewise, a person's prior experience in a similar role is assumed to be a predictor of being a high performer in a new company. Many weight selection heavily on such drivers.

'One of the ways organisations fool themselves is by hiring people with enormous, but not the right, talent'

The idea that smart people with good grades are a sure thing is a bad one. Those with good grades are often shunted into respected professions like medicine, finance or law. Just because we've got the smarts does not mean we can perform in a role, or that we should. These individuals have a set of strengths that will enable them to compete in most professions. However, being smart helps people to grind, cuff, or blag their way through, but not necessarily excel.

'The idea that smart people with good grades are a sure thing is a bad one'

Unless their interests and values also align with a role, they end up flat, minimum effective dosing their work, and dependent on external motivation to prompt them into action. They are reliant on carrots and sticks versus an internal compulsion to excel. The real risk with the smart and competent approach is that we turn away a lot of potential elite performers whose concordance was not reflected or ignited by academia. Likewise, being qualified is not necessarily predictive of superior performance. Just because a person did the same job somewhere else, doesn't mean they should do it for the rest of their life, or for this organisation.

We can train competency in a certain role, but we can't train psychological fire-power. Possessing the right qualifications or experience is not enough to achieve results unless the psychological factors are also right. The level of performance ultimately achieved is proportionate to the performer's level of concordance with the role.

'We can train competency in a certain role, but we can't train psychological fire-power'

It's not just true in business. The NFL Combine is where the potential of America's greatest talent (the top 300 players) is tested. All the tests are designed to examine each performer's competencies, such as their speed, strength, and power. Millions are at stake; the whole event is filmed live on TV, as the experts predict the stars of the future. The process is almost completely useless. A mere one in ten players with the fastest 40 yard dashes (one of the highest weighted screening tests) have ever made a pro bowl. The candidate with the record bench press was never even drafted. Then there is the Wonderlic Cognitive Ability Test, which has close to zero causal relationship with success on the football field.

It is easy to be seduced by culturally impressive achievements, but much of the time they are irrelevant. If you've completed a marathon or triathlon, then power to you. At Mandara we didn't care; we were looking for super traders not Iron men, fellowships in piano or Sandhurst graduates. These have zero causal links to success in trading so why would we?

'Concordance is specific to the role, domain, and organisation in question, not a bunch of impressive stuff. '

At Mandara, we wanted the candidate that had read every book on trading they could get their hands on, who had traded their own personal account since they were ten years old, who listened to Chats With Traders podcast religiously, who played online poker until 03:00 every night and who was sports betting all weekend.

Limitation three - Superficial screening

In most organisations, screening tends to be haphazard and based on chaotic superficial scans instead of rigorous examination of a candidate's strengths, interests and values in relation to the specific requirements of the role. Much of the time CEOs and hiring managers hand out jobs expecting elite performance without acquiring any evidence of the characteristics (strengths, interests, values) that we know accurately predict elite performance.

Worse, these managers who have conducted superficial scans have the audacity to then moan about how their employees don't perform to the level they expect. Their natural next step is to implement leadership training, management workshops, team building and morale-boosters to motivate and appease weak talent identification. Instead, they should pre-emptively allocate the time, effort, and thought required to make sure they have the right people chasing the right goals in the first place.

Limitation four - Ego

Too many organisations complain about not having enough talent. Many talent identification programmes are blinded by egotistical assumptions about how special the role they are hiring for is. That's just an excuse. Talent is not the problem. It's our approach to finding talent that is the problem.

The challenges of talent identification stem from a weak strategy, not a lack of talent. Talent exists everywhere. It is the owner, CEO or manager's responsibility to identify, develop, and retain it. I don't care if you are trying to identify potential Premier League footballers, surgeons, or pop idols. As we map out what excellent talent identification looks like, we will uncover where our talent identification process is breaking down.

'The challenges of talent identification stem from a weak strategy, not a lack of talent'

Limitation five - The interview problem

We can't spot superstars by sitting behind a desk chatting. In business, amongst other domains, too many are hired based on talking a good game. Interviews are the default in traditional talent identification. When asked the question the interviewer has read in Fifty Questions to Guarantee Great Hires, the candidate will respond with what they've read in How To Ace Interviews. 'What is your biggest weakness?' Their aim: to find out how humble and honest you are. 'I can be a bit of a perfectionist' is sufficient evidence that the candidate has at least read How To Ace Interviews and turns the weakness into a positive. Behind the scenes it becomes a futile competition between hiring managers as to who can come up with the most creative questions. Unfortunately most talent identification opts for this type of chitchat over specific, repeatable, objective testing.

'You can't spot superstars sitting behind a desk chatting'

The problem is that talking about performing is not performing. We can bullshit talking, but we can't bullshit doing. There are very few roles where the ability to interview well is causally related to superior job performance beyond the general ability to communicate.

'We can bullshit talking, but we can't bullshit doing'

We have all, at some point, been forced to work with the individual who is incompetent and yet presumably flew through the interview with flying colours. Likewise, we have almost certainly let potential superstars slip through our fingers. So, if interviews are useless, and pretty much all the available evidence shows this to be true, why do we insist on using them?

The answer is that our brains are story making machines and interviews provide a more interesting narrative about candidates. The issue is these narratives are highly inaccurate and riddled with bias. We have an addiction to fiction and are really good at making up stories to confirm our own subjective and often useless first impressions. Plus, interviews are easy and they are the way it's always been done. It's much harder to do the thinking required to produce and operate an evidence-based talent identification process. So most of us don't bother.

Limitation six- Bias

Imagine two police officers, sitting by the side of the motorway, using their eyeballs to measure the speed of passing vehicles. 'He's going too fast,' judges one officer. 'No he wasn't,' posits the other. It would be absurd to ticket drivers based on this approach, but it's done day in and day out during most screening processes.

Perhaps the biggest obstacle is that we are riddled with biases about what drives success. Too many people use only their feelings, observations, judgements, and life experiences to evaluate candidates. It's akin to the scene in the film *Moneyball*, where the head of talent spouts pearls of wisdom such as, 'Ugly girlfriend means no confidence.' It would be funny except that this sort of thing is far too common.

'We are riddled with biases about what drives success'

Bias has allowed smart, well-groomed, good-looking people with polished CVs who know the right people to hack the system. Our education system is designed to manufacture such people. Inevitably, they rat-race their way towards the excellence that eludes them and the organisations they serve.

A whole host of biases make us awful at predicting future successes. There are four main culprits:

One - Natural talent bias

Here we grossly overestimate ability if we believe there are signs of natural talent. Despite the fact that we all like to think we prefer hard-working strivers, we generally opt for those we perceive to have natural gifts.

Two - The recency effect

This describes how we place more weight on the last thing we saw which is why rock stars always save the best song for last. We leave thinking that the whole gig was great. In sport the recency effect is rife after big tournaments.

Three- The halo effect

Here those who start strong are over-estimated in the future. So, for the performer who starts well, the impression is more likely to stick, even if performance subsequently drops off.

Four- Confirmation bias

This occurs when we look for proof, especially when there isn't any, to confirm our first opinion on a matter. For example in football, if the talent scout likes a player they are scouting and that player loses possession of the ball, the scout might describe the player as 'positive', or 'adventurous', for trying

> to 'unlock the defence.' The scout that didn't favour that player would describe the exact same behaviour as 'sloppy,' 'irresponsible,' or 'greedy.'

To optimise talent identification we must shift the pendulum from subjective, superficial, and biased 'good grades/ big bench press' toward a more objective evidence-based approach. We need tools, data, and facts to prove beyond all reasonable doubt that the individual possesses the strengths, interests, and values required to excel.

If we're asking someone to do something challenging for our organisation, we need to take the time to ensure they align with, and can internalise, the meaningful rationale for giving their all when doing so. Archaic organisations that rely on interviews, subjective opinion, biases, and tick-the-box qualifications will be annihilated by the organisation that uses the objective, concordance-focused, evidence-based approach we discuss in Chapter 9.

CHAPTER SUMMARY

- When we talk about talent we should do so in terms of concordance.
- Talent identification is basically venture capital. Its an investment and if we don't unearth Ed Sheeran, Mark Zuckerberg or JK Rowling, someone else will.
- Identifying the next Cristiano Ronaldo, Lebron James or Tom Brady, can convert the team from aspirational contender into championship winner.
- The challenges of talent identification stem from weak strategy, not a lack of talent. Talent exists everywhere. It's our job to find it.
- The issue with hiring the wrong people is that we end up having to live with, fix, or fire them.
- Most organisations spend a trivial amount of their time, effort and finances on talent identification and the vast majority managing their mistakes.
- Talent identification pipelines must be created by us, not discovered or outsourced to a sales team.
- We can train and pay for competency in a certain role, but we can't train psychological fire-power.
- If we're asking someone to do something challenging for our organisation, we need to take the time to ensure they align with, and can internalise, the meaningful rationale for giving their all when doing so.
- To optimise talent identification we must shift the pendulum from subjective, and superficial, to an objective and evidence-based approach.

9

HOW TO PREDICT A SUPERSTAR

What you do speaks so loudly that I cannot hear
what you say

Ralph Waldo Emerson

Mandara weren't like our rivals Morgan Stanley, Deutsche Bank, or Goldman. Neither were we like our trading house rivals Glencore, BP, and Shell, who with their herculean budgets, HR teams, and balance sheets could hire 200 graduates for fun, knowing that by chance there might be one super-trader amongst them. In contrast, we were making a very large undiversified bet and going all in. Mandara had to hire up to three traders at a time and invest everything in them. If the junior traders didn't make it, the dream was over.

Senior Mandara traders were capable of generating $100,000 a day; $750,000 plus on good days. Pulling them off the desk for days at time to (1) train hot prospects, or (2) give the hot prospects the opportunity to compete in the markets, came with a whopping opportunity cost. On top of the millions lost in opportunity cost, junior traders would often lose money to the market long before they would actually generate profit for the company.

This all made talent identification the primary focus for Mandara's success. A hot prospect that blossomed into a super-trader could generate over $10,000,000 a year in net profit. The rewards were there if we could get this right. We applied six steps to attract, vet, hire, and confirm concordant performers. These six steps are the focus of this chapter.

The objective of each step is to remove as much guesswork from predicting superior performance (concordance) as possible. The quality of our talent will be proportionate to how accurately we complete each of the following steps.

> ***Note:*** We must do everything we can to get this right not just for the sake of performance, but for the quality of life and health of those we lead.

Step one: Create an avatar

Peter Brand:

'Your goal shouldn't be to buy players. Your goal should be to buy wins. In order to buy wins, you need to buy runs.'[38]

> ***Note:*** Runs buy Peter's organisation wins. What strengths, interests, and values buys your organisation wins? This will reveal what we need to screen for.

This crucial first step is to transition from 'do they have talent?' to 'do they have the right talent?' We need to understand the dimensions of the square hole before we can go out and find the right square peg.

> 'This crucial first step is to transition from "do they have talent?" to "do they have the right talent?"'

The better we know what we're looking for, the easier it is to find it. The avatar forces us to reflect, research and form a hypothesis. There are three ways we can do so:

Option one - Model excellence

Through identifying outlier performers who have excelled and eliciting their strengths, interests, and values we can look for causal relationships between traits that are predictive of future success.

Option two - Reverse engineering

Once we're clear about the demands of the role we can reverse engineer the strengths, interests, and values that are required to excel in it:

- What strengths will be required to deal with the challenges of the role?
- What will they need to be interested in considering how they will be spending their time?
- What values will they require so that the rewards of the role are meaningful?

Option three - Post-Mortem failure

Identify what caused previous people to fail. What strengths, interests, or values could have turned things around for those individuals who didn't make the cut?

Be specific

The reality is that most roles don't need an all-purpose athlete, investor, or author. Most roles have highly specific demands unique to the organisation in question. The football manager wants a no-nonsense centre-half who doesn't stop shouting and who shores up a leaky back line. The Board might want a CEO who can inject motivation and discipline into a flat and apathetic team. In all these cases leaders are looking for people who are uniquely right for the job at hand. A great avatar should reflect this.

We need to move away from empty statements like 'intellectual distinction,' 'capacity to guide a complex institution' or 'devotion to excellence.' What does any of this even mean?

'We need to move away from empty statements like "intellectual distinction," "capacity to guide a complex institution" or "devotion to excellence'

My favourite of the empty statements organisations try to screen for is resilience. It's a cherished value at most organisations. Goldman Sachs, the NHS, and MI5 are all looking for candidates with resilience. Who isn't? The problem is that resilience is the product of an individual activating their psychological firepower-being concordant with the role. It's not a general qualification, gene or fixed entity.

'Resilience is the product of an individual activating their psychological fire-power - being concordant with the role. It's not a general qualification, gene or fixed entity'

Note: Resilience (like any aspect of psychological fire-power) is specific to the role. For the Special Forces operator this might include resisting interrogation by enemy forces. At Mandara it could have been dealing with 16-hour days and lots of negative feedback. For a junior doctor it might be dealing with the fact that their failures can result in lost lives. Therefore completing an Iron Man Triathlon is no indication of whether or not a person will be resilient in the above scenarios. Is the Iron man resilient outside a triathlon? We have no idea unless we test their concordance in these specific areas.

We need to stop matching candidates to a long list of universal traits that are too abstract and vague to accurately screen for, and instead work out the critical factors that determine a concordant fit between the candidate and the role.

Boil it down to the few specific things that matter. Avoid vagueness like 'good with numbers,' 'thick skinned' and 'confident.' What does good even mean? How good? What numbers? With reference to whom? In which environment? Under what kinds of constraints? Under how much pressure?

'Avoid vagueness like 'good with numbers,' 'thick skinned' and 'confident.' What does good even mean? How good? What numbers? In which environment?'

The more specifically we define what we want from the performer, the more accurately we can screen in the right person. This understanding enables us to match candidates against the strengths, interests, and values that are predictors for success in the role and to determine which deficits just don't matter. Plus, formulating an accurate specification of what we're looking for will give us higher conviction when we see a concordant performer.

Values are key

We want true believers. When it comes to teams, values are the glue, and when they align, the team works with blood, sweat, and tears. Most companies post artificial statements on their websites written by a PR company that have nothing to do with employees' actual values. Because they don't really mean anything, it's hard for the team to internalise them.

'When it comes to teams, values are the glue, and when they align, the team works with blood, sweat, and tears'

Instead we must to look at what the cultural architects within our organisation truly value. We need to elicit what our own winning behaviours are, the values that make our organisation unique. Then we need to find people concordant with them so that collectively we can bring the intensity we need to excel.

> ***Note:*** Avoid screening for people whose primary value is money. You will eventually lose them. Remember, there is always someone with a bigger wallet than you around the corner. Identifying and developing superstars that jump ship the moment the someone makes a higher offer is best avoided.

Step two: Increase the quality of our gene pool

Why do so many organisations go to extreme lengths to hire individuals from prestigious universities like Oxford and Cambridge, successful organisations like Google and Goldman Sachs, or sporting academies like Chelsea and Manchester United?

The demand for talent from these organisations is so high because it's so hard to get into them in the first place. In terms of producing great talent, most of the value in elite organisations is their talent identification before any education, training or skill is even uploaded.

'Most of the value in elite organisations is in the talent identification before any of the training, education or skill is uploaded'

To be considered for selection at the University of Oxford you have to achieve straight A's at secondary school, along with at least two or three additional significant achievements, like: a fellowship in piano, second or third language proficiency, or be an age-group international athlete.

So what's the message? The selection process must be hard. The challenge is that we can't make selection hard if we don't have sufficient quality of applicants to do so. Culturally elite institutions like Google, Harvard and Manchester United can make their talent identification process hard because they can attract the best talent. This is why gene pool is so important; if we don't have the right calibre of applicants then any screening is seriously impaired.

'The selection process must be hard'

Too many organisations fail to target the right quantity and quality of applicants, and even fewer measure this. This exponentially reduces our chances of finding concordant performers. It leads us to underestimate the quality and quantity of the talent pool, which causes us to panic, drop our standards and accept mediocrity.

We should never drop our standards. This is the wrong approach. If we accept talent below the minimum thresholds required to excel, we compromise performance and condemn our organisation to mediocrity from the off.

'We should never drop our standards'

We must transition from: 'who is the best of a bad bunch?' towards: 'who meets the standard?' If the answer is no one, we need to focus our efforts on maximising the quality of our gene pool, not drop our standards. Get creative, scouting where everyone else does provides no edge. We must strategically target our concordant candidates who align with our avatar, and persuade them to apply for roles with us. This involves breaking down the barriers that restrict the quality and quantity of applicants, and expanding our horizons, be it geography, status, gender, and background.

'We need to focus our efforts on maximising the quality of our gene pool, not drop our standards'

Marketing the opportunity is key. If people don't know the opportunity exists then how can they apply for it? Where might our avatar live? What social-media accounts would they follow? What might they be doing now? Go there and tell people about the opportunities that exist within the organisation. Make a song and dance about why joining our organisation is the sincere thing to do.

Note: At Mandara we cast a very wide net over a large talent pool. We advertised all over the UK, North America, Singapore, India, Sri Lanka, and Eastern Europe. We targeted traders in other asset classes (much like a commercial lawyer targeting tax or criminal lawyers). In just six months we managed to increase our applicants from 100 to 2,000, and from 2,000 to 4,000 the following year.

Communicate authentically

Mandara were competing for the same talent as Goldman Sachs, JP Morgan, and Morgan Stanley and the physical trading houses like Glencore, Vitol and BP. Those organisations could offer candidates treble the starting salary we could, exposure to all functions of the finance and commodity space, plus the kudos of working for established brands, not to mention the job security that brings.

Mandara didn't have those carrots to dangle. We couldn't offer huge base salaries, corporate hospitality, or sublime skyscraper offices. However, from a values perspective, Mandara was an organisation that offered relative autonomy, rapid progression and the opportunity to trade. So that's what we sold; rapid, meritocratic progression.

The Message: 'You will be trading from day one, you will receive personal tuition from experts daily, and if you are still here in a two years you should be expecting to earn over a million dollars. BUT. You will start on a salary half the industry standard, you will work 16 hour days, and there are seven days in our working week. You will eat, sleep, and breathe trading. Nothing else. Your social life will be the trading floor and your colleagues, you will receive lots of direct, candid feedback and be chucked so far out of your comfort zone you won't believe it's possible, and there is a 33% chance you won't make it through your first year.'

If you weren't concordant with that set-up, then you weren't concordant with the reality of life at Mandara in 2012. The right (concordant) candidates would salivate at that proposition.

Step three: Design screening tests

Looks can be deceiving, but actions aren't. The actor must step onstage. The baker must bake his cake. The teacher must teach. It's time to see, right here, right now, who brings the psychological fire-power that will drive future success. We must observe what the candidate can actually do, and most importantly how they do it. Not what they can talk about doing from behind a desk.

'Looks can be deceiving, but actions aren't. The actor must step onstage. The baker must bake his cake. The teacher must teach'

Specificity must be at the forefront of design. The best way to see who can write great code is to ask candidates to write great code. The best way to see whether someone can deal with negative feedback is to give them negative feedback. The best way to see if someone is meticulously detailed with financial accounts is to ask them to get meticulously detailed with a set of financial accounts. This ensures we are assessing concordance for the role requirement itself as opposed to the null results of smart and competent tests or biased opinions.

'The best way to see if someone can deal with negative feedback is to give them negative feedback'

Thanks to step one, our avatar, we have a precise understanding of the role and a hypothesis of what it takes to excel in it. This allows us to design accurate DCEs. These information-gathering instruments allow us to build a picture of the individual's profile versus that of our avatar. This is how we maximise the probability that the square peg fits the square hole.

To ensure the DCE is a replica of the real-world situation we must focus on three areas: Technical Capacities, Behaviours and Emotions.

Technical capacity

The DCE must accurately reflect the technical requirements of the job. It's much like requesting that an aspiring 100m sprinter performs a series of 100m training sessions to examine their capacity in this event. We need objective tests that we trust will transfer to on-the-job performance.

We must strictly avoid laboratory conditions such as how many press-ups you can do in a minute, a battery of maths questions, or how well you can write an essay on a specific subject. Laboratory style test batteries, like IQ tests, standardised fitness tests and psychometrics are too one-dimensional. They miss too much. Most roles involve lots of subtleties that fuse together to create a unique demand. This means performing several strengths simultaneously. We must accurately represent this. The more closely the DCE reflects the technical demands of the role, the more conviction we can have when the candidate owns it.

> 'Most roles involve lots of subtleties that fuse together to create a unique demand. This means performing several strengths simultaneously. We must accurately represent this'

At Mandara we built simulators of a simplified trading game that would engage the technical and psychological strengths of the actual role. In derivatives trading, yes, IQ is important, but so is dexterity, hearing, eyesight and assertive communication. Laboratory style battery tests miss all this, DCEs don't. They represent the reality of the role, with all of the subtleties included.

Behaviour

We have to ensure our assessment centre represents how things actually are. Carefully consider your environment. The question here is, what are the non-negotiable conditions performers will be exposed to in the role, and can the candidate operate effectively under these conditions? Whatever the reality entails; including interruptions, changing demands, time pressure, noise, then so must the DCE.

At Mandara, a fast-paced competitive trading floor was the reality of our culture. So we had to re-create this in our assessment centres. We over-emphasised who we were, from the way we dressed, spoke and provided feedback. This included assertive, candid communication due to the high-risk nature of the role, rapid learning trajectory and the fail-fast, learn-quick culture. Some people can thrive under these conditions, while some wilt, and we needed to know who was who for their sakes and our own.

Successful candidates would also be required to work sixteen hours a day. If they couldn't manage one sixteen-hour assessment day, how could we expect them to get through a whole year? Ultimately, we needed individuals who could take in lots of information fast, digest it faster, put it into practice, fall flat on their faces, then get up, brush themselves down and dive straight back in with a smile on their faces. So we imposed these conditions in the DCEs. The concordant thrived in these conditions.

> ***Note:*** Existing employees delivered Oscar-winning performances to act out some of the conditions the candidates would be exposed to; playing the gladiatorial senior trader, the underhand broker, or slothful colleague not pulling their weight

Emotions

The test must be performed with the candidates under the same emotional demands as the learning and performance would occur in reality. Development pathways in elite performance environments commonly involve total immersion in a competitive and assertive environment. This meant, at times, individuals will be operating with a brain full of the stress hormone cortisol-especially to begin with.

Some people are better at preventing cortisol flooding their brains than others (concordant), and some people can simply perform better with a brain full of cortisol than others. We need to find out which of our candidates were in these categories. There are multiple ways to flood a brain with cortisol. And cortisol is cortisol. Whether the performance is an exercise or the real thing.

At Mandara we would employ pre-exhaustion exercises, sensory stressors, and constant overload using biofeedback technology provided us with information on their stress response, how quickly they could stabilise after exposure, and the rate of inevitable degradation, which the process was designed to bring, then how quickly candidates could recover and go again.

Well-designed DCEs that align with the technical, behavioural and emotional demands of the role will sound any alarms about those who look perfect on paper but falter on true inspection.

'Well-designed auditions will sound any alarms about those who look perfect on paper but falter on true inspection'

Step four- The assessment

We are not searching for some wow factor moment, like who can jump the highest, which soufflé tastes best or who has the fastest mental arithmetic. Now, the traditional benchmarks of fit for purpose test scores, academic degrees or press-ups, are the supplementary warm-up act rather than the main event. We know that psychological fire-power is what demonstrates concordance. We can measure this using the following questions:

'The traditional benchmarks of fit for purpose test scores, academic degrees, or press-ups, are the supplementary warm-up act rather than the main event'

One: Who is having clicks, aha moments and is responsive to feedback (strengths)?

Two: Who is excited, engaged, and enjoying putting in the repetition (Interests)?

Three: Who is bringing the intensity, fight, and grit (Values)?

▸ Further questions might include:

- Who has a high baseline?
- Who is highly responsive?
- Who tries hardest?
- Who is most focused?
- Who demonstrates unbreakable concentration?
- Who enjoys the audition?
- Who recovers from negative setbacks?
- Who takes feedback?
- Who competes hard?
- Who pushes themselves until they drop?
- Who keeps their energy going all day?
- Who steps up when the pressure amplifies?
- Who doesn't want the day to end?
- Who grows into it?
- Who gets curious?
- Who asks great questions?
- Who sticks at it?
- Who perseveres when things don't go their way?
- Who thrives under moments of pressure?

Or from the other direction:

- Who cuts corners?
- Who starts to whinge?
- Whose brain turns to scrambled egg when the pressure amplifies?
- Who withdraws?
- Who can't follow instructions?
- Who just doesn't get it?
- Who ultimately doesn't care that much?
- Who wishes it was all over?
- Who starts off enthusiastic but gets bored quickly?

Scoring

When it comes to scoring candidates we need to swap out open questions like, 'How well did they do?' for binary yes or no answers that indicate the candidate did or did not meet the minimum threshold criteria. This helps eliminate abstract statements such as 'I don't think he's got what it takes,' or 'she wasn't confident enough.'

We need to break down what we mean by confidence to a series of questions with Yes/No answers. For instance:

- Did the candidate point out the error in the facilitator's calculations?'
- Did the candidate continue on the simulator after six consecutive errors?'

- Did the candidate communicate that their mouse wasn't working correctly?
- Did the candidate maintain eye contact and communicate clearly?

Objective binary decisions benefit candidates, too. When feedback is simple there is time to give it. Plus, the feedback will be objective.

'When feedback is simple there is time to give it'

Note: The inside person- The incognito employee or actor can play the role of undercover agent. Embedded into the assessment centre, they can acquire intelligence on the candidates' behaviour behind the scenes. This has always proved a highly useful data source for me.

Remember, the performer must meet all minimum thresholds. Candidates don't have to excel in all the dimensions of our avatar; they just can't be weak in any of them.

'Candidates don't have to excel in all the dimensions of our avatar; they just can't be weak in any'

Note: Interviews- Despite the earlier discussion on the limitations of interviews they can play a useful role, but only after the successful completion of our assessment centre. The aim of the interview should be to examine the context behind the actions we have observed. Probing to get answers to the questions asked in the appraisals in Chapters five, six and seven, to elicit supplementary data that helps us confirm or deny their strengths, interests and values match the role.

Step five: Talent confirmation

Congratulations. Candidates who meet our benchmarks are now selected for talent confirmation. Based on the DCEs, the performer is hypothesised to have the concordance to succeed in the role. Now it's time to put them to the test and observe what happens.

This should be an intensive, at least three-month talent validation process. The aim is to confirm concordance. Performers should be exposed to a carefully constructed developmental experience and their development trajectory should be tracked and benchmarked. There should be lots of tests and lots more feedback to set them up for success.

Step six: Feedback loop

At the end of the talent confirmation process we will be able to see the fruits of our labours. Hopefully some success, but most likely some failure too. Its important to post-mortem the reasons why. This enables us to optimise the design of the DCE's and how we weight them.

Change is constant. The roles we are screening for will evolve, when they do, so must our DCEs. We must ensure we are screening for candidates who are concordant with the role today, not the role ten years ago. The crest of the wave is the place to be.

As conditions change, some performers will be taken down a peg or two, others will sharpen. The question we need to answer is why? We can map against our DCEs for clues, but also re-initiate step one, updating our avatar if changes are identified. This might mean some adjustments to our gene pool too, and as our organisation grows and changes, how we advertise the role, and the values it might satisfy for potential candidates is likely to evolve.

Retaining talent

Updating our avatar might mean some adjustments to our gene pool too, and as our organisation grows and changes, how we advertise the role, and the values it might satisfy for potential candidates is also likely to evolve.

'Retention starts with selection'

Some of our values remain an essential part of who we are, some change. As we satisfy one value, a new one usually emerges. This is the things that are important to us at one stage of our life will be different at another.

The graduate, when asked what is most important to them in the context of their career might say learning, working with smart people, and the opportunity to progress. As they progress through the development curve and satisfy these values, new ones will appear. Now it might be, amongst others, compensation for hard work, freedom and autonomy or a desire to contribute more socially.

If the role doesn't evolve to reflect the emerging values of the performer then they will become less concordant with it. The consequences will be disengagement, irritability and a reduction in psychological fire-power. Eventually misalignment with values will draw the performer to something new entirely, such as a role switch or career change, and possibly with competitors.

'If the role doesn't evolve to reflect the emerging values of the performer then they will become less concordant with it'

The benefits of rigorous talent identification

Employing a robust methodology brings three major benefits to any organisation; engagement, pride and, most of all, trust.

Benefit one- Engagement

Strong talent identification gives the technical experts in an organisation the motivation, confidence, and resilience to invest time and effort into coaching. At Mandara the trading team were confident that investing the time and effort to run demanding assessment days and training sessions, even at opportunity costs of up to $100,000 a day, was a smart long-term move.

Benefit two- Pride

The harder we have to work for something, the more we appreciate it. A crazy side benefit of going through such an arduous selection process is that candidates appreciate the opportunity more. Having to earn the opportunity cultivates affection, gratitude, and a sense of pride and belonging that we made it. Things that come easy don't feel special.

'Things that come easy don't feel special'

Benefit three- Trust

Most important of all, demanding selection processes create trust internally. When we know our colleagues have also passed a meaningful and challenging test, it allows us to immediately trust them. Trust is crucial for organisational success. Without it nothing worthwhile can be achieved.

'Trust is crucial for organisational success. Without it nothing worthwhile can be achieved'

Principle-based talent identification enables us to look beyond our initial snap judgements of individuals, and beyond our biases to the components we now know drives elite performance, aspirational talent performing from their sweet spot.

It becomes crystal clear who is in their sweet spot performing the role. Hiring decisions become easy to make. If the answer isn't a 'hell, yes,' it's 'no.' The 'hell, yes' means we have an individual bursting with expandable potential. A potential superstar. To capitalise on concordance we need to acquire skills as effectively and efficiently as possible so that we can deliver elite performance.

We now transition from the hardware issue of concordance to the software issues of skill acquisition. If we could consider the concordant performer as a smart phone, then skill acquisition is the software that makes that technology functional. The concordant performer with no skill is like a smart phone with no Uber, Spotify, or Amazon. Skill acquisition is the next step in our methodology and where we now turn our focus.

CHAPTER SUMMARY

- We need to switch our mind-set from 'do they have talent?' to 'do they have the right talent?'
- We need to work out the critical factors that determine a concordant fit between the candidate and the role and create an avatar that outlines this.
- Be Specific. The reality in most roles is that we don't need an all-purpose athlete, investor, or author. Leaders are looking for people uniquely right for the job at hand.
- We need to move away from empty statements like 'intellectual distinction,' 'capacity to guide a complex institution' 'devotion to excellence.'
- Characteristics like 'resilience' are the product of an individual activating their psychological fire-power--being concordant with the role. Not a general qualification, gene or fixed entity.
- The reason talent from culturally elite institutions is so in-demand is because it's so hard to get into those organisations in the first place. We must maximise the quality of our gene pool so that we can make the selection process hard.
- We can't spot superstars sitting behind a desk chatting with them. We must have the actor step onstage. The baker, bake their cake. The teacher, teach. Looks can be deceiving, but actions aren't.
- If the candidate isn't a 'hell, yes', then they are a 'no.'
- Most important of all, strong talent identification processes create trust internally. Without trust nothing worthwhile can be achieved.

- As the demands of the roles we are screening for change, so must our selection process.

PART 3

SKILL ACQUISITION

10

WHY IT LOOKS LIKE MAGIC

We don't rise to the level of our expectations, we sink to the level of our training

Anon, Navy SEAL

Skill Acquisition: Developing the ability to successfully and repeatedly perceive, decide and execute the right techniques at the right time under the constraints of live performance

It's game six of the 1998 NBA finals between the Chicago Bulls and the Utah Jazz played in Salt Lake City, Utah. Seventy-two million tuned in, making it the most watched game in NBA history. With 17 seconds left on the clock, the Bulls are trailing 85-86. Enter Michael Jordan.

Chicago Bulls Radio Network:

'Hornacek screens across. Malone [Utah Jazz] to the post.

> Malone … stripped by Michael [Jordan, Chicago Bulls], to the floor, stolen by MJ! Michael the steal! 16 seconds left, Bulls down one...Michael against Russell, 12 seconds … 11 … 10. Jordan, Jordan, a drive, hangs … fires … SCORES! HE SCORES! The Bulls lead 87-86 with five and two-tenths left, and now they're one stop away! Oh, my goodness … oh, my goodness!' [39]

With 5.2 seconds left Michael Jordan hit a 20-foot jump shot, his 25th game-winning shot for the Bulls, now considered one of the most iconic moments in sport.

Michael Jordan had positioned himself perfectly to anticipate the action. He perceived an opportunity to strip the ball from his opponent Karl Malone's hand, and as the ball hit the floor, reacted fastest to steal it. He took a second, scanned the court, glanced at the countdown timer and considered his options. Seeing a gap, he drove to the other end of the court where he strategically paused to let the clock wind down. Then Michael exploded inside the three-point line, to the right of his defensive guard Byron Russell. He executed a quick cross-over turning back to his left while Russell slid and hit the floor. Jordan jumped, hung in the air and executed a jump shot with immaculate precision. The Bulls took the lead and won their sixth championship in seven years.

Michael Jordan was able to choose and perform the right techniques at the right time under all the constraints that live performance brings. At the end of a long season, he was carrying injuries; his team were losing and his top-scoring teammate Scottie Pippen went off injured. With less than twenty seconds to turn things around, Jordan was physically and mentally exhausted.

This is a perfect example of what skill entails. Skill is the three-dimensional ability to perceive opportunities and threats as they unfold, decide how to respond, and then execute with technical precision, just like Michael did in game six.

Perceive: To become aware

Decide: To consider and reach a conclusion

Execute: To carry out the plan

We can't talk about excellence without talking about skill. Acquiring skill is the second multiplier for progress. Elite performers like Michael Jordan have identified concordant goals and subsequently aligned their practice with the principles of skill acquisition. No matter how concordant we are, our skills just won't form as effectively and efficiently as concordant opponents who have aligned their practice with the principles we deconstruct in this section. Skill acquisition is a vital component of the performance equation and skill can only be acquired through practice.

It looks like magic

Awe-inspiring demonstrations of skill, in any field, take our breath away, leaving us to marvel at how the performer in question could possibly have acquired such divine expertise. The art of appearing to perform supernatural feats grips us the same way a magician seems to pull a rabbit from a hat. Futbal Club Barcelona striker Lionel Messi, the Little Magician, bamboozles defenders, turning them inside out with his sublime twisting and turning, leaving bodies in his wake. Norwegian chess genius Magnus Carlsen, dubbed the Mozart of chess, regularly plays blind chess (playing from memory) with multiple simultaneous matches in play, a feat hardly imaginable to any normal mind. Then there is the Oracle of Omaha, investment genius Warren Buffet, who has amassed a ninety-billion-dollar fortune through his investing skills. He regularly dispenses wisdom and witticisms, dubbed 'buffetology', to his legions of disciples across the world.

Breathtaking demonstrations of skill might look like magic to you, and even feel like magic to them, but they're not. There is a repeatable set of skill acquisition principles behind these awe-inspiring demonstrations from our concordant magicians.

'Breathtaking demonstrations of skill might look like magic to you, and even feel like magic to them, but they're not. There is a repeatable set of skill acquisition principles behind these awe-inspiring demonstrations'

The expert mind sees the world differently from the untrained mind. Experts like Messi, Carlsen and Buffet need look at very little to see an awful lot. They can recognise patterns in data that would overwhelm and confuse their less-developed adversaries. The effect is similar to slowing time, like the bullet-time scenes in The Matrix, that are slow enough to show normally imperceptible data, such as bullets splitting the air and the micro-expressions of the enemy.

Messi, Carlson, and Buffet don't literally slow time, they perceive, decide, and execute faster. The experts' experience differs from their less-skilled counterparts. Their internal processes run quicker, which is why the world outside seems to be moving more slowly. The expert's brain works faster so responds more readily; perceiving the environment meticulously, deciphering the data to make effective decisions, and then executing with technical precision. This results in a clear competitive advantage. Yet again. The game is rigged.

But how do they do it? This is a question that has puzzled managers, scientists, and the public, not to mention the competition, who struggle to match these outliers' incredible grasp of their craft.

The answer is that experts' minds have been exposed to training conditions that enable them to perform skills in time frames that are too small to be perceived by the untrained mind. This is why expert performance can appear as an act of divine inspiration to us mere mortals.

> 'Experts' minds have been exposed to training conditions that enable them to perform skills in time frames that are too small to be perceived by the untrained mind'

Why do we find it so difficult to imagine ever acquiring the ability to perform such skills? The reason is that we default to thinking that these skills are all down to IQ, dexterity, or photographic memory. We think in terms of hardware, when thankfully acquiring skills is all about software, and we can always upgrade software.

> 'Acquiring skills is all about software, and we can always upgrade software'

Warren Buffet did not generate billions in profit because he has an exceptionally high IQ. Lionel Messi doesn't glide past defenders because he has better eyesight or faster reflexes. The secret to Magnus Carlson's ability to play multiple blindfold games simultaneously is not because he has a photographic memory. What they have is a set of more advanced mental structures that allow them to seize opportunities their counterparts with less sophisticated mental structures can't see.

Mental structure: A conceptual system we use to process, understand and use information

The saving grace is that, while these individuals are one of a kind, they use an ability that we all have: the ability to form and develop advanced mental structures through the right type of practice.

'While experts are one of a kind, they use an ability that we all have: the ability to form and develop advanced mental structures through the right type of practice'

Our mental structures have the potential to overcome the edge that someone with higher IQ or natural talent has when it comes to progressing fast. Understanding the powerful effects of our mental structures and how they can be leveraged will shift your perception of your potential to acquire skill. The rest of this chapter is dedicated to understanding this mechanism.

Note: Obviously natural talent plus advanced mental structures are optimal.

Mental structures

Skills are stored in our brains as mental structures. They act as short cuts where multiple pieces of information are assimilated into one big chunk of information. Luckily, they aren't just for Ballon d'Or champions, chess masters, and hedge fund billionaires; we all use them.

Think about learning to drive. The steering wheel, gears, mirrors, display screen, lights, and pedals controlling a one and half ton metal monster. The first time we sat in a car, the process of driving was alien. An unrelenting series of conscious evaluations of our actions and their impact on the environment around us. It's no surprise that very quickly we can become overwhelmed. But, with practise, driving eventually becomes second nature. That's because we develop mental structures that reduce the input needed from our brains' working memory.

The steering wheel, gears, mirrors, display screen, lights, and pedals all become one big chunk, labelled driving. The individual pieces become part of an interconnected body of information that provides context, meaning and information, instantaneously, resulting in superior performance.

What novice drivers find overwhelming can be handled with ease by expert drivers who have developed one large mental structure for 'driving'. The expert can drive, within reason, while multi-tasking: holding a conversation, finding and drinking from a bottle of water, or thinking about what to have for dinner. At this point we generally stop trying to improve unless the goal is to excel in driving. Those who decide to excel and become Formula One drivers, like seven-time World Champion Lewis Hamilton, are able to do all of this at speeds of over 350k/ph.

Whether it's learning to drive or to produce game-winning

jump shots like Michael Jordan, acquiring skill is like completing one big jigsaw puzzle. When we begin the puzzle, we only have separate pieces in one big pile of chaos, with no meaning or context. As we start the puzzle, we combine the corner pieces or edges to create small chunks, forming a frame which contains a bit more meaning making the puzzle easier to complete. We convert these pieces of information into one bigger chunk of information. Each chunk can be thought of as a filing card which stores information in the brain.

As we progress, we get to a point where eventually we have a complete puzzle. Random chaos is superseded by one clear picture. Through glancing at that one chunk, our completed puzzle, a complex latticework of information is instantly accessible. Like a firework that explodes into a thousand particles of light followed by a roar that conquers the sky- but in our brains. The more advanced our mental structures, the more impressive the firework and louder the roar. This is why experts are fifty moves ahead of us and everybody else.

Benefits of mental structures

There are eight key benefits advancing our mental structures brings, the synergy of which enable us to acquire skills faster and make them stick for longer. The amount we benefit is proportionate to how sophisticated our mental structures are.

Benefit one: Free up working memory

The principle benefit is that mental structures bypass the limitations of working memory. Working memory is a cognitive system that can hold and store information temporarily, and it can only hold approximately seven sets of information at a time. This is why, when we're learning new skills, the information can quickly overwhelm us.

Executing complex skills requires the brain to process an immense amount of data. For example, if we are presented with the following sequence of words:

Structure the mental best concept way
the to of learn about is to structures develop
mental a good.

As a novice in an area, any data we acquire appears unrelated, like the set of random words. In this scenario we attempt to store each word as an individual piece of information. But when trying to recall those words, the limitations of working memory kick in. This is why we struggle and only remember around a maximum of seven words.

When the same words are rearranged into a sentence:

The best way to learn about mental
structures is to develop a good mental
structure of the concept.

Here we might remember all the words in perfect order. What's the difference? The words mean something. When we have a mental structure for the pieces of information, 18 random words can be chunked up to one single set of information. The connections between the words that form a sentence mean that we can remember and understand them. We can now make sense of the words using our pre-existing mental structures.

The more advanced our mental structures for the task at hand, the more we can sidestep the usual restrictions that working memory places on mental processing.

Benefit two: Simplify complexity

Mental structures simplify complexity by shaping the connections and opportunities that we see. A good example is the ability to read and write. Through practice random shapes acquire meaning and become letters. Next we learn to combine them into a new concept called words. Eventually, we discover that groups of words can form sentences, which can form stories. Before we know it, we have formed the near mystical ability to read and write. Where once was randomness and chaos is now order and utility. The only reason that reading isn't considered magical is because so many of us can do it.

Benefit three: We can consider more data

Mental structures enable us to consider more data when it comes to solving problems, which means we can consider options others just won't see. This is why our experts can respectively glance at the opposition defence, the chessboard or a portfolio of investments and immediately sense the strengths and weaknesses, and what a good or bad move for them might look like.

Lionel Messi doesn't see 22 random players chasing a bag of wind. Magnus Carlson doesn't see 32 isolated pieces of ivory, and Warren Buffet doesn't see 15 three-letter acronyms of random companies. Instead, these elite performers receive an instant three-dimensional bombardment of information enabling them to act fast.

The bonus is that, because complex skills are reduced to one chunk, more information can occupy the remaining working memory slots, allowing for more advanced connections and even deeper analysis.

Benefit four: They alert us faster to opportunities and threats

The more sophisticated our mental structures, the faster we're alerted when something unexpected arises. As our mental structures alert us to opportunities for action, we slow down, double check, consider the options, and adapt accordingly.

Messi's, Carlsen's and Buffet's eyeballs will, without warning, perform a handbrake turn, alerting them to vital opportunities for action. Just like sunlight flickers off a diamond and grips our attention, a simple gap in the opposition's defence causes Messi to salivate, an opponent's botched move sets off alarm bells for Carlsen, and an undervalued stock grips Buffet's attention like a flare pinpoints someone in distress.

Benefit five- They help us detect and correct mistakes

Mental structures also help us detect our mistakes and find solutions. Like a clairvoyant staring into a crystal ball, advanced mental structures allow experts to simulate the future by playing it out in their heads. This enables them to deconstruct how subsequent actions might impact their performance. Experts can quickly examine strings of possible moves and counter-moves in great detail, looking for the killer pass, devastating attack or game-changing opportunity for action.

Benefit six: They make it easier to learn

Mental structures are not just the product of learning; they make it easier to learn, they are like mental hooks we can hang future learning on.

If you've ever tried learning a foreign language, you'll know some words are easier to recall because they sound familiar to the same word in your native language, compared with words that do not. This is why the English meaning of a Spanish phrase like *acelerar excelencia* (accelerating excellence) is easier to remember than the meaning of words like *rendimiento deportes* (human performance).

The reason that learning a new language is so hard is because our brains have to construct a new mental structure for it. As we learn enough words and the rules of the language, we can communicate with locals, and learn more through doing so, and that's when we start to compound our learning.

Benefit seven: There is no thinking

Another benefit of mental structures is that there is no thinking involved; in fact, thinking is one of the few things that can interrupt an expert in flow.

These structures enable outliers to quickly recognise the challenge in front of them without having to do any conscious calculation. Just like when I ask you to calculate 2x2, the solution: 4 lands in your head. Your mental structures are sophisticated in this area, and so the answers are instantaneous. On the other hand, when asked to calculate 23x17 we are forced to engage in slow, effortful, conscious work (unless we have advanced mental structures for double-figure multiplication). This ability to bypass thinking is why experts move faster than their opponents who remain stuck calculating what to do next.

> ***Note:*** Whenever a skill feels mechanical and deliberate, the mental structure isn't advanced enough for the task at hand. This is why we are left consciously examining the options that exist before we can confidently act.

Benefit eight: More opportunities for action

The opportunities experts see in their environments are enhanced by their ability to act on them. The more advanced the quality of the mental structure, the better the quality of our opportunities for action. If our mental structures are less advanced than our competition then we can't see, act, or predict the opportunities they can. When Messi takes a shot at goal, the perceived opportunity to shoot is relative to the precision with which he can strike the ball. The opportunities Lio sees appear invisible to a player with less sophisticated mental structures which can't relate the circumstances to a goal-scoring opportunity. Such a player lacks the advanced software Messi has acquired which affords him such advanced opportunities for action.

The extent to which we capitalise on the benefits outlined in this chapter is proportionate to the sophistication of our mental structures. The synergy between them creates a powerful compounding effect, which accelerates how we acquire skill and ultimately, dictates the level at which we perform.

The reason elite performers appear as magicians, or oracles of their craft is because we mortals can only reference their superior skill against our own limited mental structures. This is why it feels like magic. If we cant see how the magician pulled the bunny out the hat then, yes, it will look and feel like sorcery is at play.

Through the right type of practice, experts have changed the neural circuitry of their brains to produce highly specialised mental structures, which results in the extraordinary perception, decision-making and execution needed to demonstrate unequalled skill.

Whether your concordant goal is to become a stock-market wizard, hit a two-inch ball with a stick into a two-inch hole 400 yards away, or to combine 100,000 words to create a Pulitzer Prize-winning novel; world-class experts, in any field, align with the same principles to advance their mental structures in their craft.

Now we understand that superior mental structures enable exceptional performers to acquire such extreme levels of skill, we can discuss where skill acquisition tends to go wrong for most us and, most importantly, how we can get it right.

CHAPTER SUMMARY

- Skill is the three-dimensional ability to choose and perform the right techniques at the right time under all the constraints that live performance brings.
- The experts' minds have been exposed to training conditions that enable them to perform skills in time frames that are too small to be perceived by the untrained mind.
- Skills are stored in our brains as mental structures. They act as short cuts where multiple pieces of information are assimilated into one big chunk of information.
- The sole purpose of skill acquisition is to advance our mental structures.
- Mental structures have seven benefits, they:
    - Bypass the limitations of working memory
    - Simplify complexity by shaping the connections and opportunities that we see
    - Enable us to consider more data when it comes to solving problems
    - Alert us faster to opportunities and threats when something unexpected arises.
    - Help us detect our mistakes and find solutions
    - Make it easier to learn
    - Enable outliers to quickly recognise the challenge in front of them without having to do any conscious calculation
- The extent to which we capitalise on these benefits is proportionate to the sophistication of our mental structures.

- The more advanced the quality of the mental structure, the better our opportunities for action.

11

PERCEIVE, DECIDE AND EXECUTE

Football is played with your head, your feet are just the tools

Andrea Pirlo

The University of Oxford was founded in 1096.[40] It is a unique and historic institution and the oldest university in the English-speaking world. Back then the lecturer would use a large blackboard to explain things to the whole class in one go, and students would sit with smaller blackboards, recording what they saw and heard. Aside from lecturers now using PowerPoint and whiteboards, and the students using laptops, not much has changed. The expert at the front leads the aspiring experts who listen intently. Lecturing has been the predominant form of teaching since it began in the tenth century. The challenge is that most lectures aren't just boring, they're ineffective too. The lecturing method was great in the industrial age where the objective of British schools was to train children to go on to work in factories, but it's not so effective for preparing aspiring experts to excel in the digital and knowledge working world of today.

In a similar vein, six partners from one of London's most prestigious law firms come trickling out of a conference room for coffee and pastries at the Four Seasons Park Lane. They are at an exclusive leadership training off-site. Later that day, sipping a glass of champagne, they rank the experience with five stars. The human resources manager who organised the workshop has a smile on their face and a bounce in their step, they are thrilled the training went so well. Despite the fact everyone seems delighted with the workshop, one month later, 90% of the content was forgotten, and close to zero acted upon.

Even in elite sport, English Premier League clubs recruit thousands of aspiring footballers into intensive programmes, training four times a week from the age of eight. The majority of these academies have thousands of players performing drill after drill honing techniques. They stand in line dribbling balls around cones, racing between speed gates, then practising free kicks and penalties. Unfortunately, approximately 1% of the aspiring footballers end up with a professional career in the game, so why are so few making the cut?

The short answer is that most universities, corporate development programmes and sporting academies conduct technique, not skill, acquisition. The issue is that technique acquisition includes regurgitating information, copying others, and lots of repetition, but doesn't produce sophisticated mental structures.

'Most universities, corporate development programmes and sporting academies conduct technique, not skill, acquisition'

To optimise our skill acquisition it is critical we understand the difference. In this chapter we start to deconstruct the limitations of the traditional approach to practice, and finish by outlining the new way. We will begin by dispelling two misconceptions that hold us back.

The traditional approach: One-Dimensional training

Skill acquisition starts the second we're born. We immediately engage in skill development, much of it by trial and error, copying behaviours, along with guidance from mum and dad. As we grow we find something we're motivated to learn, get some instruction from a friend, teacher or YouTube, and we practise. Perhaps we play our guitar in the basement, kick a football against the garage door, or engage in a throw-down game of chess in the park. Plus, the recite, remember, regurgitate lecturing we experience at school. This is how most of us begin to practise.

Misconception One: doing the job makes us better

Making the transition from play to competition, eventually we enter the professional world. In most organisations the methods that exist, such as play the game training, shadowing or watching and learning, tend to be semi-organised and produce unpredictable results. Most organisations lack standardised and sophisticated approaches to training and, as soon as we're good enough to do the job, usually we're left to our own devices. It's a case of hit the clock, buckle down and play the game.

As we progress through our careers, the natural assumption is that continuing to do the job leads to improvement. Which makes sense. Undeniably we improve by doing the job, to a point, but not very efficiently, and we very quickly reach a ceiling. After reaching good-enough, additional years doing the job tend not to lead to improvement. The doing the job approach is a recipe for slipping backwards, not accelerating forwards.

'After reaching good-enough, additional years of doing the job tend not to lead to improvement'

The reason is that doing the job does not expand the complexity of our mental structures. Automated abilities deteriorate over time without conscious intentional efforts to maintain and improve them. Anyone who has done the same park run for the last five years knows what I'm talking about.

Misconception two: Consuming knowledge makes us better

The next assumption is that, as long as we update with new developments, in the form of articles, conferences and journals, we will continue to get better. The gold standard of training in many organisations is the almighty workshop, like the one our lawyers attended. These are often delivered to staff at a glamorous, off-site location over a few days. We are wined and dined, while experts instruct us on the latest information. The big question is: did anyone improve? The reality is that we are more likely to remember how many bottles of wine we put away than the innovative techniques the expert shared.

The issue is that information is not the problem. If information changed behaviour then we would all be teetotal millionaires with six-packs. Workshops might be great morale boosters, but they are expensive, and seldom lead to lasting change. The same goes for conferences, articles and journals. They might refresh our knowledge, but they don't expand our mental structures. And after a certain point, nor does learning by having a go, osmosis or doing the job.

'If information changed behaviour then we would all be teetotal millionaires with six-packs'

Doing the job and consuming knowledge, along with the examples of training provided in the introduction to this chapter, are all what I like to call one-dimensional training.

One-Dimensional training

One-dimensional training: Learning techniques that focus purely on execution or knowledge

To sum up one-dimensional training, the approach is to learn a method, recipe, and procedure for how to do something. An example might be the aspiring chef who copies recipes from the expert's latest cookbook. The aim is fast, automatic technical perfection. We read a recipe. We memorise it. We repeat it. We carry on repeating until we get it.

One-dimensional training requires hard work, lots of repetition, and lots of corrective 'don't do this, do that' feedback. We are given the test and the answers. Detecting and correcting errors is the job of coaches who adopt a cookie-cutter mode, as they attempt to drill technique into their students.

The reason one-dimensional training is so popular is that it's the quickest way to teach and to learn. When we are given a very specific recipe to follow, we are able to produce superficial results fast. We feel like we're doing well and the coaches look good.

Ignoring the true chaos that elite performance brings allows for systematic, mass-produced training that can manufacture performers fast, it's also cheap and easy to organise and this all appeals to performers, managers and owners. So, what's the problem?

Picture the aspiring chef plying his trade at Gordon Ramsay's Michelin-star flagship restaurant, Petrus. It serves elegant modern and classic French cuisine and is located on Kinnerton Street, Belgravia in London. With the one-dimensional approach, our aspiring chef can very easily re-create the 'Wild mushrooms, smoked cheddar veloute'. Chef diligently follows Ramsay's recipe; based on lots of repetition, hard work, and plenty of their boss's most remorseless verbal beat downs for feedback.

The product of this one-dimensional training is that the aspiring chef can follow Gordon's recipe, assuming everything goes to plan. However, one missing ingredient, a lapse in time keeping, or faulty equipment can land our aspiring chef in trouble since they lack the sophisticated mental structures required to improvise and solve the problem. They are now left wide open to a character assassination from a frustrated Gordon Ramsay.

The one-dimensional approach to training can build great techniques, but does not build great skills. Following Gordon Ramsay's recipe is a technique our chef has acquired that provides a specific way of accomplishing a specific task, but not much skill.

Techniques and skills are different. A technique is a specific set of actions that produce a specific result. If techniques are tools, then skills are the tool-box. A skill is the ability to choose and perform the right techniques at the right time, successfully and repeatedly in a competitive setting. We can't excel with a bunch of techniques, only with skills.

'If techniques are tools, then skills are the tool-box'

Technique: A specific set of actions that produce a specific result

Skill: The ability to choose and perform the right techniques at the right time, successfully and repeatedly

Ramsay has sophisticated mental structures that enable him to create novel gourmet meals, improvise and adapt if something goes wrong, or to seize an opportunity to innovate if one presents itself.

When we employ the one-dimensional approach, we end up with individual chunks of knowledge that we don't know how to connect to each other, giving us a bunch of techniques but no skills. The message here is that we can read, watch, and repeat the techniques of elite performers but unless we develop the perceptual and decision-making skills that dictate how, when, or why to use a certain technique we wont. One-dimensional training omits all of this.

'We can read, watch, and repeat the techniques of elite performers but unless we develop the perceptual and decision-making skills that dictate how, when, or why to use a certain technique we wont'

This is not a war on one-dimensional training. It can be useful. One-dimensional training allows us to perform in a controlled environment, assuming optimal conditions where no improvisation is required. If we are just starting out in our craft, or working on techniques that are breaking down in competition, or learning to change our brake pads in our car, then one-dimensional training is a great way to do so. But, when we enter the real world it brings with it uncertainty and variability, and the one-dimensional solution is unlikely to fit the situation. There is no perceiving and no decision-making and therefore the end product is an incomplete mental structure and a technically perfect, but practically useless performer. At this point the risk is that we malfunction. If our ambition is to excel in our craft then one-dimensional training won't cut it.

The way forward: Three-Dimensional training

Three-Dimensional Training: Learning to perceive, decide and execute (skill) effectively in your craft

When the media, public, and experts themselves describe moments of extreme skill, the focus is almost exclusively on execution. The way Messi struck a pinpoint pass from forty yards, Carlson cornered the King, and Buffet demonstrated superior stock picking. This focus omits a vital preamble, that the execution is the product of lots of perceiving and decision-making. In short, elite performance is about great perceiving, great decision-making and only then, as the icing on the cake, great execution.

Perception

We often talk about athletes reading the game, or traders reading the market, or an artist's emphatic brushwork. Way before any action, the first thing experts do is acquire information. They must perceive their environment. This enables them to focus on the right opportunities and threats.

'Way before any action, the first thing experts do is acquire information'

Experts like Messi, Carlsen, and Buffet are constantly scanning their environments for data. Messi will stand in specific areas of the pitch, watching, switching his line of sight; you will see lots of head turning as he picks up information. This allows him to anticipate the action. Perceiving is always the first step in the process that culminates in a sudden eruption into action.

In art, painting techniques are not the reason da Vinci, Picasso, and Van Gogh are revered, but rather their ability to perceive. An artist must perceive edge, space, relationships, light and shadow. This comes way before putting brush to canvas.

In the knowledge-working world, traders don't just stare at screens. Their eyes are searching for information, vigorously tracking multiple sets of information, up to twelve screens at a time, which are populated with thousands of numbers, online feeds, plus eavesdropping on sales teams, brokers, colleagues, and live news reports. Yet again, it all starts with great perceiving.

Decision making

Upon perceiving the environment, the next thing the elite performer does is process the data. This involves problem solving, recognising patterns, and retrieving information from memory to uncover opportunities for action, before ultimately deciding on one.

Lionel Messi has the technical ability to land the ball on a drawing pin from 40 yards, but before that skill can be executed in a game he must first perceive the opportunity to do so. Football is fundamentally a game about space and movement. Through deciding to stand in the best areas of the pitch, Messi can enhance his ability to perceive the game. Now he can use the decision-making dimensions of his mental structures to recognise patterns of play to deduce how each player's movements will create space for him and his teammates. He starts problem-solving making rapid calculations. Then he decides on the optimal course of action and begins to retrieve the right techniques from memory. Messi turns his shoulders and hips towards where he has decided to play the ball before he has even received it. This means he can take fewer touches and get a head start on the opposition's defence. This decision-making means Barcelona's play moves faster.

Even in highly artistic domains like oil painting, arguably one of the world's greatest living painters, Gerhard Richter, must recognise patterns, problem solve and make decisions. He must decide which are the most dominant shapes and make them as strong and simple as possible, while ensuring the shadow describes the form in the correct level of warmth, considering whether the addition of foreground material might deepen the space, making sure the half-tones properly relate to the background and that the symmetry stays in the correct perspective.

Traders must weight information against other information, processing vast quantities of numeric data and contrasting it against subjective information to identify patterns that might predict over- or undervalued assets. The trader is required to calculate their live trading positions in the split of a second and devise ways to exit risk should unforeseen events impact the strength of these positions. This requires rapid calculations and instant decisions made on the basis of incomplete information.

Note: Experts stand with their shoulders back, chests out, and chins high; they appear to have extreme conviction in their actions. That's because generally, they do. The conviction is the product of their advanced perceiving and decision-making skills. The aim in elite performance is to acquire superior perceiving and decision-making so that the right pass, play, or portfolio becomes obvious, commanding you to act with complete conviction. Only three-dimensional training can develop these aspects of our mental structures.

Execution

Once the expert has perceived the environment and chosen a course of action, they must execute with technical precision. Once Messi has decided on the most dangerous pass that takes out as many opponents as possible, he must execute it with technical precision, all that great perceiving and decision-making counts for nothing. Once executed he leaves his opponents frantically attempting to catch up.

Likewise, Richter must demonstrate meticulous dexterity and fastidious control over the brush as he executes each stroke on the canvas. And the trader must make multiple multi-million-pound transactions in a matter of seconds before the opportunity passes and is gone forever.

The perceptual elements of a mental structure provide experts with an extensive view of their opportunities for action. The decision-making aspects allow them to zero in on the right course of action. The execution aspect of the mental structure enables them to strike with technical precision to devastating effect. Each phase alone is not particularly awe-inspiring, but put them together and the compounding effect leaves us with can look and feel like magic. This is why three-dimensional training focuses on all three dimensions of skill acquisition.

This is a book about excellence, and to excel, training techniques must never come at the expense of developing skills. My objective is always to develop great perceivers, confident decision makers, and slick executers. For this we need three-dimensional training.

The question we need to answer now is, what are the principles of the three-dimensional training that allows us to form the advanced mental structures fastest we need to excel?

CHAPTER SUMMARY

- Misconception One: Doing the job makes us better - After reaching good-enough, additional years of practice tend not to lead to improvement.
- Misconception Two: Consuming knowledge makes us better. If information changed behaviour then we would all be teetotal millionaires with six-packs.
- Too many organisations conduct technique, not skill, acquisition. Technique acquisition includes regurgitating information, copying others, and lots of repetition. It doesn't produce sophisticated mental structures.
- We can read, watch, and repeat the techniques of elite performers but, unless we know why one method over another was used, we will lack the knowledge to deploy that advice in our own contexts.
- We can't excel with a bunch of techniques, only with skills. If performers don't have the perceptual and decision-making skills that dictate how, when, or why to use a certain technique, then they won't use them.
- Perception: We often talk about athletes reading the game, or traders reading the market, or artists' emphatic brushwork. Way before any action, the first thing experts do is acquire information.
- Decision making: the next thing the elite performer does is process the data. This involves recognising patterns, problem solving and retrieving information from memory to uncover and select opportunities for action

- Execution: Only once the expert has perceived the environment and chosen a course of action, can they execute with technical precision.
- To excel, training techniques must never come at the expense of developing skills. The objective is always to develop great perceivers, confident decision makers, and slick executers. For this we need three-dimensional training.

12

PRINCIPLES OF THREE-DIMENSIONAL TRAINING

Education is what society does to you, learning is what you do for yourself

Joi Ito

Like any elite performer, the Royal Air Force's (RAF) new $80million F-35 fighter jet has situational awareness second to none. It can see trouble coming ahead, behind, or below far enough in advance to avoid a threat or kill it.

The RAF's mission is to train world-class F-35 pilots. The F-35 provides the pilot with a three-dimensional picture of the battle space, but the pilots must attend to the right information and then use it correctly to recognise patterns and problem-solve to generate solutions. They achieve this through a revolutionary training system. With state-of-the-art simulation, the RAF F-35 is redefining how pilots train.

The simulator is an exact replica of the real thing. There is air traffic control with a replica flight tower including flight-test engineers monitoring all the parameters that are analysed in live sorties. All personnel involved are Royal Navy staff with fleet experience (have done the job for real at sea). Pilots can train to land an F-35 loaded with weapons onto Britain's flagship aircraft carrier, the Queen Elizabeth II. When things go wrong on Naval carriers, they go wrong fast. The training team are constantly adjusting the conditions from the aircraft handling, the way the ship rolls, the wind, waves and ship speed. There is even a simulator that can tank in a fuel pump to the replica jet to train pilots in aerial refuelling.

The F-35 Full Mission Simulator trains everything from the most basic skills, all the way up to teaching and assessing students in complex tactical formations against potent enemy threats. Pilots can train air-to-air, air-to-ground and electronic warfare missions collectively in large virtual environments. Every mission is different from the last.

The simulator means that pilots can operate independently without the RAF having to cough up $25,000 an hour to keep the jet in the air, and avoids risking death or crashing the $80million asset. It also means that if the pilot makes errors, then they have to opportunity to detect and correct them independently, without co-pilots jumping into fix things.

The RAF are a pioneering example of how outlier organisations align with the principles of three-dimensional training as this chapter explains.[41]

Elite performance requires lots of perceiving, deciding and executing, therefore, so must training. This enables us to form one big three-dimensional skill where all three aspects are integrated into one comprehensive mental structure. This product is that we know what, when, and how to call upon an armoury of techniques.

'Elite performance requires lots of perceiving, deciding and executing, therefore, so must training'

It is not the time spent training that matters, but rather the time spent training under the principles of three-dimensional training that is the most important predictor of our development trajectory. We maximise the rate at which we acquire skill and the amount that skill sticks by aligning our training with the following seven principles.

'It is not the time spent training that matters, but rather the time spent training under the principles of three-dimensional training that is the most important predictor of our development trajectory'

Principle one: A broad-to-narrow approach

> To be successful you don't have to do extraordinary things, you have to do ordinary things extraordinarily well
>
> Jim Rohn

When building a skyscraper, the foundations must go in first, then the footing to disperse the weight. Next you raise the frame, before the concrete core and staircases go in, then the electrical systems and plumbing. Once this is complete you can start to embellish with interior design. But fail to follow this broad-to-narrow process, and one storm can topple the whole thing. The mastery of the basics provides the foundation from which all masterpieces are built. Excellence will elude us if we have shoddy foundations.

When we are full of energy and excitement, we often sprint towards learning more and more, faster and faster. The problem with this is that we don't acquire or digest anything in a deep or meaningful way. We can kid ourselves into thinking we're doing well, but the foundations of our mental structures are fragile. The risk is of becoming the child who can perform astonishing playground tricks with a football, but who is hopeless in Saturday's big game.

The stuff that is sexy, exciting and looks good is important, it's fun, playful, and it primes us for the skills we might need further down the line. But it is extra-curricular. So, do it for pleasure, a break, and enjoyment; just don't expect it to send you to the top. The impressive tricks never come at the expense of the internalisation and mastery of the most basic principles.

'The impressive tricks should never
come at the expense of the internalisation
and mastery of the most basic principles'

Principle two: Games over drills

Drill: A technique repeated over and over again

Games: A multi-faceted dynamic burst of activity ending with a final result

When we repeat something over and over again, like when Lionel Messi dribbles the ball in-and-out of cones, Magnus Carlson memorises opening moves, and Warren Buffet recalls a company's statistics, we are practising drills.

Drills are a defining theme of one-dimensional training. When performing drills, the information comes at us in a consistently one-dimensional way and not much changes from repetition to repetition. There is usually only one option. Messi dribbles the ball around the cone and then shoots. Repeat. Carlson memorises the twenty-move opening full of traps. Checkmate. Repeat. Buffet regurgitates the company statistics. Repeat. There is no perception nor decision-making here.

The positive is that drills allow us to hone technical execution. We can focus on form, get the feeling and acquire comfort with the movement. Which is useful. We need to spend some time drilling technique. But as little as necessary. The more automated our training, the less we're learning.

'The more automated our training, the less we're learning'

The solution is to focus our training on the problem, not the tools. If the aim is to teach people how engines work, one-dimensional training would have us drill, memorise, or attend a course on what screwdrivers, wrenches and hammers do. Three-dimensional training asks us to participate in the take-the-engine-apart game, where we are forced to experiment, think and ask questions about the purpose of each tool. Here, we would have lots of moments like 'Aha! That's what the screwdriver is for' and 'Eureka! That's what the wrench is for,' and there is a click as we work out what the spanner can do. The aim is to understand not regurgitate.

'The aim is to understand not regurgitate'

Games like this mirror the realities of live performance,

replicating the same thinking, doing and feeling that performance demands of us. We must train amid the chaos that live performance brings with it if we want to excel. Like reality, games are dynamic and information is constantly changing. This forces us to adapt our skills to be effective in different conditions. It prepares us to perceive, decide and execute under the constraints of the actual event. This ensures we develop the ability to pick the right tool from the toolbox.

'We must train amid the chaos that live performance brings'

Knowing a lot about pianos doesn't mean we can play one. It's what we can do, not what we know, that sets us apart. In three-dimensional training we swap recite, repeat and regurgitate for think, do and produce. Instead of memorising opening moves, Magnus Carlson can play them, engaging in simplified simulations of his problem areas before pausing to engage in discussion and forcing him to think, converse, challenge and articulate his understanding of his actions.

'In three-dimensional training we swap recite, repeat and regurgitate for think, do and produce'

Permanent gains are locked in faster when thinking and doing occur together. Unless we can actively link knowledge with behaviour, theory has limited impact on performance. This is why an ounce of practice is generally worth more than a tonne of theory.

Principle three: Work things out for yourself

It's our development, our future, and our responsibility, therefore we must take the lead in it all. Too much support can develop a childish dependence and create performers who depend on others to fix their problems. The feelings of ease, comfort and security become addictive. The risk is we fail to cultivate that vital habit of doing the thinking ourselves which is necessary to develop advanced mental structures. Plus, life will be a disappointing experience if our expectation is to be given the answers for every challenge we face.

'It's our development, our future, and our responsibility; therefore we must take the lead in it all'

When we're fed the answers, such as in one-dimensional training, there are fewer breakthrough moments that fire and wire our mental structures. Instead we just receive information. The problem is that information won't advance our mental structures and therefore change our behaviour.

Advanced mental structures cannot be taught, they must be discovered. When we have to summon our own solutions, the practice changes us. Having to think for ourselves forces brain cells to communicate with each other, and eventually they connect to become a bigger network, permanently changing our mental structures. This neurological change is why skill retention is higher with three-dimensional training.

'Advanced mental structures cannot be taught, they must be discovered'

Coaches can explain it to us but they can't understand it for us. With three-dimensional training, we are accountable and responsible for our problem-solving. This can range from the incidental, like deciding what time to set our alarm, to life-affecting, highly specific technical skills, such as the Special Forces operator deciding to pull the trigger (or more importantly, when not to). Here, when we make errors, we also do the thinking, reflecting, and experimenting required to solve them.

'Coaches can explain it to us but they can't understand it for us'

We switch out daydreaming, humdrum, and blank stares, and we replace them with a braced body, locked gaze, and a galvanised mind as we search to find our own solutions. This might involve opening our mouth to answer a question then stopping, experiencing uncomfortable silences, and feeling exposed and judged. We must get comfortable with these experiences if we want to excel.

There will be lots of time for reflecting, sitting in silence thinking, tilting our heads, rubbing our chins, while our eyebrows knit together as we attempt to detect and correct our own errors. It will feel awkward and uncomfortable at first and we will be tempted to fill the silence. We must resist.

The general pattern is to get actively involved in the challenge, think through the problem, make a decision, try it out, analyse what happened, devise a plan and then seek verification on that plan. This way we learn how to learn and become a self-sufficient, self-improving performer.

As we work things out for ourselves, concordant solutions emerge, which means we stay in sync with our sweet spot. Carving our own minds ensures that we nurture the concordance with our craft. This concordance will enable us to express ourselves through our expertise. This is how Cristiano Ronaldo and Lionel Messi have both achieved similar outcomes to excel by winning five and six Ballon d'Or (the trophy for world player of the year) respectively, despite having contrasting styles of play. Three-dimensional training equips them to leverage their unique qualities to overcome the same problems. One-dimensional cookie-cutter training on the other hand suffocates our innate feelings for our craft and churns out robots.

'Carving our own mind ensures that we nurture the concordance with our craft'

Coach can give us a hand, but not hand-outs. To provide more opportunities for breakthrough moments, there should be less corrective feedback and more questions. We are questioned about our decisions and actions and encouraged to take the time to explain our thought processes, to consider alternative ways to accomplish the same aims.

The downside is that we are required to do more mental slog; it takes more time and more operational effort. The upside is cultivating ownership, self-awareness and sensitivity to what is and isn't working, and the ability to develop solutions. These are all crucial psychological skills we require to maximise our development.

Note: Self-Correction- If coach constantly jumps in to correct us, we lose the ability to self-correct in our craft; we become dependent on coach to fix things. Too often, if we make a mistake in training, the coach will stop everything and fix it. Or, if we crumble five minutes into a presentation, we stop and start over. In three-dimensional training, the rule is that we do the fixing. Just like we would be required to in competition. We don't get to start again. Here, we let the play, repetition, or task continue until the skill is completed.

Principle four: Training is hard

The more you sweat in peace, the less you bleed in war

Norman Schwarzkopf

When things are easy early on, we establish the illusion that they will continue to be easy. Then one day, when the intensity or pressure cranks up, we receive an almighty, and often shocking reality check. Easy training can delude us when it comes to our actual ability. In addition, we can end up going with the flow, which leads us to hang onto goals we aren't really concordant with, just because they are easy.

When things are easy we block the development of vital psychological skills necessary for long-term progression. Think about it. Is it reasonable to expect a performer to handle the challenges they might encounter on the pitch, stage or battlefield if their training is easy? Of course not. Hard practice in which demand exceeds capacity, forcing failure in safe, controlled environments, teaches us to deal with the emotion, challenges, and failure we will experience in reality.

'Hard practice in which demand exceeds capacity, forcing failure in safe, controlled environments, teaches us to deal with the emotion, challenges, and failure we will experience in reality'

We need challenge to change. When we increase our demands beyond our current abilities we create a performance gap. Exposure to this gap is the stimulus to adapt to a higher level. We call it the adaptive zone. This is the spark that activates genes that expand our capacity, so we can rise to the demands imposed. It's how we get comfortable with the uncomfortable. To maximise our developmental trajectory, we need to spend as much time as possible in the adaptive zone.

When things are too easy, we end up smiling, tapping our fingers, as our minds drift. We need to shift to the adaptive zone, where we're sitting upright, mouths wide open, hands clasped, raising our eyebrows and squinting our eyes. We feel our hearts pound as our minds churn. In the adaptive zone our eyes should be burning holes through anything placed in front of them. We don't improve without giving our full attention. Whatever we're doing, we need to be all there.

'In the adaptive zone our eyes should be burning holes through anything placed in front of them'

Note: Panic Zone - If we're on edge, hyperventilating and feel an overwhelming sense of dread, then the challenge is excessive, and negative adaptation like injury, burn-out and disillusionment can occur. Excessive avoidance, defensiveness, and aggression are indications we might be heading that way. Some of the less obvious signs are the hasty conclusion that it's all a waste of time, or that we don't care anymore. When this happens, we're trying to do too much too soon, and we need to reduce the challenge.

If our mind is somewhere else, we're not learning. If the instruction is sending us to sleep, stop. If we're thinking about what we're going to have for dinner, leave. In all these situations we aren't getting better. Day-dreaming, a wondering mind and having a laugh are all natural occurrences before and after training, but never during.

If we're concordant with the goal, the train-hard-from-the-off approach will stimulate us, and if not, then we have valuable feedback we can use to inform our future goal selection.

> ***Note:*** Praise- Too many coaches praise all their performers' actions good or bad. No doubt they have the best intentions of building confidence. This approach is wrong. Constant praise can churn out fragile, egotistical performers. This is why sixth-place trophies are a ludicrous idea. Constant praise discourages objectivity and creates a false sense of reality that sets their performers up for failure. Praise should be reserved for good perception, decision-making and execution along with the demonstration of proactive behaviours and effort. That's it.

Principle five- Be specific

If it doesn't happen on the pitch, then it shouldn't happen in practice. Unless our training activities reflect the specific dimensions of the skill in play during live performance, it won't make us better, no matter how long we do it for and how hard we try.

'If it doesn't happen on the pitch, then it shouldn't happen in practice'

An unbreakable rule in three-dimensional training is that we need to keep it real. Fifty-round volleying in tennis is not specific to any tennis match in history. So don't do that in practice. In basketball, eliminate rules like not being allowed to leave the court until you have hit ten free throws in a row. At most, there should be two shots in a row because that's the most we could take in an actual game. To do more, intersperse activities that simulate the reality of the game between each set of two free-throws.

Training should not be general as in the examples above; it should be specific to where performance is breaking down in competition. The aim is to identify the problem areas we see breaking down on the pitch, in the office, or on the range. This enables us to re-create these problems in training.

The question is, which skills are failing? If we're not sure where our skills are breaking down, go as hard as we can until we break. Just like holding a punctured football under water, this shows where the leak is; failure points to gaps in our mental structures that are causing the skill to break down.

'Failure points to gaps in our mental structures that are causing the skill to break down'

Let's assume that Messi has problems with long-range passing in matches. At this point, one-dimensional training would have him repeat the long-range passing drill. The problem is that this only advances his execution, which might not be the issue. With three-dimensional training we can go a level deeper and identify in which dimensions the skill is breaking down.

Our skills will always break down in the dimensions in which our mental structures are weakest. In most cases, the limitations of one dimension will cause the whole skill to deteriorate. Not seeing the pass, being slow to decide, or not executing accurately. This is why people can fail at the same skill due to errors at different dimensions.

The skill might be breaking down for Messi because he doesn't effectively see his teammates' runs. This is a perceiving problem that results in poor long-range passing (the skill). To make training effective we have to isolate this perceiving dimension of the skill. We achieve this through recreating games that encourage him to fix these specific limitations of his mental structures.

TIP: Spend 1% of the time on the 1% situations.

Principle six: There is lots of uncertainty

When there is certainty, things are predictable, and we feel comfortable with the day-to-day feeling of going through the motions. This is not the reality of performance. When reality hits and things inevitably become less certain, we quickly become uncomfortable.

Great training involves preparing for the worst-case situations. In most fields, elite performance is full of unexpected minefields. Extreme situations are valuable since they manifest the most demanding of dilemmas, from which we can maximise learning. When we prepare and train in extreme conditions, we are less intimidated when we encounter them in the real world. We inoculate against the risk, pressure, and fatigue that live performance brings through progressive exposure to them in training.

'When we prepare and train in extreme conditions, we are less intimidated when we encounter them in the real world'

Creating uncertainty involves exploring the dark side of what can go wrong. One of the extremes our RAF F35 pilots might experience is enemy capture. This must be factored into training. Pilots will undergo practices such as hooding, sleep deprivation, time disorientation, humiliation and deprivation of warmth, food and water. During interrogation sessions, the performers' objective is to maintain self-control regardless of what's being inflicted on them. Most of these techniques are against international law if used in interrogations; however, these performers must be prepared for the extremes. In unlikely extreme scenarios such as enemy capture, this means that operators are equipped with the mental structures that enable them to resist these techniques.

Injecting some uncertainty can range from overwhelming a performer in a training session, throwing spanners in the works, to even ensuring performers never assume their place in the starting line-up, and everything in between.

Principle seven: Variability

Here's how this works: Let's say we want to understand the deeper principles and master skill A. A could be a baseball player hitting a pitch clean, a doctor diagnosing a medical condition, or an investor conducting perfect analysis on a stock. Approach 1 is the three-dimensional approach to training, while Approach 2 is the one-dimensional approach.

APPROACH 1	APPROACH 2
A A A A A A	A A A A A A

Which approach prepares the performer best? Each A in Approach 1 gives an insight into what stays and what differs between them. By comparison, each A in Approach 2 gives us limited insight.

By experiencing lots of variability we are forced to adjust our skill to the changing situation. This requires lots of perceiving and decision-making. We begin to intuit what does and does not provide opportunities for action. Suddenly, not only can we cope with variability, we unlock the superpower of being able to throw together unique solutions in these moments.

This is exactly why the training team adjust the waves, wind, speed and rocking of the ship at each and every attempt the F35 pilots make to land the jet on that carrier. If we want the ability to unlock our skill under all the angles that reality might entail, then we must prepare accordingly by introducing variability to our training.

Almost every team, individual and organisation I have worked with spends too much time engaged in one-dimensional training. If we want to maximise the rate at which we acquire skill, and how well we retain those skills, then we need to shift to aligning with the principles of three-dimensional training. Like concordance, skill acquisition is a game of better, not perfect. If we can move a bit further along the continuum than our rivals, then we gain a competitive edge over them.

Remember, it's not the time spent training, but the time spent training in alignment with these principles that is the biggest predictor of development trajectory. We can take these principles and build out a comprehensive three- dimensional training syllabus with state-of-the-art simulators that cost millions, like the RAF. But the reality is, all we really need is time, effort and a bit of creativity. We can make small tweaks to our existing training tasks, the people involved in them and the environment we train in to align our skill acquisition programme with the principles of three-dimensional training. All of which costs us nothing. In Chapter 13 I show you how.

CHAPTER SUMMARY

- Elite performance requires lots of perceiving, deciding and executing, therefore, so must training.
- It is not the time spent training that matters, but rather the time spent training under the principles of three-dimensional training that is the most important predictor of our development trajectory.
- Work things out for yourself: It's our development, our future, and our responsibility; therefore we must take the lead in it all. Coaches can explain it to us but they can't understand it for us.
- Games over drills: We need to swap recite, repeat and regurgitate for think, do and produce. Games are multi-faceted dynamic bursts of activity ending with a final result that force us to perceive, decide and execute.
- A broad-to-narrow approach: To be successful you don't have to do extraordinary things, you have to do ordinary things extraordinarily well.
- Training is hard: We need challenge to change.
- There is lots of uncertainty: Great training involves preparing for the most extreme situations that might occur. We inoculate against the risk, pressure, and fatigue that live performance brings through exposure to them in training.
- Variability: Forces us to adjust our skill to the changing conditions, which hones the perceiving and decision-making aspects of our skill.

- Be specific: Unless our training activities reflect the specific dimensions of the skill in play during live performance, it won't make us better, no matter how long we do it for and how hard we try.
- With time, effort and a creativity anyone can make small tweaks to their existing training to align with the principles of three-dimensional training

13

THE POWER OF CONSTRAINTS

If you don't look back on yourself and think wow how stupid I was a year ago then you must not have learned much in the last year

Ray Dalio

The Navy SEALs, form one of the United States elite special operations units. SEALs are tasked with capturing or eliminating high value targets, or gathering intelligence behind enemy lines. One of most crucial skill-sets the SEALs' possess includes conducting small-unit special operation missions in urban environments.[42]

A fundamental skill in urban warfare is Close-Quarter-Combat (CQC). CQC involves clearing buildings and structures of enemy combatants using carbines, pistols, and hand-to-hand fighting. In combat, enemies, hostages, civilians and fellow operators can be closely intermingled, so CQC demands rapid and precise application of lethal force. The operators need acute perceptual awareness, the ability to make split-second decisions, and expert proficiency with their weapon systems, to ensure mission success.

As part of their CQC skill acquisition training, special operations units like the SEAL teams will conduct a series of very fast and violent takeovers of a simulated enemy structure to rescue hostages. The CQC instructors will force lots of perceiving, decision-making and executing from their operators.

This all usually starts sitting in the HELO [helicopter], the smell of kerosene filling their lungs and the rotor-blades thudding as the operators conduct their final weapon checks before they hit the venue.

This time, on the first run-through the team leader goes down within seconds, which they have deliberately been assigned to do by the training team. The rest of the team is required to attend to the casualty, but also to take charge of the perceiving and decision-making functions. This constraint forces them to improvise, adapt and overcome.

Next time around, the team find the door to the room the hostage is in is barricaded shut. It's a new problem. Again, the Instructors have put pressure on the team, challenging them to expand their mental structures and emerge with solutions by pulling different tools from the toolbox.

On the third run, upon entering the building the team realise they have been given incomplete intelligence. Should they proceed, and if so, how? Or is the risk too high; should they abort the mission? Again, the team are forced to perceive their environment, think about the situation, recognise patterns, make decisions and uncover solutions.

On the final run-through, sixty seconds before starting, the urgency of the operation is heightened and the team are told they have only five minutes until the hostage will be executed. They have half the time they anticipated to achieve mission success. Just when they were beginning to get comfortable, this time constraint pens them back in the adaptive zone.

The Instructors use of constraints ensures aligns them with the principles of three-dimensional training, maximising the transfer, rate and retention of their skill acquisition.

Constraint: A boundary which encourages the learner to emerge with certain behaviours

In this example, the different venues, the team leader going down, the barricaded door, the incomplete intelligence and the time limit are all constraints that have been applied to accelerate learning. Constraints direct the performer to acquire specific solutions. They provide the boundaries within which the performer can search for their own unique solutions to their own unique problems.

'Constraints direct the performer to acquire specific solutions'

Constraints are not random. The objective is to apply the constraints that will channel the performer to expand their mental structures in the specific dimensions their skills break down during live performance. We use constraints to pressure the performer to solve the problem through amplifying the problem, narrowing their attention to it and forcing them to search, find and internalise solutions. The performer's job is to place their sole focus on adapting their skills to the constraints imposed.

There are three types of constraints we can manipulate to expand our mental structures: we can constrain the task, the performer, or the environment.

Task constraints

Task constraints concern the rules of the game. We can constrain:

Deadlines (tight or slack)

If we assume one of our F-35 pilots' limiting factors is that they take too much time to make decisions, then we might apply a series of tight deadlines, which forces either faster decision making, or failure. We can recreate the type of high-pressure situations where their skills tend to fail on the simulator, and progressively tighten the timings to provide the pilot with opportunities to find their own solutions.

> ***Note:*** The training team can support the performer in finding solutions by asking questions.

Severity of consequence (for success and failure)

Let's assume Lionel Messi's long-range passing is still breaking down because he isn't perceiving his teammates' runs effectively. In training we might reward him every time he perceives correctly (scans his teammates' runs), even if he then decides to make the wrong pass, or fails to execute with precision. Simultaneously, we could also punish him for failing to scan, even if he successfully completes a pass based on good decision-making and execution.

> ***Note:*** While increasing the severity of consequences can deter a specific behaviour, reducing the severity can encourage more exploration of that behaviour.

Speed of the session (speed it up, slow it down)

For Messi, we could also adjust the time he has to perceive (more or less). We might pause the game just before he receives the ball, or perform the session in slow motion, to provide him with opportunities to scan.

Set specific points

For our F-35 pilot who is taking too long to make decisions, we can set specific points for them to problem-solve during the exercise. We could provide periods where we pause the exercise and have the pilot transition to the air traffic control tower to draw their focus to how their indecision impacts the mission for the rest of the squadron. We could also set reflection points and have the pilot watch recordings of their performance between run-throughs to provide opportunities for self-detection and correction of errors.

> ***Note:*** If the performer is slow in overcoming a constraint, we can amplify the pressure by intensifying the existing constraint or adding a different type of constraint that narrows their focus to where they will find solutions.

Purpose of the task (the why)

If we instruct the F-35 pilot that the purpose of the session is to make sure the mission is completed as fast as possible, we will obtain a different set of behaviours than if they are instructed to focus on making perfect decisions. In this case, decision-making under pressure is the focus and therefore the former is advantageous.

Resources (restrict or permit)

We might restrict Messi from passing to his favourite teammate, Antoine Griezmann, which forces him to explore other options, like the runs of his other teammate, Philippe Coutinho.

Pre-requisites (patterns of work/play)

We could instruct Messi to make visual contact with at least three teammates in the five-second period before he receives the ball; this would force him to take more time to scan (perceive) the environment.

Information (withhold/overload)

For our F-35 pilot, we could have air traffic control withhold some information to prompt them to be more proactive and assertive in retrieving the information needed to make good decisions.

> ***Note:*** The solution must come from the performer, not from the constraint. If we want Lionel Messi to perceive his teammates' runs more effectively, then opportunities for him to do so must be provided. It is paramount that the desired action is not the only available opportunity. The right pass must not be the only available choice for him. Messi must generate his own 'aha!' moments, leveraging his own unique resources. This ensures he is concordant with the solutions that emerge.

Performer constraints

Performer constraints relate to the individual's unique characteristics. We can constrain:

Anthropometry (height, weight, and limb lengths)

To effectively prepare a Team GB boxing gold medallist to become a WBC (World Boxing Council) Champion, we need to ensure they spar a variety of opponents with a range of tactical attributes. This includes short, stockier, short-range, high-pressure fighters, but also tall and lean, tactical long-range fighters; and everything in-between. This forces our aspiring champion to perceive, decide and execute against opponents with differing height, weight, reach and styles.

Fitness (strength, aerobic capacity and flexibility)

If our boxer struggles with fatigue, we might rotate their sparring partners with fresh opponents each round to challenge their aerobic fitness, and skill under fatigue. Our boxer must come up with the solution to the constraint. They might decide to dedicate time to build aerobic fitness, learn to box more efficiently, or maybe a combination of both.

Cognitive ability

We can overload the high-IQ chess players Magnus Carlsen by having them play multiple games simultaneously. We could pit them against a 'centaur' where a human is paired with a computer to create a synergistic chess IQ and highly challenging opponent. Our chess star must become more efficient, resourceful and creative by exploring new tactics and aspects of generating wins against a superior opponent.

Personality

Aspiring traders at Mandara (see chapter 8) would often struggle with the idea of risk-taking in the form of making large bets. We would constrain the trader by setting a minimum bet size and making it compulsory to always place a trade.

The trader was forced to reconcile what was holding them back and find a way to overcome that obstacle. Some had to confront their fear, some the fact they weren't prepared enough, some had to divest some of the comfort they were unconsciously seeking, while others had to question whether the risk-taking that comes with trading was for them at all.

Likewise, paper targets don't return fire, and this is why Navy SEALs conduct force-on-force training with non-lethal training rounds that (piercing skin) hurt, or use live ammunition.

> ***Note:*** The more closely training reflects the emotional component of competition, the more prepared we will be for the real thing.

Sensory (sight, sound, feel, touch, taste, and smell)

Another constraint we can apply to help Lionel Messi perceive better is to prescribe his teammate with the right run to stay silent and the teammate who is the wrong option to scream for the ball. This forces Lio not to rely on just auditory perception.

We could also clothe players in camouflage tops or the same colour kit to force him to expand his perceptual skills. He could even wear a pair of special goggles that restrict his peripheral vision, forcing him to scan his environment deliberately by conducting lots of head turning.

For our F-35 pilot, we can tell air traffic control to mumble, and even release smells into the cockpit that might indicate a technical malfunction. This prompts our pilot to communicate more assertively and pick up on sensory information, which could be the limiting factors causing the slow decision-making.

Emotional control (impulse)

If a performer tends to lose their temper during a game with opponents or officiators, then we should present opportunities in practice to overcome this. We can assign players in training to antagonise, or deliberately give bad decisions against them, forcing a volatile performer to emerge with an internalised way to keep it together instead.

Environmental constraints

Environmental constraints relate to the differences between the environments in which we compete, recover and train. Things we can constrain include:

Location (geographic, socio-cultural, public/private, light, noise, altitude, weather, time zones)

Elite performers change the venues in which they train, forcing them to perceive, and adjust to, the various scenarios they may encounter in live performance. This is exactly why the world-number-one golfer Rory McIlroy doesn't putt on the same green, and why Navy SEALs conduct their training in Arctic, desert, jungle, mountain, marine and urban environments, and why our F-35 pilots land the jet on the aircraft carrier in all sorts of light, weather and speeds.

Culture (aggressive versus passive)

To create an aggressive environment, coaches, management and peers can be hyper-critical, zero-tolerance assertive and pushy. We can prescribe teammates to be vocal with their disappointment when mistakes are made.

Alternatively, for a more passive context, we can have support staff adopt a relaxed, calm and supportive attitude toward the performer. If the objective is to encourage zero errors, then the former is optimal. If the objective is to encourage experimentation, then it is the latter.

Resources (support staff, facilities)

We could increase the quantity and quality of data and sports science support to provide Messi with a comprehensive suite of statistics on the perceiving aspects of his long-range passing. This could highlight his successes and failures providing him with metrics depicting the number of times he scans (head turning) his teammates and the opposition's players in each game.

People (over/under rely on)

To develop better sensitivity to error detection and correction, we could deprive access to external feedback and provide Messi with extra time to review video footage in feedback periods independently, to prompt him to detect and correct his own errors. Alternatively we could have the coach, his teammates and a performance psychologist engage in these sessions to help generate solutions.

Technology (limit or overload)

At times we can just turn the technology off and force the traders to develop their own internal sense of their current risk exposure, the conviction of the buyers and sellers in the market, the direction the market is trending, and the opportunities that exist to capitalise on without the luxury of a suite of technical indicators.

Logistics (things go smoothly, things go wrong

Buses break down, equipment gets lost, the opportunity to compete is brought forward or delayed, and we must factor all these constraints into our training.

> ***Note:*** We need to make training as real as possible. Special operations medics use amputee actors and Hollywood make-up artists to accurately simulate the casualty evacuations that occur in war. They go the extra mile to bring blood-and-guts realism that helps ensure they are technically and psychologically prepared to deal with the realities of war.

Skill acquisition is not mindlessly repeating solutions; it is the mindful search for solutions, repeated over and again. Found a solution? Then adapt the problem through adding a constraint, and repeat. If we're not adjusting the constraints, we're developing technique, not skill. The aim is to get it right and move on. As soon as we do the same thing correctly twice, add a constraint. The progressive evolution of the right constraints is what pins us firmly in the adaptive zone and maximises our development trajectory. Our brain will start to churn again and our senses will sharpen as we re-enter the adaptive zone, maximising our potential for progress.

'Skill acquisition is not mindlessly repeating solutions; it is the mindful search for solutions, repeated over and again'

CHAPTER SUMMARY

- A constraint is a boundary, which encourages the learner to emerge with certain behaviours. The objective is to channel the performer to expand their mental structures in the specific dimensions in which their skills break down in competition.
- Task constraints concern the rules of the game. We can constrain: *Deadlines (tight or slack), Severity of consequence (for success and failure), Speed of the session , Set specific points, Purpose of the task, Resources (restrict or permit), Pre-requisites (patterns of work/play), and Information (withhold/overload)*
- Performer constraints relate to the individual's unique characteristics: *Anthropometry (height, weight, and limb lengths), Fitness (strength, aerobic capacity and flexibility), Cognitive ability, Personality, Sensory (sight, sound, feel, touch, taste, and smell), Emotional control (impulse)*
- Environmental constraints relate to the differences between the environments in which we compete, recover and train. Things we can constrain include: *Location (geographic, socio-cultural, public/private, light, noise, altitude, weather, time zones), Culture (aggressive versus passive), Resources (support staff, facilities), People (over/under rely on), Technology (limit or overload), Logistics (things go smoothly, things go wrong (limit or overload.)*
- All solutions must come from the performer! Generating our own breakthroughs ensures we are concordant with the solutions that emerge.

- Learning is not mindlessly repeating solutions; it is the mindful search for solutions, repeated over and again.

14

COACHING FEEDBACK AND THE ENVIRONMENT

A great coach can lead you to a place where you don't need him anymore

Andre Agassi

The skill the trader must master is to identify patterns within complex sets of information, make rapid calculations, manage risk, dominate communication, and seize opportunities to generate capital that may present for seconds.

Vitol: '10 BID 4-7 JUNE!'

Shell: '30 OFFER!'

BP: 'JOIN THE OFFER!'

Glencore: 'JOIN THE BID FOR 10!'

Note: Mandara need to gauge which direction the market is going in order to ride the price movement when things kick off. The aim is to act faster with more conviction than the competition.

Mandara: 'From a numbers perspective things are balanced. I need to test the market to get a better sense of who is going to win in moving the market their direction. My gut tells me the sellers are bluffing, so I'm going to test the sellers by showing a strong bid and see how they react. "20 BID!"'

Vitol: [Silence]

BP: [Static. Silence. Static. Silence again.]

Glencore: '35 OFFERED ONLY'

Note: The big players show their hands. Vitol and Shell fail to improve their offers and BP backs off. Now Mandara must go for the kill.

Mandara: 'BUY SHELL AT 30!'

Note: Mandara react in an instant. The order given is clear, loud and precise, so there can be no doubt the deal will stand. Mandara buys all Shell have.

Mandara: 'BID ON. MORE SIZE!' [Split-second pause.] 'TAKE BP!'

BP: 'Fine. 100 done [He says to the broker reluctant at getting hit]'

Note: Another sign Mandara have made the right decision. They press the advantage.

Mandara: 'WHERE IS THE FOLLOW? I NEED VOLUME!'

Broker: 'I have ENI at offer +35 for 400.'

Mandara: 'TAKE THEM!' *

Walking onto the Mandara trading floor was like stepping into the Colosseum. The digital version of what used to be one big open bear pit of Cockney barrow-boys. As the trading window approaches, the tension in the air starts to build, like the clash of thunder and flash of lightening before a tropical storm hits. Then suddenly, the trading floor erupts; screaming, shouting, rapid head-turning, knees jerking, they even use hand signals to transfer information. Controlled chaos at its finest.

The large open trading floor is surrounded by desks, with a sales team in the middle. Each desk is enclosed by 14 screens; speed is critical in trading, and you don't want to waste time toggling between windows. You need to monitor market data, major headlines, transactions, pricing applications, and technical platforms to execute trades.

After the European window closes (at approximately 17:30) everyone in the company, excluding the trading team, begins to wind down their day. The traders on the other hand are just about to start expanding their mental structures. They have a three-hour

* This is a hypothetical example based on real-life events.

break before the US window, an opportunity to get better, and the aspiring super-traders seize it.

Glance across the trading floor at 18:00 and the first thing you'll notice is the concentration on the face of the alpha (senior) traders' faces. They sit in silence and immediately engage in reflection as they complete their trading diaries.

In the meeting room adjacent to the trading floor you will see the head of trading sitting with two aspiring traders from one of the teams. On the big screen they replay the European trading session from beginning to end. Their aim is to analyse their perception, decision-making and execution. They wrack their brains, scanning the screen; thinking hard before seeking verification of their learnings. The head of trading pauses the video strategically to provoke insight, asking questions and encouraging traders to think harder. There is lots of uncomfortable silence.

In the training room next door, junior traders compete in an exercise that simulates the window. The session is run by one of the senior traders. He gives clear, precise instructions and controls the exercise, fighting the urge to jump in and correct the juniors' mistakes. He trusts the process and manages to restrain himself. The games are extremely competitive but between rounds the traders reflect in silence, before giving each other feedback, talking through their problems and strategising for the next round. Their scores on the simulators are displayed publicly in rank order on the trading floor.

In the adjacent room another mid-level trader is running a pit-trading game that simulates open outcry oil trading. Back on the trading floor, a group of new recruits sit discussing live trades they have placed as part of another game where they get to risk $50,000 in teams of three. The winning team splits the profit between them.

The challenge at Mandara was getting these concordant performers to switch off and go home. This type of training provides an example of what characterises great talent-development environments. In this chapter we explore why.

We're now going to deconstruct three things: the role of the coach, the feedback process, and what the optimal environment looks like. This chapter outlines what to look for from a coach and from the environment. Most importantly, it illustrates how using these principles we can become our own coach, maximizing the quality of our feedback and optimising our developmental environment.

Coaching

Coach: A person who influences training
[to include the performer, peer, manager,
parent or friend]

Traditionally, we think of coaches as screaming maniacs, pointing frantically while shouting instructions on the side of the pitch, in the meeting room or trading floor. We think, 'Wow, what a great coach, they really know they're stuff.' There is an underlying expectation that a coach is not earning their money unless they're saying something or giving answers.

Most coaches are very good at 'do more of this' and 'do less of that' one-dimensional training. In fact, if given the option most coaches would use a joystick to control us. Whilst joy-sticking is all well and good for a video game; it isn't for our development.

'I know what you need to know' coaches can't help jumping in and solving the problem themselves; the problem is that this deprives us of our opportunity to grow. We can't learn about things after the solution has been revealed. Learning occurs while the answer is in the process of being discovered.

'We can't learn about things after the solution has been revealed. Learning occurs while the answer is in the process of being discovered'

Too often, coaches make connections and point out patterns for students without realising they are teaching them to imitate what they do, rather than to construct their own meaning for themselves. Then the coach wonders why the performer cannot find patterns in their craft.

The traditional focus in sport, business and the military (amongst other domains) has been too much on what, versus how, to coach. In fact, leadership, management and coaching training rarely includes any skill acquisition training. Instead the focus is usually on acquiring techniques and tactics. Now we will discuss the real role of the coach, with emphasis on how to coach, versus what to coach.

The great coach

The first thing a great coach does is laser in on the specific dimensions in which skills are breaking down in competition. Their primary role is to initiate breakthrough moments through setting the right constraints. The learner's job is to adapt to and overcome those constraints.

'The first thing a great coach does is laser in on the specific dimensions in which skills are breaking down in competition'

Coach will pressure action, constraining and amplifying, forcing us to raise our game and find solutions. They don't need to know the solutions, that's our job. They just need to know what to constrain so that we are forced to emerge with concordant solutions. Coach will progress things when we do.

The great coach will layer learning, prescribing the right progressions at the right times. They will carefully manage the intensity, and when we get too comfortable, they dial it up. When it gets too much they will tone it down, keeping us penned in the adaptive zone.

The great coach is there to facilitate the learning curve, but we are responsible for it. They impart ownership onto the performer and hold us to account when we make excuses or start to attribute blame.

'The great coach is there to facilitate the learning curve, but we are responsible for it'

They will provoke insight through asking the right questions and create opportunities for reflection by drawing out pertinent information and encouraging exploration. Then coach highlights and rewards our solutions reinforcing the process.

Great coaches also know how to tailor practice to an individual's capacity, intuiting when we need to practice more, take a break, or break sessions into sets. Acquiring the skills it takes to excel is an exhausting process, so to increase focus and conserve motivation, the great coach limits practice sessions to a time frame that matches our levels of attention and motivation. This keeps us hungry. Coach knows that quality beats quantity. It also helps avoid injury, burnout, and excessive loading, all of which can de-rail a concordant performer.

Coach has to be great, respective to our level right now. As our skills and abilities advance, so must the quality of our coach. There will probably come a point we have absorbed all that our current coach can teach us. When this happens, we have to find a coach at the next level.

> ***Note:*** Just because the coach can do it, doesn't mean they can teach it. The best way to assess a coach is to observe them, or acquire references from former students. Pay particular attention to their development trajectories.

Feedback

Feedback: Information that can be used as a basis for improvement

Our rate of skill acquisition is proportionate to the quality of feedback received. Feedback contains potential for improvement. We need to know whether we're on target, and if not, where we're going wrong. Feedback allows us to modify future efforts, not just when things are going badly. No matter how good an outcome, there are always opportunities for improvement.

The questions are: How should we give and receive feedback? Who should be involved? And what are their roles? We'll answer these questions now starting with our role in the feedback process.

Step one: You

Feedback begins and ends with you. We know that, when we generate those 'aha!' moments ourselves, the learning sticks. We need to take the time to process our own thoughts and feelings about what we did well, what we didn't, and what new questions came up.

'Feedback begins and ends with you'

Coaching ourselves in this manner, even by reading this book, should be done before we let our coach interfere. This is exactly what was going on during those moments of silence in the Mandara training room.

We should always start by focusing on ourselves. Keep the focus internal to begin with; on our own mind-set and our performance, not the outcomes.

▶ We ask ourselves questions like:

- What were my aims?
- What did I notice?
- What options were available?
- What actions did I take? What made me choose that option?
- What did I do correctly? How specifically was it good/bad?
- What did I do incorrectly? How specifically?
- Are there any immediate actions I can take?
- What adjustments can I make next time?
- For what reasons am I choosing those adjustments?
- Repeat these questions over and over again.

Then we can switch our attention to the external. Now our focus switches to the outcomes and the effect we are having on our environment.

- Now we ask questions like:
  - Did I impact my teammates performance (emotions/ tactics/ opportunities)? If so, how?
  - How did my actions effect the competition (emotions/ tactics/ opportunities)? If so, how?
  - What was my impact on the customer/product/audience?
  - How was my experience with the equipment?
  - Did the report/ presentation/ pass hit the target?
  - What was my effect on the referees, sub-ordinates and super-ordinates?
  - Repeat these questions over and over again.

Remember, learning only happens when we think and work things out for ourselves. The more we take responsibility, the better.

> ***Note:*** Perceiving and decision-making come first, and execution second. Maybe we created an opportunity but the execution didn't come off? If we are getting opportunities to execute, it means our perceiving and decision-making is going well. Recognise and reward this. Fine-tuning execution is where one-dimensional training comes in. The drills are like homework; we can go away and get on with it independently. If we saw an opportunity but failed to execute it, then we can stay late and drill, repeat and regurgitate that technique until the execution is second nature.

Step two: Peers

In elite performance environments everyone is a coach. After we've exhausted our own brains, we can request feedback from peers, colleagues, or teammates. We should be exchanging information with our peers before, during and after training. There should be lots of peer-to-peer coaching, supporting, questioning, and challenging. Sharing information and provoking insight is the aim.

'In elite performance environments everyone is a coach'

At this point in the feedback process, the great coach has still not uttered a word. The aim is to have performers coaching themselves and each other. Everyone should be involved designing training. This expands our mental structures for learning, as well as our craft.

- ▶ Coach will ask questions like:
  - Where is their skill breaking down?
  - What constraints could we amplify those areas?
  - Which zone are they in (comfort, adaptive, panic)?

'The aim is to have performers coaching themselves and each other'

When it comes to peer review, the optimal group includes a range of experience and ability: plus, minus and equal.[43] This principle ensures we get continuous feedback about what we know and what we don't. We want feedback from someone more advanced than us (plus) to learn from them and strive to close the performance gap between us. We also want someone with similar ability (equal), so we can compete against them. Finally, we want someone we can teach (minus). Teaching what we know, known as the protégé effect, consolidates and expands our own mental structures, adding layers of complexity. This information sharing improves our retention of those skills and can facilitate learning breakthroughs.

Step three: Coach

Once we've completed all the above, we can finally involve coach. But even here, the great coach will apply the 'guess before given' rule.

Guess before given:
The performer must anticipate coach's response to their questions before being provided with answers

Before the coach answers our questions, we will be required to predict their response. This squeezes out an ounce more thinking and reflecting, forging these crucial abilities. Our objective is to receive verification, not answers. It is our job to bring well-thought-out questions along with potential solutions and only then, go and ask for coach for feedback. This way we don't just get information on the actual problem, the swing, the loss of sales, the play you made, we get feedback on our whole decision-making process. This hones our ability to self-improve.

'Our objective is to receive verification, not answers'

Bandwidth Feedback: A method for determining when to assist in the learning process

Imagine turning a dial to achieve the right frequency on an

old radio. If the signal is all but there and just needs some fine-tuning to remove the last bits of static, then the great coach will get out the way and let you do the fine-tuning. However, if there is no whisper of a signal and the radio is starting to melt, crack or smoke, coach can jump in and get more involved, pushing and prodding, pointing the antenna in a different direction, and lend a hand. Remember, the aim is that we, rather than coach, come up with as many of the solutions as possible, because this ensures they stick.

'The aim is that we, rather than coach, come up with as many of the solutions as possible, because this ensures they stick'

Support roles

The optimal development environment consists of three key supporting roles. The ideal set up involves a combination of mentors, arse-kickers and cheerleaders:

Support Role One: The mentor - acts as a sounding board, a source of expertise and helps to identify resources.

Support Role Two: The arse-kicker - reminds us of the realities of performance and holds you accountable to the standards elite performance demands, they will be radically transparent with you and are not afraid of conflict. They remind you that pursuing excellence is a privilege and that you need to align with the strategy and bring the effort, or you will be ejected from the programme.

Support Role Three: The cheerleader - provides the

encouragement and motivation we all occasionally need. This is someone you can vent to with no fear of reprisal or judgement, and who provides social support during the inevitable challenging times.

Note: These support roles don't have to be made up of professional coaches, psychologists and mentors. Friends, colleagues and even family can perform them perfectly adequately.

Step four: Data

Now it's time for data, Key Performance Indicators (KPIs), Global Positioning Systems (GPS), metrics, heat maps, heart rate variability (HRV), and so on. Data must be preceded by thinking for ourselves. When we use data we should use the guess-before-given rule. We have to estimate what the data will be before we calibrate it with the facts. This exercises our ability to calibrate with the numbers and develop our own accurate internal data suite.

'Access to data is a right we should have to earn, and it comes after thinking for ourselves'

The reason data comes last is that it can take the focus away from us and we lose our ability to feel. For example, the athlete might lose sensitivity to their fitness levels if they constantly subordinate their training loads to data alone. We need to develop our own sense of what's going well and what's not. If we don't use the feeling, we lose it.

Intense debriefs where we can watch video or access data to eliminate the subjectivity that can accompany retrospective recall are a great asset. But even with the data, we need to keep things interactive so that we keep perceiving and decision-making. Freeze-frame, ask questions, engage, pause and think, just like the Mandara traders. This can help identify the skills that are breaking down, and where they are breaking down. It also provides an opportunity to train our mental structures without having to set up a complex game-style activity that can involve a lot of resource.

The environment

I am not talking about multi-million-pound training complexes, hyperbaric chambers, sleep pods, float tanks and walls plastered with motivational quotes. Instead the focus on the environment concerns the people, behaviours and opportunities within it. Coaching environments should have high levels of connection, competition, autonomy and opportunity.

Connection: An energy exchange between people
Competition: Striving to go beyond others within the group
Autonomy: Self-government
Opportunity: The chance to compete

These terms can be described as the winning behaviours (amongst the others that will be unique to your organisation) that act as catalysts for enhancing skill acquisition and performance. These behaviours should be set and enforced by the cultural architects within the environment and organisation.

Cultural Architects are leaders, champions, or advocates who influence, motivate and engage others to align with the principles that drive success and the values of the organisation.

'Cultural Architects are leaders, champions, or advocates who influence, motivate and engage others to align with the principles that drive success and the values of the organisation'

On the other hand, we have the negative, destructive forces of the cultural assassins who make excuses, complain, blame, go through the motions and work to their own agenda. When it comes to dealing with cultural assassins, the most decorated manager in the history of football, Sir Alex Ferguson, says it best during a conversation with British Cycling legend Sir Dave Brailsford.

Sir Dave Brailsford: 'What is your secret to constant success and longevity?'

Sir Alex Ferguson: 'Get rid of the c****'[44]

We'll now explore each characteristic starting with connection.

Connection

Aspiring financiers flock to New York, hopeful start-up technologists to Silicon Valley, and would-be actors go to Hollywood. The reason is that our skills develop best in response to like-minded human beings. Feeling connected to others is a fundamental need and a catalyst for developing any skill. The more in sync we are with our teammates, peers, or colleagues, the more satisfaction, knowledge and skill we are likely to acquire.

'Our skills develop best in response to like-minded human beings'

There should be a sincere and meaningful sense of unity. This is one of the reasons why picking the right organisation to work with is so important. When we fail to align with the interests and values of the group, we are dragged from our sweet spot and experience an exponential reduction in psychological fire-power.

One of the best ways to sustain concordance is to surround ourselves with supportive people who share our ambition and values. Spending time with those who understand our commitment to develop helps us to create and sustain our motivation. The desire not to let teammates we respect and care for down can be another motivating factor. Plus, it provides us with a support system in response to the inevitable ups and downs.

Competition

Iron sharpens iron. Our development accelerates in competitive, enthusiastic, and high-effort environments where learning and winning are the aims. In elite performance environments this is business as usual.

'Iron sharpens iron'

The more advanced the mental structures of our colleagues, peers, and teammates, the more advanced our own will become. We want to embed ourselves in a supportive yet challenging environment. We should be glad for our peers when they do well, and we should be disappointed when we don't.

Internal competition is very often the spark that incentivises us to reach that next level, and a competitive environment leads us to train hard. Anything void of direct competition means there are no objective criteria for superior performance. Competitive environments keep us in the adaptive zone, and can be interspersed with lots of fun.

Autonomy

Autonomy is the right to decide our own courses of action; one of the defining themes of three-dimensional training. The opposite is authoritarian instruction, traditionally associated with one-dimensional training. This includes excessive threats, surveillance, and constant evaluation. Too much of this makes it impossible to enjoy learning, suffocating our psychological fire-power. When we feel like our life is at stake every time we train or compete, we're less likely to engage in the session. Questions emerge like: What will happen if I make a mistake? Will I look stupid? Will I be humiliated? This can lead to fear of failure causing individuals to play it safe, hiding their deficiencies instead of addressing them.

'When we feel like our life is at stake every time we train or compete, we're less likely to engage in the session'

In elite performance environments the standards are communicated clearly and it's our job to meet them. There is no one yelling at us to get our act together because getting our act together is our job.

'In elite performance environments there is no one yelling at us to get our act together because getting our act together is our job'

The message here is not about isolation; it's about developing independence, so that we have the freedom and discretion to take ownership of our own training and development.

> ***Note:*** We know by now that to excel we must possess concordance with the role. If we need threats, surveillance, and constant evaluation to push us, we might be pursuing the wrong goals.

Opportunity

Perhaps the most critical factor when it comes to maximising progress is the opportunity to compete. Ultimately we have to perform our roles. We learn to write by writing, to play football by playing football, and to soldier through soldiering. Assuming we are technically and psychologically prepared, we must have the opportunity to compete in the real world.

The market, the pitch, and the battlefield will give us feedback that no textbook, drills, nor games in the training room can ever provide. The stressors experienced in the real world are the most powerful form of feedback and the purest in terms of optimising our mental structures.

'The market, the pitch, and the battlefield will give us feedback that no textbook, drills, nor games in the training room can ever provide'

Now we know what the optimal talent development environment looks like, it's time to acquire concordant skills using an Individual Development Plan (IDP). Our IDP can be used independently or with a coach. The types of skills we need to acquire, and the way to develop those skills, are addressed through a six-step process. Once complete, this plan of action will evolve as we advance our skills and accomplish our goals.

CHAPTER SUMMARY

- Anyone who influences training can be considered a coach (performer, peer, manager, parent or friend).
- Traditionally, we think of coaches as screaming maniacs, pointing frantically while shouting instructions. Coaches that jump in and solve the problem themselves deprive us of opportunities to grow.
- We can't learn about things after the solution has been revealed. Learning occurs while the answer is in the process of being discovered.
- The first thing a great coach does is laser in on the specific dimensions that skills are breaking down in competition, then initiate breakthrough moments through setting the right constraints.
- The great coach is there to facilitate the learning curve, but we are responsible for it. The real job of the coach is to encourage the performers to coach themselves and each other.
- Feedback begins and ends with you. After we've exhausted our own brains, we can involve peers. Only then can we seek out coach for verification.
- Access to data is a right we should have to earn, and it comes after thinking for ourselves.
- We need a mentor to acts as a sounding board, an arse-kicker to reminds us of the realities of performance and a cheerleader to provide encouragement and motivation.
- Coaching environments should have high levels of connection, they should also be competitive and we should have the autonomy to decide our own courses of action.

- Assuming we are technically and psychologically prepared, we must have the opportunity to compete in the real world.

15

INDEPENDENT DEVELOPMENT PLANS (IDPS)

> You are what you do, not what you say you'll do
>
> Carl Jung

92% of people who set new year's goals never achieve them and 80% fail by February.[45] That leaves 8% in a very elite category of achievers. What do they do differently that 92% of us are missing out on?

The answer is that elite performers manage themselves exceptionally well. Whether we're aspiring artists, athletes, or CEOs, we are not robots. Anyone giving single-minded, determined, ambitious people like us sets of orders, expecting us to execute like a machine would is in for a surprise.

You may have noticed that you don't always do what you say you will. Every morning on which you hit snooze on your alarm clock you break a promise you made to yourself only eight hours ago. That's how bad we are at this. We're not our own servants; instead we are complicated individuals we have to learn to negotiate with.

This is about personal leadership. We must start with setting a plan that we will actually follow. We know that ambition isn't the problem, follow through is. That's why maximising our motivation is at the forefront of design with the IDP method. It's our development plan and therefore we take the lead in all of it. We drive everything in individual development planning, the goals we set and the method for achieving them, this ensures we have complete volition with the process, maximising the probability we stick to the plan and achieve our objectives.

The IDP gives us the carrots and sticks along with the opportunity to learn how to use them. We know the answers most of the time, and the times we don't represent vital opportunities to develop our ability to work them out. The aim is to become a self-sustaining, self-improving, and self-regulating elite performer.

'Volition is everything when it comes to follow through'

Traditionally development-planning sessions resemble a medical consultation. The coach makes their assessment and decides on what was good and bad before offering a prescriptive, vague, off-the-shelf improvement plan. We play a minor and passive role in the process. Inevitably the plan ends up a mundane, ineffective, gutless piece of paper that never sticks. We need to do everything we can to avoid these prescriptive packages.

Your learning and development needs are specific to you. Remember, we each have a unique nature, and to get the most out of ourselves we must align with it. The more individualised our development plan, the more we will maximise each moment's potential for progress. We need to address our own biggest obstacles rather than the general pattern of error within a group. This means assigning specific practice drills that target the dimensions where our skills break down in competition.

A plan we don't stick to is a waste of everyone's time. Here we set our own goals, and the method for achieving them. This maximises our volition, alignment and the probability we will stick to the plan and achieve our objectives.

The IDP makes statements like 'get better' actionable by forcing us to clarify what excellence looks like to us, pinpointing our strengths and weaknesses, setting the training outcomes we will strive to achieve, and eliciting the strategies that will take us there. It applies to all aspects of performance: technical, physical, and psychological skills (and even lifestyle skills). This maximises our preparation for competition.

The IDP can also sharpen communication with peers, coaches and managers provoking insight by prompting serious thinking, which means we can extract more value from these individuals, should we wish to involve them. The critical stipulation is that we do all the decision-making. To be clear, the IDP does not require external involvement and remains an effective tool even if used in isolation.

> ***Note:*** Coaches - This is an elite development tool, not an HR or management whipping mechanism, therefore the performer drives everything. If you're the coach and you want total buy-in from your performers, you can use questioning to expand options, challenge, and prompt consideration, but you must let the planning flow from them.

Creating an Individual Development Plan

The IDP process breaks down the very complicated and all-encompassing concept of achieving excellence into smaller units, specific enough to be measured. Dividing up what looks like an infinite amount of material into digestible chunks means that we can decompose our pursuit of excellence into a series of achievable sprints, as opposed to an unrelenting marathon.

Creating an IDP comprises six steps:

- Step 1 - Model excellence – What are we trying to build?
- Step 2 - Rate importance – What are the highest value activities?
- Step 3 - Identify a baseline – Where are we now?
- Step 4 - Aim at a target – What outcomes do we want to achieve?
- Step 5 - Develop a process – What actions will achieve our outcome?
- Step 6 - Steps 1-6 calibration – 360-degree feedback on the above

Step 1 - Modelling excellence: 'What are we trying to build?'

Have you ever tried to complete a puzzle with no picture? Could you put a puzzle together if the title just said 'NFL quarterback,' 'CEO' or 'Published Author'? Not impossible, but much more bothersome than the puzzle needs to be. One of the simplest tips for completing a puzzle is to check the image on the box lid. This keeps us focused on what we are trying to build.

The IDP starts with the end in mind. We need to identify the fundamental qualities or characteristics of elite performance for our role. We start by listing the qualities or characteristics we have determined are important to performance. For example:

Roger Federer is a professional tennis player who has won 20 Grand Slam titles, the most in history.[46] His IDP might include technical, psychological and physical skills (amongst others) like:

	CONSTRUCT
Technical	First Serve
	Second Serve
	Return Serve
Psychological	Confidence
	Re-focusing after errors
Physical	Nutrition
	Family Time
	Sleep

Note: As an athlete, he might include physical capabilities (amongst others) like; Strength, endurance, flexibility, etc...

Step 2 - Rate importance; 'What are the highest-value activities?'

Now we know what puzzle we're trying to build, and we have found all the pieces. We don't set out to complete a 10,000-piece puzzle all in one day. We need to start with small but important sections that make the next section easier to complete. These are the most important parts of the puzzle. We must identify the edges, group pieces of similar colour together, and arrange the corner pieces into a large square.

We can't develop everything at once. Performance requires trade-offs and we must prioritise our efforts. Development needs to be structured with clear focus on the most pivotal skills. We must never work on the small things at the expense of the big things. Now we must rank each skill on a scale of 0 (not at all important) to 10 (extremely important) based on the importance ("I") of each skill.

	CONSTRUCT	IMPORTANCE
Technical	First Serve	9
	Second Serve	9
	Return Serve	9
Psychological	Confidence	9
	Re-focusing after errors	9
Physical	Nutrition	7
	Family Time	7
	Sleep	7

Pareto's Law states that 80% of the effects come from 20% of the causes. In tennis, the serve, the return serve and the second serve dictate approximately 80% of points won. Therefore an aspiring Wimbledon champion's development plan should reflect this and be scored higher for these areas.

> ***Note:*** The objective here is to identify our equivalent first serve, return serve, and second serve skills so that we can devote our training resources to these high-

value skills that have a disproportionate impact on the results we produce.

Step 3 - Set a baseline

Before we jump to setting targets, we need to understand where we are today and why. A better understanding of the problem allows us to develop more effective solutions. We need to rank each skill on a scale of 0 (poor) to 10 (excellent), based on our current perceived ability in each skill.

> ***Note:*** The actual scale isn't important; it's just a mechanism through which we can establish where we are and where we are not. If you prefer 0-100 that's fine.

The crucial step is to elicit the content behind the number to keep things objective and to get you to demonstrate your thinking. So if Roger Federer has re-focusing after errors as one of his disproportionately important skills. The next step is to baseline this skill.

> ***QUESTION:*** On a scale of one to ten how would you score your ability to re-focus after errors?
>
> ***Roger Federer:*** '6'
>
> ***QUESTION:*** Why not 5?
>
> ***Roger Federer:*** [might respond by saying something like…](1) Most of the time I dust myself down and get

on with it. 70% of the time it's not a problem.
(2) I never completely lose my temper or let my opponents recognise I'm frustrated.
(3) I never let it spiral, it's only ever two or three errors max.

Note: This process of questioning can be done with this script. We don't need a coach for this.

This step provides us (and coach, parents, or teachers) with critical insights into self awareness. More specifically it shows how we perceive our current competencies, how hard on ourselves we are, and what our perceptions of good look like.

	CONSTRUCT	IMPORTANCE	BASELINE
Technical	First Serve	9	9
	Second Serve	9	9
	Return Serve	9	9
Psychological	Confidence	9	7
	Re-focusing after errors	9	6
Physical	Nutrition	7	7
	Family Time	7	7
	Sleep	7	7

Step 4: Set a target - 'What outcomes do we want to achieve?'

Outcome: The result we want to achieve

We need a target to aim for. It's hard to score without any goalposts. Without a scoring system that determines what constitutes good or bad performance, it becomes very difficult to improve. There is always a way to measure performance, even if it's just a simple subjective 1-10 rating scale from as illustrated here.

The point is to establish objective outcomes that will clarify when we have or have not achieved the target that we set. We can use experts, peers and others who utilise the skill in question from different domains to benchmark ourselves against. For example:

> ***QUESTION:*** 'Where do you want to want be on that scale of 1-10 in one, three or six months from now?' [Roger Federer currently rates himself a (6)]
>
> ***Roger Federer:*** '7.'
>
> ***QUESTION:*** 'Why aren't you a seven now?'
>
> ***Roger Federer:*** (1) 'I'm not patient enough, and I forget that one error means nothing in the context of an entire game.'
> (2) 'I get insecure about my opponent sensing he's getting to me when I make a mistake.'
> (3) 'I don't take enough time between serves [because he's anxious] and sometimes this makes me angry with myself.'

Now Roger has some explicit outcomes to work with: More patience, be secure in himself, and eliminate rushing.

	CONSTRUCT	IMPORTANCE	BASELINE	TARGET
Technical	First Serve	9	9	9
	Second Serve	9	9	9
	Return Serve	9	9	9
Psychological	Confidence	9	7	7
	Re-focusing after errors	9	6	7 (+1)
Physical	Nutrition	7	7	7
	Family Time	7	7	7
	Sleep	7	7	7

Now Roger knows where he wants to go (7), and where he wants to move away from (6). Having something to move away from and something to move towards maximally activates our brain's predator and prey circuitry, maximising our motivation. This scoring mechanism provides him with explicit criteria for progress, a way to judge whether the development plan has been a success, and which provides a realistic expectation of improvement.

Outcomes are important, like being patient, less insecure and to eliminate rushing, but what enables Federer to acquire these skills is his process for achieving them. Outcomes are important, like being patient, less insecure and to eliminate rushing, but what will ultimately enable Federer to acquire these skills is a precise set of actions for achieving them- a process. We must make sure our goals are actionable if we are to achieve them.

Step 5 - Set a process- 'What actions will achieve our outcome?'

Process: A series of actions or steps to achieve an outcome

We have to come up with a specific set of actions to enact that will result in achieving our target.

QUESTION: 'What do you need to do day to day, week to week, month to month, to ensure you achieve each of your outcomes?'

Roger Federer:
Outcome: Being patient
Process: A ten-second countdown after each error

Outcome: Less insecure
Process: Wear polarised glasses like poker players do between sets

Outcome: Eliminate rushing
Process: Set a sixty-second performance routine to enact between serves

CONSTRUCT	IMPORTANCE	BASELINE	TARGET	
Re-focusing after errors	9	6	7 (+1)	• A ten-second countdown after each error • Wear polarised glasses between sets • Set a 60 second performance routine to perform between serves

There are four key benefits to a well-thought-out process:

Benefit One- A process keeps us sane

A focus on outcomes rips us from the present into a state of constant failure until we eventually achieve and can then enjoy success. On the other hand, a process provides an opportunity for daily success, because every time we execute the process, we succeed. This means we get to feel good and this makes us want to execute the process more.

Benefit Two- A process can be upgraded as we go
The daily focus means we have a finger on the pulse. Fine tuning as we go, we can test and adjust the process each time we use it. If, after a couple of games Roger Federer's ten-second countdown doesn't work, he can try something else. Failure becomes feedback providing an opportunity to optimise our process. This is way more effective than realising we have an ineffective approach three months down the line when it's time to test the outcome.

Benefit Three- A process makes things less personal
If the result is failure, then our process failed and we just need to improve it. This moves us from the 'I'm not good enough' mentality to: 'My approach isn't good enough.' Subsequently we spend less mental effort wallowing in self-pity, and more on understanding where to improve our process. A much healthier, more effective place to be.

Benefit Four- With a process there is no need to think
Thinking prohibits action. Once the process is set, all we have to do is execute. There is no need for thinking. This means that we can save mental effort for high-value activities.

Step 6 – Calibration

Jigsaw puzzles are not just a solitary activity; peers and coaches are ideal companions. So, if you want some company while you ponder, get them involved and complete the puzzle together. Four eyes are better than two - especially if those eyes have more advanced mental structures than yours.

When people know our aims, they are better able to support us to achieve them. Plus, rating ourselves can be difficult, so input from peers and coaches can help balance out our personal biases. We can have coach, teammates, or friends carry out their own assessments of us in relation to (1) agreed skills (2) our importance ratings (3) our self-evaluation and (4) our target level.

> 'When people know our aims, they are better able to support us to achieve them'

As a coach, we can't be effective if we don't know where our performer is at and where they want to go. If we want to influence their behaviour then we have to accurately understand their perceptions. The coach-performer relationship is stronger when vision, goals and targets are shared and agreed. Any differences can be highlighted and addressed in advance of investing resources.

> ***Note:*** It can be nice to present the data in a spider diagram, excel sheet or bar chart to create a visual representation of our IDP.

Once the IDP process has been completed it is time to put our process to work. We can measure the effects as we periodically check in to score our progress. As we make progress we will need to scan through the six steps, updating them as we go to reflect how new demands emerge forcing us to adapt our development plans in response.

We can have the best three-dimensional training, the greatest coaching, an optimised development environment, and the perfect IDP in place, but now we have to go and put all of that to work. This is where fear of failure can potentially de-rail all our great work. With concordant goals, and well-designed development plans, this is unlikely. But just in case, chapter 16 shows you how to summon the confidence to really go for it.

CHAPTER SUMMARY

- 92% of people who set new year's goals never achieve them and 80% fail by February.
- We are not robots. We're single-minded, determined, ambitious people who can't just be given a set of orders and be expected to execute like a machine would
- Maximising our motivation is at the forefront of design with the IDP. It's our development plan, our responsibility, our future, and therefore we take the lead in all of it.
- Volition is everything when it comes to follow through. The IDP gives us the whip and the opportunity to learn how to use it. We know the answers most of the time, and the times we don't represent vital opportunities to develop our ability to work them out.
- Creating an IDP comprises six steps:
  - Step 1 - Model excellence - What are we trying to build?
  - Step 2 – Rate importance - What are the highest value activities?
  - Step 3 - Identify a baseline – Where are we now?
  - Step 4 – Aim at a target – What outcomes do we want to achieve?
  - Step 5 - Develop a process - What actions do we need to take and when?
  - Step 6 – Calibration of Steps 1 - 5
- A clear process; keeps us sane, can be upgraded as we go, makes things less personal, and eliminates the need to think.

- Calibration is key. The coach-performer relationship is stronger when vision, goals and targets are shared and agreed. When people know our aims, they are better able to support us to achieve them.

16

THE F WORD

The maxim 'Nothing but perfection' may be
spelled 'Paralysis'
Winston Churchill

Disaster was the first thought that entered my mind as I watched the window smash for the second time. The event went viral, bringing immediate worldwide attention. Luckily, the general consensus was that Musk's latest idea - the Cybertruck - is genius.

Elon Musk: You want a truck that's really tough, not fake tough...You want a truck you can take a sledgehammer to, a truck that won't scratch, doesn't dent.[47]

Note: To prove it he directed Tesla Chief Designer, Franz von Holzhausen, to strike the all-electric Cybertruck's door with a sledgehammer.

Franz von Holzhausen: WHACK! [He smashes the side of the truck]

Note: The result… no damage, not even a scratch. The audience gasped and applause ensued. Next up, Musk instructs him to throw a metal ball at the driver's side window which is made of armoured glass.

Elon Musk: Oh my f****** God.

The window shatters. Silence.

Elon Musk: [Drawing laughs] Maybe that was a little too hard'.

With a sense of humour, humility and irony he carried on with a highly entertaining product launch.

Elon Musk: Oh man, At least it didn't go through. That's a plus side.

Elon Musk's staggering success as he grew Paypal, Tesla, and SpaceX into the trailblazing companies they are today contains an equally staggering amount of failure. Whatever future success he has will likely be accompanied by still more failure.

Musk's portfolio of failures include being rejected by Netscape, being fired as CEO of his own company while on honeymoon, and watching both Tesla and SpaceX hover on the brink of bankruptcy. The first SpaceX launch failed at a cost of $30million. The second failed at a cost of $60million. Third time lucky the launch was successful and won the company a billion-dollar contract from

NASA.[48] As much as his highlight reel inspires, Musk's gift is learning from his failures and emerging from them stronger than he went.

Was Musk afraid of failure? Most likely. Did it stop him in his tracks? Absolutely not. He has a unique outlook that stops fear of failure from breaking his stride. Instead of trying to avoid it, Elon Musk considers failure part of the process.

Elon Musk:
'Failure is an option here. If things are not failing, you are not innovating enough.'

This chapter deconstructs the biological role of fear, the two mind-sets we have the option of bringing to the table, and most importantly, how to generate the confidence to give it all we've got.

Fear of Failure (Atychiphobia): When fear stops us performing the actions that move us towards our goals

We all possess an innate ambition to acquire skill. As babies we develop the most challenging skills like learning to walk or talk. We never contemplate whether it's possible or worry about making mistakes. So, what puts an end to this? Judgement. As soon as we realise we are being judged, many of us develop fear of failure. The reality is that whilst we need to know what people really think of us, it can be a bitter pill to swallow.

The biological role of fear

We know that our two-million-year-old brains were built for survival. Failure back then often resulted in death, and fear prompted us to avoid it. This all made perfect sense, but flash forward two million years and we have a problem. Our challenge now is to excel, not survive. The fear that served our ancestors can deprive us. Avoiding uncomfortable situations is a rational thing to do, but when we deny failure altogether, we bring progress to a standstill.

> 'Avoiding uncomfortable situations is a rational thing to do, but when we deny failure altogether, we bring progress to a standstill'

The good news is that, if we're failing we're in the adaptive zone, creating that performance gap that sparks us to adapt to a higher level. Plus, the failure gives us clues to how we can move forward. It shows us what skills and dimensions are breaking down, and thus where to focus our efforts. There are always lessons in mistakes. And lessons are what we need to propel us forward.

When fear leads to patterns

The emotional brain is the oldest part of the brain; it is where fear is triggered thanks mainly to adrenaline. There are three behaviours this hormone instinctively prompts us to engage in: fight, flight, or freeze. These hangovers from our caveman ancestors can impede our ability to acquire skill. When we feel the threat of failure upon us, one of three potentially destructive behaviours can emerge.

One: Avoidance

> Avoidance: When a person changes their behaviour to avoid thinking, feeling or doing difficult things

The first danger is that, when fear sets in, we stop trying and switch off. The voices of judgement can lead us to procrastinate for as long as possible. After all, shirking challenges is a guaranteed way to avoid humiliation. We can sidestep all the discomfort through avoidance, we take flight from the situation.

When we fear failure and flee, avoid or procrastinate, results inevitably suffer. This confirms our initial belief. 'See, I told you I couldn't do it. I knew this was a waste of time.' This amplifies the problem. We invest even less effort and our results get even worse. This strengthens our initial belief 'that we can't' and the cycle repeats. This can lead to spiralling negativity that culminates in a total character assassination: 'I'm lazy.' 'I have no willpower.' 'I hate myself.'

When we flee from failure, the unconscious message we reinforce is that we are unable to deal with challenges. Our level of confidence is determined by how we unconsciously judge our own behaviour. The unconscious mind presides over our actions twenty-four seven passing judgement. If the judge (unconscious mind) observes us saying 'I am going to try hard today' but by the end of the day we avoided the challenge altogether, the verdict will be that we are a fearful person who avoids challenges. We end up trapped with this invisible, critical judge; our own brain. The danger is that we self-criticise, chipping away at our own confidence until there is nothing left.

Two: Victim mentality is born

Perhaps the most destructive pattern that emerges from fear of failure is Ego. Ego arises from our brains' attempts to preserve confidence artificially. Ego is confidence on credit with extortionate interest. Payment comes in terms of a complete halt to our development. While we might say we want the truth, all we really want is to be reassured that we're right, and that we are hidden from failure. We freeze.

Ego puts the nail in the coffin of progress by denying altogether that our mistakes exist. We start to pretend we're better than we are. Very quickly we become our own worst enemies. Here, looking good comes before improvement. The number one priority is to deflect criticism.

> 'Ego puts the nail in the coffin of progress by denying altogether that our mistakes exist'

Ego blinds us to reality; we make excuses, refuse to accept responsibility, and blame others. 'If only my coach could communicate better,' 'if only my colleagues understood me,' 'if only the board weren't so impatient.' If it weren't for everyone else, life would be great. We search for ways to make us feel better about our own failures; like attributing the success of others to luck, being well-connected or winners of the genetic lottery. Excuses relieve the guilt we feel for surrendering to our fears.

> 'Ego blinds us to reality; we make excuses, refuse to accept responsibility, and blame others'

Freezing, concealing or hiding from our failures means we

cannot correct them. The person, organisation, or team that cannot self-correct cannot excel across time. We end up powerless victims unable to adapt to the challenges that impede our growth.

'The person, organisation, or team that cannot self-correct cannot excel across time.'

Three: Overcompensation

Overcompensation: Taking excessive measures in an attempt to correct for (perceived) deficiencies

The final response is to fix our bayonets and fight. Here we plug away like a world champion. The problem is we don't tend to have the conditioning of a world champion. 'I will not accept failure,' is the motto, but our training hasn't prepared us for the demands we start to impose on ourselves. We become perfectionists. If something isn't perfect, it's a disaster. Here it's all-or-nothing. We stay on the perfect diet or we binge. We train for three hours a day and then nothing for weeks. We work eighteen-hour days one month, then we're last in, first out the next.

A high work rate is commendable, but if the intent is to compensate for deficient confidence through becoming a workaholic, we are in for a losing battle. The inevitable product of an all-guns-blazing approach is that we break down, blow up or burn out.

When our expectations are perfection we set ourselves up with an impossible task that always ends in failure. Nobody, not even outliers, can live up to perfect.

How to build confidence

Confidence: The sincere belief in someone or something

Outlier performers don't remove fear; they grow confidence. When our confidence exceeds our fear we experience forward motion towards our goal. To excel we must have the confidence to step into our adaptive zones as much as possible. This comes with the risk of failing. The question is how do we generate the confidence to really go for it?

'Outlier performers don't remove fear; they grow confidence'

Some are born with confidence. Most must cultivate it. There are no supplements and just saying, be optimistic and believe in yourself, is pop-psych rubbish. Similarly, an exaggerated sense of self-importance or mantras that insinuate that we're better than we are, or that our problems don't exist, do more harm than good and are not the answer.

Fear of failure and confidence are mind-sets that can be demonstrated on a continuum. The good news is that mind-sets are just beliefs held in our minds, and we can change our minds.

'The good news is that mind-sets are just beliefs held in our minds, and we can change our minds'

	MINDSET	
	FEARFUL ←	→ CONFIDENT
WHEN FACED WITH FAILURE	I'M USELESS	NEED MORE EFFORT OR BETTER STRATEGY
FEEDBACK IS	AN INSULT	POTENTIAL FOR IMPROVEMENT
THINK THEY ARE	UNABLE TO CHANGE	A WORK IN PROGRESS
THEY FEEL GOOD WHEN	WHEN I'M PERFECT	WHEN I CAN DO SOMETHING I COULDN'T DO BEFORE
COPING STRATEGY	BLAME	DETERMINATION
RELATIONSHIP WITH CONFIDENCE	I HAVE TO PROTECT IT	I GAIN CONFIDENCE AS I OVERCOME CHALLENGES
WHEN FACED WITH DIFFICULTY	I'M NOT GOOD ENOUGH	SMART THINKING AND EFFORT CAN GET ME THROUGH THIS
WANT OPPONENTS WHO ARE	SMALLER, SLOWER, WEAKER	BIGGER, FASTER, STRONGER
WHEN THINGS GET CHALLENGING	LOSE INTEREST	SWITCH ON
GET THEIR THRILL FROM	AN EASY WIN	A HARD CHALLENGE

This model was inspired by both: Carol S. Dweck's million-copy best-seller- *Mindset: The New Psychology of Success* [49] and, Tal Ben-Shahar's insightful book- *The Pursuit of Perfect*. [50]

We need to think about where we are, what we want to achieve and what mind-set will take us there. Understanding how our mindset impacts our behaviour means we can put this into practice for ourselves and others, so that we notice when we feel threatened by feedback, discouraged by something that requires effort, or we evade the truth.

There are seven principles that accelerate the rate with which we build confidence. We'll deconstruct each of these now.

Principle One- Reward and effort process

The default in high performance is to reward results, not effort. This makes total sense seeing as the external rewards of competition are based on the results we produce. The challenge is that rewarding outcomes implies that we are winners because we won, and losers because we lost. This outcome domination can lead to the idea that our results are a literal indication of who we are and what we're capable of. This adds fuel to the fire when it comes to fear of failure.

With this mentality, low grades means we're not smart. Struggling to pick up a skill means we lack the gift. And our failing start-up indicates we don't have what it takes. Failure becomes part of our narrative rather than a transient experience. 'I failed' transitions to 'I am a failure' and if we're failures, why bother trying?

Obsessing on outcomes breeds the need to appear gifted, transforming failure into a fire-breathing dragon to be avoided at all costs – at the expense of our development.

To cultivate confidence, we need to trade out the infatuation with outcomes, and reward doing what it takes to excel; investing effort and aligning with the right strategy. No matter how gifted we might be, effort and strategy are the catalysts that ignite our potential. Outliers align with the principles of three-dimensional training and invest enormous amounts of effort to acquire their expertise.

'Obsessing on outcomes breeds the need to appear gifted, transforming failure into a fire-breathing dragon to be avoided at all costs'

The extent to which we align with the principles of three-dimensional training like; solving our own problems, engaging in peer-to-peer feedback and adapting to the right constraints will dictate our development trajectory. Then the effort we put in which includes; how often we train, how hard we focus, and the level of challenge we take on in training will dictate how far that strategy takes us.

Rewarding effort and strategy, can reconstruct behaviour. Rewarding the alignment with the right type of practice reinforces adherence to it. Praise for great perception and decision-making, even if the execution isn't quite right, increases the chances the performer perseveres and ultimately masters the skill. Likewise, rewarding the performer for stepping into the adaptive zone cultivates the cravings for taking on challenging problems that offer the most opportunity for progress, as opposed to the ones that make them appear talented.

'Rewarding the alignment with the right type of practice reinforces adherence to it'

Rewarding effort also means we invest more, which inevitably increases the quality of the outcomes we produce. 'I knew there was something there!' We invest even more effort. Our results improve even more. We start to galvanise our belief, and our perception of potential expands. This cycle becomes an upward spiral that feeds itself.

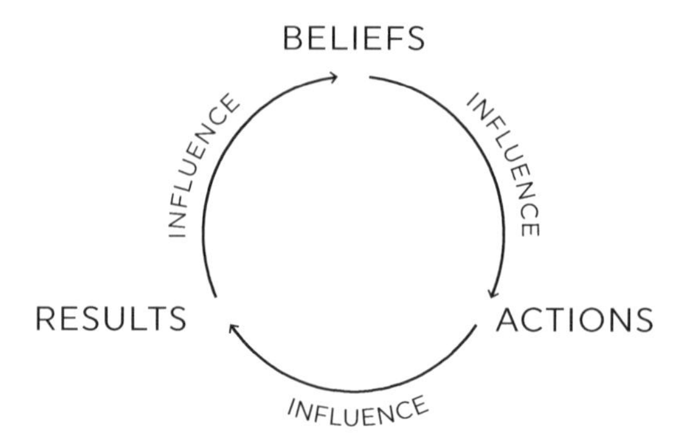

We begin to perceive that through effort, we can overcome our challenges and expand our potential. Once we internalise that effort offers a solution to our problems, it's easy to summon it when the going gets tough. This ability to stick at it, especially when it's not going well, is one of the defining characteristics of elite performers.

Does rewarding effort and strategy produce performers who believe that anyone can become Cristiano Ronaldo, Elon Musk or JK Rowling? No. We know that some have inconceivable strength in certain areas, or fanatic interest in others. But we also know that our potential is expandable and that incredible skills can be acquired given the right effort and strategy for improvement.

Principle Two- Permission to be human[51]

No one excels and gets to avoids failure. We need to accept this. Michael Jordan was cut from his high school basketball team. J.K Rowling's Harry Potter was turned down by 12 publishers. Warren Buffet was rejected by Harvard University.

We must give ourselves the permission to be human. The reason we are engaged in skill acquisition is to learn how to acquire new skills. This comes with the understanding that we do not know everything we need to know. Yet. We will fail at times. People will doubt us. At times, we're going to look bad. And that's ok. It's completely natural to make mistakes, fail, and feel scared, anxious, or sad. Throughout the development process we will encounter euphoria, joy and elation but also anger, frustration and doubt. There is not one outlier in any endeavour that hasn't intensely encountered these emotions.

'The reason we are engaged in skill acquisition is to learn how to acquire new skills. This comes with the understanding that we do not know everything we need to know. Yet'

When we give ourselves the permission to be human, we instantly reduce the intensity of these emotions when they inevitably strike. This reduces their power over us, increasing our potential to excel.

'When we give ourselves the permission to be human, we instantly reduce the intensity of these emotions and experiences when they inevitably occur'

Principle Three- Progressive exposure

I see this all the time. People set a goal and come out of the gate fast and furious, only to run out of steam five minutes in. The mind-set of go big or go home, needs to shift to slow and steady wins the race. Remember, slow is smooth and smooth is fast. We need challenge to change us, but we only level up when we're prepared to do so, otherwise the risk is that we blow up.

'The mind-set of go big or go home, needs to shift to slow and steady wins the race'

We need to chop up our challenges until they are small enough that we are prepared to take them on. The key to building confidence is to start with something we are capable, and motivated to cope with. Through progressive exposure we gradually increase the size of the steps we decide to take, inoculating against the fear of failure as we go. There is no rush. The small steps will compound. Instead of procrastination, we get iteration. As we experience failure and learn from it, our confidence grows and we begin to perceive failure as potential for improvement.

When we say to ourselves: 'I'm going to give it a try today,' and we grit our teeth, give it a go, and fail, but we accept the failure. The judge inside us will start to internalise motivation, confidence, and bravery. Now we can begin to see ourselves as someone who is confident, capable and can cope when things don't go to plan.

Principle Four- It's not that bad

Impact bias: The tendency to over-estimate the intensity of future emotional states

Fear of failure is exactly like our first kiss, cycling without stabilisers, or swimming in the deep end; all unknown petrifying experiences. Clinging to the side of the deep, dark pool for hours, suddenly we just do it, and seconds later we're thinking, what was I so worried about? Even if it didn't go perfectly.

The funny thing about failure is that it's not until we fail that we realise it's not that bad. The dragon we feared is never nearly as terrifying as we thought. Psychologists call this impact bias. Our evolutionary programming, designed to keep us alive, overestimates how bad things are. Consequently we fear failure more than we should. The failure itself is never as bad as we anticipate. But unless we fail, we never learn this.

'The funny thing about failure is that it's not until we fail that we realise it's not that bad'

When we think about potential failure, we imagine the whole event, all of the pain, the embarrassment. We focus on the failure and forget the things in our lives that haven't changed. The other 99% of life remains more or less the same. Failure impedes the task at which we fail, not us as a person. HBO will still churn out great series, beer will still taste refreshing, and our family and friends will still love us.

I am not saying failing doesn't hurt; it does. There is nothing fun about failure. Nor am I saying that we should aim to fail; that would be idiotic. The message is that it's way less painful than we think.

Principle Five- Harness your psychological immune system

We're way tougher than we think. We are built to compete, take on challenges, and cope with the inevitable hits that come with failure. We are the product of millions of years of evolution. Our in-built ability to recover from trauma is hard-wired into our DNA.

'We are built to compete, take on challenges, and for the inevitable hits that come with failure'

In the same way, our physical immunity depends on exposure to germs, viruses, and bacteria. This also happens on a psychological level. When we put in the effort, take a risk, and fail, we start to build immunity to fear of failure. Our psychological immune system kicks in.

Taking on a challenge and exposing ourselves to fear is how we strengthen our psychological immune systems and forge confidence. We have to learn to fail, and trust in our psychological immune system to get over it, this doesn't mean we never get sick, but it means we get sick less and recover quicker.

'We have to learn to fail, and trust in our psychological immune systems to get over it, this doesn't mean we never get sick, but it means we get sick less and recover quicker.'

The catalyst of all mankind's greatest achievements is the ability to have a go, fail, get over it and go again.

Principle Six- Compare you to you

Comparing our own behind-the-scenes with everyone else's highlight reel is why so many of us struggle with confidence. The most common way to measure progress is by comparison to others. To some degree or another, we all care how we compare to the rest. That's fine. But, when our confidence is completely dependent on how compare to the rest there is a problem. Although glory can be a powerful motivator, the problem is that there is little room at the top and inevitably we will fall short at times. It is in these moments our confidence runs dry.

'Comparing our own behind-the-scenes with everyone else's highlight reel is why so many of us struggle with confidence'

Those at elite academic institutions, law firms, and sporting academies were selected for these elite institutions because they were number one in their previous schools, universities and teams. But now, in these elite organisations 99% of those who were used to being in number one position, no longer get to stay there. If their confidence had relied on being number one and suddenly they're not, they suffocate in terms of confidence and fear takes hold.

To forge confidence that sticks, it is paramount that you compare you to you. The questions we need to ask are: 'Am I stronger today than I was yesterday? Will I be smarter a year from now? Am I making progress?'

When we compare ourselves to ourselves, we bring our focus to what we can change to improve our own situations. We are in control and this brings ownership. This is one of the most empowering characteristics of any winning individual or organisation. With ownership our problems no longer have anything to do with anybody else. If it impedes our progress it's our responsibility. This means we can focus our energy on finding solutions, instead of trying to figure out who or what to blame for our shortcomings.

'If it impedes our progress
it's our responsibility'

Principle Seven- Set a clear 'win' or 'development' agenda[49]
Thriving on competition, nurturing the desire to win, and learning how to win under pressure are vital skills. Competitive events, challenging competition, success or disappointment will often trigger us to shift to the next level. But the thing we crave so much, winning, can also hold us back if it's not managed properly. After all, we can win today by relying on skills we know won't work at the next level. This means there are times where we must sacrifice winning today to prioritise developing the capability we need to win tomorrow.

'There are times where we must sacrifice winning today to prioritise developing the capability we need to win tomorrow'

For example, raw athletic ability in football or a photographic memory in trading are skills that enable us to produce winning results in the earlier stages of our development. The snag is that the effectiveness of these attributes diminishes as the standard of competition increases. At the elite level, everyone has these skills. Suddenly new skills like spotting the pass are key for the footballer and connecting information fast and under pressure is key for the trader. If the sole priority has been to win at all costs, and we have relied purely on the skills we know don't work at this new level - raw athletic ability and photographic memory - we won't have formed the mental structures we need to progress and compete at the top.

The good news is that there is a time and place for winning and a time and place for development. We can classify certain competitions or time periods with either a development or win agenda. We can set clear development periods which give us opportunities for experimentation without fear of failing.

Win Agenda: Win at all costs failure is not an option

Develop Agenda: Risk off safe time to experiment

We can intersperse these periods with clear win agendas. The win agenda reminds us that things are real and there are times we have to decide to become confident, grit our teeth and grind out a result. There are consequences for the results we produce, and we have to be able to turn it on when it counts. So, if we're developing new skills then it's the development agenda. If we have three months to keep our job, then it's the win agenda.

> 'If we're developing new skills then it's the development agenda. If we have three months to keep our job, then it's the win agenda'

With minor adjustments to our mind-set failure is transformed from something we fear to potential for improvement. Failures still frustrate us but they no longer turn us to stone. It's never fun hearing that our work doesn't measure up but when we're no longer terrified of negative emotions, judgement and failure, we experience less threat. We can begin to perceive incrementally stepping out of our comfort zone as a way of moving forward. We will start to internalise optimism, bravery and courage. Suddenly we start getting our kicks from taking on hard challenges, putting in the effort becomes worthwhile and when things get tough, we get determined.

At this point in our pursuit of excellence, we have identified and set concordant goals and optimised skill acquisition through aligning with the principles of three-dimensional training. We know what to do and how to do it. Whatever it is to you. The next question is: can we deliver all that technical ability on demand and under pressure when it counts? Concordance and skill acquisition count for nothing if we can't turn it on when it matters most – in competition. From here on out, it's a total head game.

CHAPTER SUMMARY

- When fear stops us performing the actions that move us towards our goals we suffer from fear of failure.
- Fear of failure instinctively prompts us to engage in one of three destructive behaviours:
  - We fight- We fix bayonets and attack with all guns blazing and we inevitably break down, blow up or burn out.
  - We take flight- We sidestep discomfort through avoidance- we flee.
  - We freeze- Ego emerges as we deny altogether that our mistakes exist, we hide from failure.
- Outlier performers don't remove fear; they grow confidence. When confidence exceeds fear we experience forward motion towards our goal.
- Fear of failure and confidence are just beliefs held in our minds, and we can change our minds by:
  - Centring praise on doing what it takes to excel- the amount of effort we put in and the strategy we align with.
  - Giving ourselves the permission to be human- the reason we are engaged in skill acquisition is to learn how to acquire new skills. This comes with the understanding that we do not know everything we need to know. Yet.
  - Progressive exposure- we need challenge to change us, but we only level up when we're prepared to do so, otherwise the risk is that we blow up.

- Realising failure is never the beast we feared: Our evolutionary programming, designed to keep us alive, overestimates how bad things are.
- Trusting our psychological immune systems- we're way tougher than we think. Our in-built ability to recover from trauma is hard-wired into our DNA.
- Comparing you to you- the reason so many of us struggle with confidence is because we compare our behind-the-scenes with everyone else's highlight reel.
- Classifying certain time periods with either a development or win agenda- development periods give us opportunities for experimentation without fear of failing. The win agenda reminds us that competition is real and there are times we have to grit our teeth and win at all costs.

Recommended Reading

Carol S. Dweck - *Mindset: The New Psychology of Success*
Tal Ben-Shahar - *The Pursuit of Perfect*

PART 4

EMOTIONAL CONTROL

17

IT'S A HEAD GAME

In the midst of chaos, there is also opportunity
Sun Tzu

EMOTIONAL CONTROL: The ability to monitor, evaluate and modify your emotional reactions to the ever-changing demands that elite performance (and life) brings

Super Bowl LIV in February 2020 was passing Patrick Mahomes by. The twenty-four-year-old quarterback with a rocket launcher for an arm and a league MVP award already in his locker had just 8 minutes and 33 seconds remaining in the game. Mahomes's team, the Kansas City Chiefs, were trailing 20-10 to the 49ers. He needed to flick the switch and turn the game on its head. Flick the switch he did. The moment the opposition thought they finally had him in their grasp, Patrick Mahomes rocket-armed the ball 44 yards to wide receiver Tyreek

Hill, setting the Chiefs up to score for the first time since early in the second quarter. In a blink of an eye, the Chiefs scored 21 unanswered points and won the Super Bowl. Mahomes was named Super Bowl MVP.[52]

Nerves of steel and calm under pressure are not reserved for sport. For undercover agent Alex Anderson* and his team, the pressure came through a text message. There has been an incident, it's bad. His cover has been blown and his location compromised. Members of a terrorist organisation are en route to take his life. What to do? Hide? Hope? Capitulate? All understandable human reactions. Yet, there is another, more powerful option, the one that Anderson chose. He flicked the switch. Resisting the urge to panic, keeping his composure, and countering with devastating effect. A cool, calm and collected Anderson retraced his steps meticulously. The conclusion he came to was that his actions were faultless. The enemy were bluffing. With his head high and mind clear he executed the operation, acquiring vital intelligence resulting in the team thwarting a would-be devastating terrorist attack costing countless innocent lives.

Perhaps one of the most nerve-wracking experiences any of us could imagine is catastrophic engine failure at 32,000 feet. This is exactly what happened in July 2000 on a routine flight from New York La Guardia airport to Dallas, Texas. The Southwest Airlines Boeing 737-700 was rocked by a huge explosion. An engine on the plane's left side blew, smashing a window and causing cabin de-pressurisation. The aircraft dived and shook vigorously as metal debris sheared off and was flung into the aircraft, smashing a window and sucking a passenger into the hole where the window had been. Passengers reported thinking they were going to

* The performer's name has been changed to maintain their confidentiality.

die and many texted goodbyes to relatives and friends.

Captain Tammie Jo Shults, a former Navy fast-jet fighter pilot (one of the USA's first females to perform the role), was the pilot in charge that day. With oxygen masks dangling and passengers screaming, things looked grim aboard the Southwest Airlines flight. But, listening to the recording from air traffic control, we would never know the grave danger they were all in. As the plane descended abruptly, Captain Shults engaged in cool, calm and controlled communication to her passengers, reassuring them she was going to land in Philadelphia. When it mattered most Shults flicked the switch bringing the aircraft safely into land at Philadelphia International Airport. She then, very calmly, thanked the air traffic control team before walking through the cabin thanking all the passengers, checking that they were ok. In the midst of chaos Captain Shults kept it together to save hundreds of lives.[53]

Elite performance without pressure? No such thing. The two are inseparable. If we want to excel, pressure is inevitable. What Patrick Mahomes, Alex Anderson and Tammie Jo Shults demonstrate is the art of not panicking. Perhaps the most unique characteristic of elite performance is that, when the going gets tough, outliers flick the switch, regulate their emotion and fight the urge to panic. They emerge from crisis triumphant, stronger than when they went in.

> 'When the going gets tough, outlier performers flick the switch, regulate their emotion and fight the urge to panic'

Ten years of work can come down to ten crucial seconds, whether in cup finals, major tournaments, product launches, live television, the leading role, or final exams. We may have spent months getting to that point. Ultimately, we will be judged on our ability to deliver a single performance. To perform when it counts is the measure of elite performance.

Few of us have played international sport, built a billion-dollar company, or flown fighter-jets, but we can all relate to choking under pressure. Every one of us, from school to college student, from novice to Olympian, graduate to CEO, one time or another has choked under pressure. When the stakes are high, sometimes the only thing we do effectively is hit the self-destruct button. The way our minds commit acts of mutiny against us can be an enigmatic experience.

'When the stakes are high, sometimes the only thing we do effectively is hit the self-destruct button'

Too many of us experience frustration over not consistently performing the way we are capable. Emotional control, the third stage in the four-tiered process of accelerating excellence, is about understanding what goes on inside our heads that causes us to perform so poorly or so well; why we are inclined to mess up at the precise moment we need our skill the most. Why we are so prone to fail when we most want to succeed? The pressure isn't the problem; it's how we react to it that can be. Do we stay calm and collected, or start to over-think our performance and capitulate?

'Too many of us experience frustration over not consistently performing the way we are capable'

When the stakes are high, our biggest fear is choking. And we cannot simply train harder to prevent it. As we advance to the competition stage in our performance journey, psychology trumps technique. In those crucial moments, the focus is no longer on getting better, but on delivering. Now it's time to compete on demand and under pressure.

'The focus is no longer on getting better, but on delivering'

This chapter examines how those at the top of their games keep it together and deliver all their technical ability when it matters most. When it comes to negative emotions like doubt and uncertainty, we have two options: to be their master or their servant. A key difference between those who cave and those who climb is what goes on between the ears: the confidence, composure and conviction required to deliver success. Those who climb control their emotions best under the highest stakes. They have mastered emotional control.

Emotion control is the ability to monitor, evaluate and modify our emotional reactions to the ever-changing demands that elite performance brings. To simplify it, I explain it as a set of switches. The aim is to flick the right switch for the right emotion, at the right moment.

The three brains

Performance at the highest level is largely a psychological challenge, it's a head game. Acquiring emotional control starts with understanding how our brain works. After all, if we don't know how the brain works, it's only natural to feel like the victim when negative emotions strike. The question then becomes what goes on between behind our eyes?

In fact, we have three brains, the unconscious, the frontal and the emotional, and at any point in time they compete for control. Outlier performers excel at plugging into the correct brain at the right time.

The unconscious brain

The unconscious brain is the source from which peak performance flows. Elite skill execution is an unconscious process, occurring automatically when the unconscious brain is in the driving seat. Patrick Mahomes's brain automatically computes the angles of his teammates' runs, calculating the most promising option to execute the throw with the precision and slant to fall into his team mate's hand. In live performance, situations unfold so fast there is no time for analysis. Our unconscious brains already know what to do. These are where our advanced mental structures are stored for automatic and rapid deployment.

> 'In live performance, situations unfold so fast there is no time for analysis'

The frontal brain

From time to time, elite performance requires some conscious thinking, like when Alex Anderson took the time to analyse his response to the terrorist threat using data, facts and logic. This is where your frontal brain comes in. In the event that any challenges or unusual circumstances appear that require some conscious thought, the frontal brain, the default back-up in elite performance, wakes up and takes over from our unconscious brain. When we are thinking in a calm, rational manner, the frontal brain is in control.

The frontal brain is the CEO of our lives, the part of us that thinks about what we're doing before we do it. Its central focus is to achieve the things we want to achieve. It is ripe with common sense, interpreting information based on objective data in search of the truth, which in turn leads to informing a plan. When in control, we stick to logic, reason and the plan. Just like Captain Tammy Jo Shults did to bring Southwest Airlines Flight 1380 to land safely.

'The frontal brain is the CEO of our lives, the part of us that thinks about what we're doing before we do it'

The emotional brain

Then we come to brain number three, the real culprit, the emotional brain. Obstacles, uncertainty, and life can make us panic. There is no avoiding this. When we feel or perceive a threat, our blood supply diverts from our unconscious and frontal brains to the emotional brain. The do-it-yourself lobotomy. It's the emotional brain that blurts out drivel, while the frontal brain is left thinking, 'Why the hell did I just say that?' Any time we have irrational thoughts or feelings, the emotional brain is running the show.

When the switch that channels the power supply to our emotional brain is left on, we lose access to the highly sophisticated mental structures encoded in the unconscious part of our brains. When this happens, unconscious execution of the skill is interrupted; logical thinking stops, and the skill breaks down completely causing us to choke. The worst part about choking is that it tends to spiral. As we fixate on worst-case scenarios, adrenaline shoots through us. We second-guess skills that have been honed through years of practice. The grace of our talent disappears and temporarily, we perform like a novice again.

'When the switch that channels the power supply to our emotional brain is left on, we lose access to the highly sophisticated mental structures encoded in the unconscious part of our brains'

The emotional brain has evolved over two million years as a survival mechanism whose primary purpose is to keep us alive. For our caveman ancestors, failure meant death. Whether that was escaping giant bears, African crowned eagles, sabre-tooth tigers, or failing to be accepted by the tribe and propagating the species. Either way, our emotional brain alerted us to the danger. This is why it has evolved such a heightened sensitivity to threat and such an enormous capacity for negative emotion.

The emotional brain is constantly scanning for threats and is prone to paranoia, drawing conclusions from limited data. After all, anything is better than being ostracised by society or being eaten alive. We can end up entangled with unpleasant emotions and misleading thoughts. Classic examples are excessive worrying, saying things we regret in the heat of the moment, hitting the snooze button on our alarms, or more generally acting disproportionately to the circumstances at hand.

The amount of our technical ability that we concede or access is proportionate to our level of control over the emotional brain.

'The amount of our technical ability that we concede or access is proportionate to our level of control over the emotional brain'

Flicking the switch: Performance routines

As mentioned earlier, if a switch were connected to each of your brains, you'd have the power to flick them on or off. In fact, emotional control is the ability to flick these switches, and we do so through executing performance routines that engage the optimal brain for the task at hand. Routines are not just weird habits; they are a deliberately choreographed set of thoughts and actions that change our brain on a chemical level. It's genius.

'Routines are not just weird habits; they are a deliberately choreographed set of thoughts and actions that change our brain on a chemical level'

In the midst of panic, we're often told to stop worrying, relax, or calm down, but never in the history of being told to calm down has anyone ever calmed down. Easily said, a lot harder done. The good news is that our emotions are not hard-wired and uncontrollable brain reactions. We can control our emotions because we create our emotions. If it's in our heads, we have the option of being in control.

'In the midst of panic, we're often told to stop worrying, relax, or calm down, but never in the history of being told to calm down has anyone ever calmed down'

Emotions are built by us, not built into us. We possess an unbelievable tool, the brain, which can make us confident, move us from panic to calm, and switch us off from the world completely if and when required. The question is how do we flick the switch and seize control when chaos strikes?

If we want to develop routines for emotional control, then we can use the following formula:

T(houghts) + A(ctions) = E(motion)

The sequence of our thoughts and actions is what generates the emotions we experience. If we change the routine (the type and sequence of thoughts and actions), we can change the results (which brain we switch on). Just like tuning a radio to that perfect frequency, executing a routine tunes us into the optimal emotions that performance requires.

'If we change the routine (the type and sequence of thoughts and actions), we can change the results (which brain we switch on)'

The best thing about routines is removing the need for thinking. With routines everything is automatic and effortless. They eventually become a set of habits as opposed to a to-do list we battle through on willpower.

Routines grip our attention, reducing the urge to succumb to distractions. Having a clear process to follow mitigates the tendency to dwell in the moment and over-think, which prevents the power supply from diverting to our emotional brain. Routines put us in charge, switching from reactive to proactive, bringing focus and calm even when the outside is chaos and disorder.

Outliers like Patrick Mahomes, Alex Anderson and Tammie Jo Shults possess three switches: *on, control, off*. The on switch is where they plug into the unconscious brain and fire on all cylinders. The control switch is activated when they notice the emotional brain taking charge, and when flicked this hands back the power supply to the unconscious or frontal brain. The final switch outliers possess is the off switch. This unplugs all three brains completely so they can reap the benefits that true rest bring.

Most of us don't operate in the on or off position, like outlier performers do. Instead we tend to hover, recoil, and bounce around somewhere in the middle. We never completely fire on full cylinders, nor do we ever fully switch off and enjoy true recovery.

'Most of us don't operate in the on or off position, like outlier performers do. Instead we tend to hover, recoil, and bounce around somewhere in the middle. We never completely fire on full cylinders, nor do we ever fully switch off and enjoy true recovery'

These switches are as important as any technical skill, and not only for the purposes of performing well, but also for the sake of having a life. When we learn to flick each switch, we maximise our performance, along with our quality of life and health.

Flicking the switch is a skill, and like any skill, it can be developed. When practised we can supersede our natural impulse to panic and become the master of our emotions instead of their servant. The paradox is that we very rarely think about training psychological skills in the same way we train technical or physical skills. We must remind ourselves that emotional control is a skill, and we must invest methodology, time and energy to develop and maintain it. In Chapter 18, I show you how.

'We must remind ourselves that emotional control is a skill, and we must invest methodology, time and energy to develop and maintain it'

CHAPTER SUMMARY

- Elite performance without pressure? No such thing. The two are inseparable. If we want to excel, pressure is inevitable.
- Ten years of work can come down to ten crucial seconds. The focus is no longer on getting better, but on delivering. To perform when it counts is the measure of elite performance.
- Emotional control is the ability to monitor, evaluate and modify our emotional reactions to the ever-changing demands that elite performance (and life) brings.
- We can control our emotions because we create them. If it's in our heads, we have the option of being in control. Our emotions are built by us, not built into us.
- When the going gets tough, outlier performers flick the switch, regulate their emotions and fight the urge to panic.
- We can develop performance routines that act as switches we can flick using the following formula: T(houghts) + A(ctions) = E(motion). If we change the routine we can change the results.
- Outliers possess three switches: *on, control, off*:
  - The on switch is where they plug into the unconscious brain and fire on all cylinders.
  - The off switch unplugs all three brains completely so we can reap the benefits that true rest brings.
  - The control switch is activated when they notice the emotional brain taking charge
- Most of us don't operate in the on or off position, like outlier performers do. Instead we tend to hover, recoil, and bounce

around somewhere in the middle. We never completely fire on full cylinders, nor do we ever fully switch off and enjoy true recovery.

- We must remind ourselves that emotional control is a skill, and we must invest methodology, time and energy to develop and maintain it.

18

FLICKING THE SWITCH

An abnormal reaction to an abnormal situation is
normal behaviour

Viktor Frankl

Emotional control begins with awareness. Without awareness there can be no routine. Just like weather forecasters using a barometer to measure air pressure we can create our own barometer to report on and expand our awareness of our emotions. The barometer senses what we are feeling, to what degree we are feeling it, and whether the feeling is appropriate or not for the situation. This barometer is the focus of this chapter.

The four zones

Our barometer has four zones in which, at any point in time, we can find ourselves: blue, red, black and green. Only one zone is optimal for performance. Each zone has a unique in-built psychological and biological function that dictates how we think, feel, act and ultimately, perform. They are all interconnected, but being in the wrong zone at the wrong time causes us to leak ability just like a high-performance sports car crunches and grinds when we select the wrong gear. If we want to deliver our A game on demand, firing on all cylinders when it matters most, we need to develop the skills to ensure we're in the right zone at the right time.

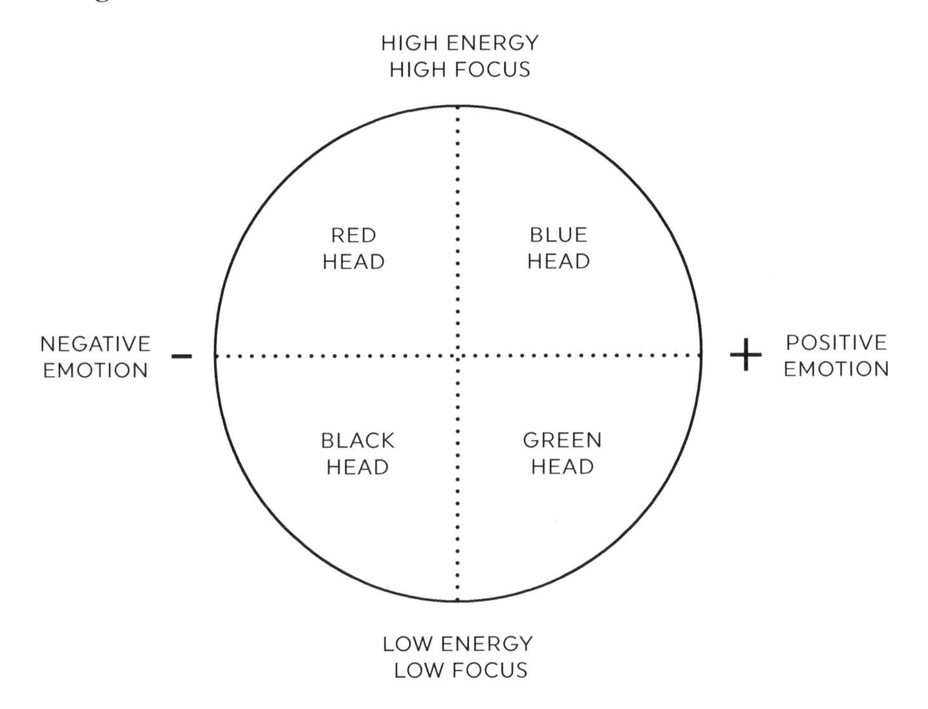

Note: We can check in on the barometer in acute situations, like during a game, working day or series. We can also check in chronologically, across tournaments, seasons and careers.

Model adapted from: Russell, J.A. - *A Circumplex Model of Affect.*[55]

Blue head

Psychologists call it flow, athletes call it the zone and I call it blue head. When we're in blue head we just know. There is lightness, energy radiates through our bodies and we totally commit to the moment. The distant unfocused smile, crisp nod, and glint in our eye says it all. For England cricket hero Ben Stokes, blue head is when a 99mph fast bowl seems the size and speed of a beach ball. For the Navy SEAL sniper it's when his second shot keyholes his first. For swimmer Michael Phelps, it's when he cuts through the water as if he is powered by a nuclear reactor.

Mihaly Csikszentmihalyi
(Hungarian-American psychologist):

> 'Flow [blue head] is a harmonious experience where mind and body are working together effortlessly, leaving the person feeling that something special has just occurred... It lifts experience from the ordinary to the optimal, and it is in these moments we feel truly alive and in tune with what we are doing'[54]

Blue head is accompanied by feelings of excitement, confidence, and motivation among others, or as one outlier confessed to me, 'I feel like a god in here.' It's the place in which we channel all our energy with laser focus on the task at hand, and feel damn good about it. This is the cool, controlled, elite performance state, where all of our technical ability is available to us; the zone where our potential becomes expandable. The blue zone represents the grace, majesty, and synchronicity of elite performance. Our presence in blue head is exclusively in the here and now, there is zero worrying about the past or anxiety about the future. Blue heads are calm, clear, and task focused, locked into the moment.

If you're like me, you dream about these moments; the true thrill of excellence.

'Blue heads are calm, clear, and task focused, locked into the moment'

Blue zone is where all the magic happens. The blue zone prompts the secretion of the super six neuro- chemicals that drive elite performance: norepinephrine, dopamine, serotonin, endorphins, anandamide and oxytocin. They release in perfect symphony, in the right sequence, right concentration, and at the right time.

The super six not only make us feel good, but narrow our focus to the task at hand, while accelerating our ability to think quickly and broadening awareness. This makes us more skilled in complex analysis and enhances our ability to see and invent new ways of doing things. This is another reason quarterbacks like Patrick Mahomes, intelligence agents like Alex Anderson, and pilots like Captain Shults, and are fifty moves ahead of the rest. They know how to flick the blue switch.

Blue head is no accident. There is an evolutionary reason behind this chemical symphony of indestructibility and flow. We call it broaden and build theory; this elusive state helps broaden our behavioural repertoires when it comes to acquiring skills, maximising resources, and developing innovative solutions to overcome challenges that impede our growth. This enables us to evolve by shifting the baseline of our capabilities and the opportunities they afford us. It's the total opposite of the fight, flight or freeze response. When it's time to train or compete, we need to know how to flick the switch and plug into blue head.

When it's time to train or compete, we need to know how to flick the switch and plug into blue head.

> ***Note:*** Without concordant goals it is difficult to activate the psychological fire-power to access blue head. This is why concordance comes first when accelerating excellence. Simultaneously, if we don't possess the technical ability then we can't deploy it. This is why skill acquisition also precedes emotional control training.

Red head

So we're up in blue head, all is going well and then whack, we hit a wall. This comes in a myriad of forms; a bad call from the referee, the market crashing, the sight of the audience, or bullets cracking and thumping past our skull. When perceived demands outweigh perceptions of our capacity to deal with them, our emotional brains trigger stress and send us into red head.

The colour red is associated with threat, fear, and danger. Terms like 'red mist,' 'red-lining' and 'seeing red' represent anger, shock and frustration. Red head is the precise opposite of blue head. The flaring nostrils, sweeping arms and sharp gestures say it all. In the red zone we run too hot, burn up, and become overwhelmed and tense. Our emotional engine is smoking, our perception is slowing, the game is running away from us, our decision-making is rushed and irrational and we are close to meltdown.

In the red zone we run too hot, burn up, and become overwhelmed and tense. Our hearts begin to pound, our teeth grind and our bodies tense up. When stress hits, our emotional brains will always act first. The emotional brain is more powerful and reacts faster than the unconscious or frontal brain, we trade in our steely blue head for an emotional freak-out. There will inevitably be times at which life triggers red head. It's impossible to stop this. When the blaze of negative emotions indicating red head rip us out of blue head, accepting reality is a sure-fire way to reduce the intensity of the emotions when they strike.

Over the last 100,000 years we have seen technological advancements including quantum computing, space rockets and virtual reality. Despite this incredible scientific evolution, we are still walking around with what is essentially the same nervous system as our caveman ancestors. In any situation in which we perceive threat we summon the same fight, flight or freeze stress response that evolved to avoid being eaten alive by sabre-tooth tigers, is triggered. We are shunted into red zone.

From a hormonal perspective, red head trades the rejuvenating and motivating super six for the frustrating three stress hormones: cortisol, adrenaline and nor-adrenaline. When these stress hormones flood our bodies, the power supply is pulled from our unconscious and frontal brains, forcing them to shut down. Here our emotional brain is running the show; constantly scanning for threats, conjuring up catastrophic images, such as getting fired, markets crashing, or messing up a key presentation. Our inner caveman wants to come out. Our instincts kick in and all we want to do is fight, flight or freeze.

Fight enables us to lash out and execute a primal attack on the perceived threat, sometimes with unfathomable strength or speed; we become argumentative, confrontational and aggressive. Flight is opting to avoid the problem, refusing to face it, and running away; often hoping that someone else will solve it. Flee behaviours can manifest in modern society in the form of escapism, drugs, tobacco, alcohol, promiscuity and eating everything in sight. When we freeze under stress, we're basically denying that the stress exists and hoping the problem will vanish on its own; we withdraw, avoid and drag our feet.

The emotional brain hijacks the nervous system at the expense of our aspirations and prioritises pursuing its instinctive drives. Everything we know we need to do goes out the window. Our survival instincts win at the expense of clear thinking, meaningful relationships, good sleep, healthy eating, and a positive outlook, which digs a deeper hole in a head red-hot with negativity, frustration, and despair.

'The emotional brain hijacks the nervous system at the expense of our aspirations and prioritises pursuing its instinctive drives'

When we panic and allow those survival (stress) hormones to take over, we increase the probability of making mistakes, overriding our operating procedures, and deviating from the plan. We lose track of what's in front of us and focus on future threats and past mistakes. We replace doing with thinking and risk becoming unresponsive. Remember, elite performance happens so fast there is no time to think. This is what makes performing in red head costly to those we care for, compete with, and most importantly those we serve (defendant, hostage, or customer, amongst others).

Most of the time, the event we initially anticipated that sent us into red head never materialises. Consequently the stress hormones summoned, that are linked to virtually every major disease we know of, continue circulating through our body. So, spending time in red head is not just to the detriment of our performance but, more importantly, to our health.

We need to consider the obstacles that trigger red head our biggest competition. If we don't let them take control of our emotion and therefore our next move, we win. Inevitably life will drag us into red head at times, so expect it and accept it. Our objective is to ensure that, when we do enter red head, we identify it fast. As soon as we're aware we can flick the control switch and bounce back into blue head as soon as possible, just like Patrick Mahomes, Alex Anderson and Tammie Jo Shults did when disaster hit (See chapter 17).

Black head

Vacant stares, slack expressions and bent necks say it all. When we are unable to detoxify after a stressful event, and are then exposed to more stress, the brain and body will eventually break down and burn out- welcome to black head. The brain and body can become so drained they just give-out. Here, there is no energy left, no focus, and we feel awful.

Black head doesn't just hit us, like the kick in the groin red head delivers. We don't wake up one morning and suddenly feel burn-out. Instead black head is insidious, creeping up on us over time. This can make awareness challenging.

> 'We don't wake up one morning and suddenly feel burn-out. Instead black head is insidious, creeping up on us over time'

The emotions that engulf us in black are, amongst others, helplessness, hopelessness, detachment, and misery. We lose interest, isolate, withdraw from responsibilities, excessively procrastinate, feel we have failed, doubt ourselves and our roles in life, and are riddled with anxiety and neuroses about things that never previously troubled us. We feel overworked, undervalued and may even temporarily fall out of love with our concordant goals. Our symptoms are now pathological: chronic fatigue syndrome, strokes, heart attacks, high blood pressure, anxiety, depression, sleep disorders, thyroid shutdown, migraines and autoimmune disease. Feeling beyond caring, we become apathetic, nihilistic and struggle to see hope of change.

The trouble is that, when we're in the darkness that is black head, it's hard to see the way out. We have to deal with burn-out immediately. Starting with calling a time-out and telling someone we trust, someone who will listen and not judge.

The good news is, that black head is a completely reversible state, through simply reversing the conditions that cause it, we can begin the recovery process immediately. Both professional and lifestyle challenges can produce burn-out. Professional causes tend to revolve around lack of concordance with, or little or no control over, work; no routine, experiencing a lack of recognition, unclear expectations, performing monotonous work, a serious lack of challenge, or operating in unrelenting chaos. Lifestyle causes of burn-out can include: lack of recovery (sleep, change, holiday, nutrition), lack of close supportive relationships, taking on too much, not asking for help, and an inability to say no.

> ***Note:*** We need to pay attention to the small things before they become the big things. If we notice there is a change in the engine noise, steering or braking of our car, we don't continue driving it. We stop, assess and check the engine, examine the steering and inspect the brake pads. More often than not, some subtle adjustments, a new brake pad, or a nut tightened here and there are all we need to stay on top of the head

> game. When it comes to our well-being many of us don't pay attention until there is loud screeching and we are well on our way to blowing up and breaking down. Prevention is always better than cure.

We must limit red head to avoid black head. The pressing question now becomes how to prevent burn-out? The short answer is, by flicking the *off* switch. Enter green head.

Green head

The off switch, when flicked, moves us straight into green head. The zone of restoration, recovery, rejuvenation, and best of all, growth. Green head is not only the antidote to red and black. It is where we sharpen the axe renewing and expanding our capacity to meet the demands performance and life imposes on us.

> 'Green head is not only the antidote to red and black. It is where we sharpen the axe renewing and expanding our capacity to meet the demands performance and life imposes on us'

Emotions that characterise this zone, include serenity, contentment and peace. The only rule here is that we're not allowed out of first gear, we're not focusing on anything, and we feel relaxed. For some it's a siesta in the sun, for others it's watching Game of Thrones on the sofa, or perhaps it's laughing and joking with friends or family.

We know that we need challenge to change. To increase our capacity to handle stress, we need to expose ourselves to it. Stress is our brain and body's stimulus to adapt to a higher level, sparking the physical and psychological adaptations that produce growth. However, growth itself does not occur in the training room, on the pitch, or in the boardroom, growth only occurs in the green zone. The hormones that power this include the sex hormones, testosterone and oestrogen, and the feel-good hormones; serotonin, endorphins, dopamine and oxytocin.

'Growth itself does not occur in the training room, on the pitch, or in the boardroom, growth only occurs in the green zone'

We need rest and recovery to adapt and improve. This is the other side of competing and training. Elite performers know this. Patrick Mahomes doesn't manage a miracle Super-Bowl comeback and then go straight into the next game. He has an off-season. This allows him to super-compensate.

Super-compensation: The advancement of our abilities that can only be achieved through rest.

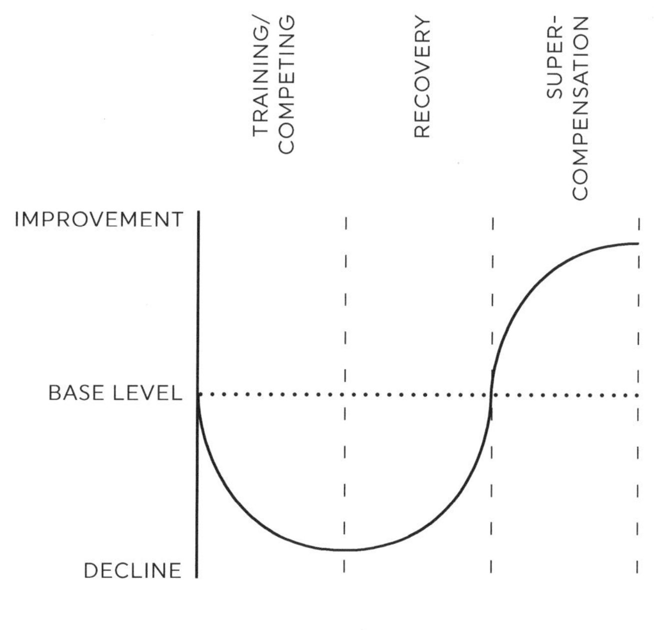

Super-compensation can only occur in green head. This is why our growth will always be proportionate to the quality and quantity of our recovery. Not only that, without insufficient recovery the next performance suffers, until we eventually break down and burn out. Not only that, without rest the next performance suffers. Insufficient green zone means that we end up red lining until we eventually break down and burn out.

To optimise performance, we need to find the correct balance between performing work (blue) and recovery (green). Maximising the quality of our recovery is just as important as maximizing the quality of our training. When not competing or training, we need to get straight into green zone and maximise the quality of our recovery.

'To optimise performance we need to find the correct balance between performing work (blue) and recovery (green)'

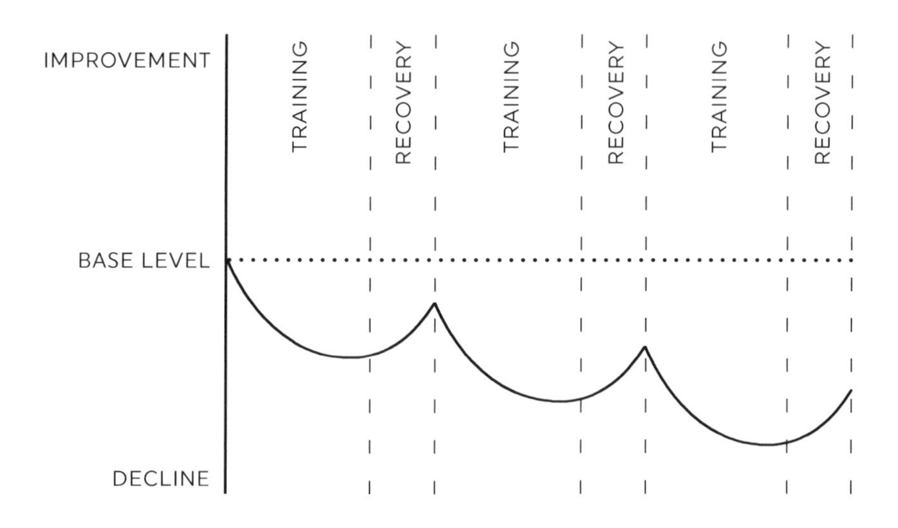

Note: The benefits and risks associated with each zone are proportionate to how deep into that zone we are. The deeper the blue and darker the green the better. The lighter the red and black the better.

A platform for common language

My favourite thing about the barometer is that it flips the normal dynamic many of us have with our emotions, namely that talking about them is a sign of weakness. Willingness to discuss our emotions is a pre-requisite for accelerating excellence. Not to mention the obvious health benefits it brings.

The barometer demystifies our emotions and provides a platform of common language for group conversation. The colours on the barometer have a specific purpose in forming a shared performance language that, like all shared languages, enables people to connect and communicate. By just saying 'I'm in red at the moment,' everyone is clear where we are emotionally, and can assist us in flicking the switch. We can also reinforce through reward a player who stays blue under pressure, just like a coach might reinforce a technical skill performed well.

▸ Reflection questions:

1. What takes you into red? Can you stop it?

   Is there a commute you can alter, a person you can stop spending time with, or a habit you can break?

2. What takes you into green? Can you schedule more of it?

   Is there an activity you enjoy, a person you like spending time with, a place you can go?

3. When are you in blue? Can you do more of it?

What tasks activate you, what responsibilities do you thrive on, and which people bring this out in you?

4. When in black, who will you let know? Is there a friend, colleague, coach or family member?

Switching on blue head when it's time to compete and train; or flicking the control switch when we're shunted into red head, or engaging the *off* switch to access green head is what emotional control is all about. This is what outlier performers do best. With this level of emotional control, successful performance becomes a series of exciting, explosive bouts of training and competing, interspersed with enjoyable periods of rest and recovery; the oscillation between blue and green.

Even if somewhat scarce or fleeting, we all experience moments where, in the midst of chaos, we are able to keep it together, finding calm and clarity. There are also moments where we switch on, and deliver our technical capabilities without a glitch. And times where we are completely switched off and reaping the rewards recovery brings. The challenge is that we don't tend to pay attention to these moments, nor capture and break them down, and then fine-tune each routine the way outlier performers do - consciously or not. Let alone to perfect the routines that we run all day.

The good news is that we can. If there was a single moment where we switched on, controlled a volatile situation, or switched off, we can have a thousand more. We can build out personalised routines that put us in the driver's seat when it comes to managing our emotions and optimising performance. Outlining examples of great routines is the focus of the next chapter. Pay attention to the tools the outliers employ to change the way they think, feel and act when it matters most.

CHAPTER SUMMARY

- Emotional control begins with building a barometer that senses what we are feeling, to what degree we are feeling it, and whether the feeling is appropriate or not for the situation
- There are four zones in which we can find ourselves: blue, red, black and green. If we want to deliver our A game on demand when it matters most, we need to ensure we're in the right zone at the right time. Otherwise we leak ability.
- When it's time to compete we need blue head. The secretion of the super six catalyse the feelings of excitement, confidence, and motivation that unlock all our technical ability.
- When it's time to compete we need blue head. The secretion of the super six performance hormones catalyse the feelings of excitement, confidence, and motivation that enable us to unlock all our technical ability.
- If we spend too much time in red head, it won't be long before we burn out and collapse, the brain and body can become so drained they just collapse, welcome to black head.
- Green head is not only the antidote to red and black. It is the zone of restoration, recovery, and rejuvenation, but best of all, growth.
- Stress is the spark that triggers all of the adaptations that produce growth but we can only expand our ability in green head.
- To optimise performance, we need to find the correct balance between performing work (blue head) and recovery (green head).

- Elite performance should be a series of exciting, explosive bouts of training and competing, interspersed with periods of rest and recovery; the oscillation between blue and green.
- If there was a single moment where we switched on, controlled a volatile situation, or switched off, we can have a thousand more.

19

EMOTIONAL CONTROL ROUTINES

Losing composure is pointless
Michael Schumacher

Emotional Control Routines: A set series of actions that generate a desired emotional state

It's hard to imagine the pressure of an Olympic final. Especially in a sport like swimming where victory can come in milliseconds. For the most decorated Olympian (28 medals, 23 of which are gold) and greatest swimmer of all time, Michael Phelps, a pre-race routine was fundamental in helping him stay calm and in control.[56] In Olympic finals athletes like Phelps cant afford to leak one drop of ability. Phelps routine enabled him to stay focused on the task at hand and to consistently deliver everything he had.

For so many it's the race day part that causes us the most problems: keeping our heads straight and our thoughts positive long enough to compete at our best. On the morning of the big race the combination of nerves, excitement and even dread can threaten to take over and that means red head potentially setting in.

Michael's race day is punctuated by a very deliberate performance routine. A simple approach with a clear purpose: to give him control over his emotions. The objective is to stay in green head until just before it's time to compete where he is then required to flick the switch, activate blue head and summon every ounce of attention, energy and technical ability to convert all his concordance and training into the hard currency of gold medals. The routine he follows enables him to box out what is happening around him and focus entirely on delivering all his potential. Phelps perceives each step in his routine as a series of small wins that give him a sense of building victory. As he approaches the event, each small step moves him from green head to blue head.

Bob Bowman (Michael Phelps's coach):

'When the race arrives, he's more than halfway through his plan and he's been victorious at every step. All the stretches went like he planned. The warm-up laps were just like he visualized. His headphones are playing exactly what he expected. The actual race is just another step in a pattern that started earlier that day and has been nothing but victories. Winning is a natural extension.'[57]

On-Switch: Green to blue

Let's deconstruct how Michael Phelps built and personalised his on switch to access blue head for the 200m Butterfly Final at the 2008 Beijing Olympics. He had won three gold medals earlier that week, and now he was gearing up for the fourth. The following is an account of how he flicked the switch from green head to blue head.

> ***Note:*** I conduct a deeper examination of the techniques that comprise our outliers' routines in the next chapter. This will enable you to build your very own set of switches to flick.

20:00 (Night before race day): The evening before a big race Michael Phelps maintains green head through watching movies or documentaries that elicit this relaxing, restorative state. During the 2004 Olympics he watched Miracle, a movie about the gold medal-winning 1980 US Olympic hockey team. In 2008 it was the documentary Planet Earth, narrated by David Attenborough.

Notice: We can almost imagine the green images of Planet Earth priming him for green head, or the triumph of the US hockey team as they overcame adversity to win gold priming him for success.

07:30: On race day Michael Phelps sat down for his regular breakfast that consists of eggs, oatmeal and four energy shakes, the first of more than 6,000 calories he consumes on a daily basis.

Notice: Specificity is key. We know that great skill acquisition should seamlessly represent the reality of competition. Phelps does exactly that; down to what time he wakes up, what he eats and how he prepares. This preparation brings calm, control and confidence. It's just another day at the office for Michael.

08:30: With his shoulders low and loose, arms limp and a weightless gaze, Michael Phelps arrived at the pool and completed the same routine of stretches he always does to prepare his body for the warm-up. Arms, back, chest, hamstrings and, last but not least, ankles, which are so flexible they extend more than 90 degrees, farther than a ballerina's en pointe. Michael targets each body part systematically, checking them off one by one. Small win after small win, the same as always.

Notice: The consistent flow of Phelps's routine leaves no time for him to get caught up in the moment and allow red head an opportunity to seize control. There is no thinking; he just flows with the slipstream of his routine, conserving all his energy for the ninety-second (approximately) race that will define everything.

09:00: Phelps takes his first warm-up lap, then swims 800metres of mixed styles, followed by 600metres of kicking, 400metres pulling a buoy between his legs, and 200metres of stroke drills. The intensity amplifies as the warm-up progresses, finishing with a series of maximal output race-pace sprints to elevate his heart rate, activate his nervous system and potentiate his muscles. This takes him precisely 45 minutes.

Notice: Michael has started to amplify his physical energy as he approaches race time. More consistency brings with it comfort and control, and represents another small victory that builds momentum.

09:45: Phelps exits the pool and squeezes into his bodysuit, so tight that it requires twenty minutes of tugging to put it on. Then he enters the competitors' ready room and performs a meditative relaxation exercise. Next he puts the tape in. 'Tape' was a word Michael and his coach Bob Bowman used to describe his vigorous visualisation process. He visualises his entire race right from the start to finish. He imagines himself jumping from the blocks and his body entering the pool at the perfect angle, imagining every stroke, every turn, every breath, right up to finishing the race, the water dripping from his face and taking off his cap and goggles. Phelps doesn't just visualise the perfect swim, he imagines a variety of possible difficulties so he is prepared for anything that comes his way.[59]

Notice: His body is activated, mobilised, and ready for competition. Now he brings his attention to his mind. Meditation brings Michael Phelps into the moment and starts to narrow his attention. The visualisation is the equivalent of the physical warm-up, activating the mental structures he is about to fire on all cylinders by diverting blood flow to these parts of his brain.

10:00: The time arrives for Michael to escape into music. The headphones, along with his expressionless face have become synonymous with the swimmer, dubbed by the media as his death stare. His hit list includes tunes by Lil Wayne, Rick Ross, Young Jeezy, and Jay-Z.

Notice: Michael Phelps is now locked in to the zone. The music helps narrow his focus even more, and mobilise his physical energy, flooding his brain and body full of the super six. At this point he is a coiled spring ready to explode in to action and capitalise on the moment.

10:29: ***Michael Phelps:*** 'After we walked out to behind the blocks, I did what I always do there. I stretched my legs on the blocks, two different stretches, one a straight-leg stretch, the other with a bent knee, left leg first. I took the right headphone out. Once they called my name, I took the left headphone out, the parka off. It's my routine to stand on the left side of the block and get onto it from that side… This is something I've done since I was a little kid.'[58]

Notice: Once Michael Phelps was up on the blocks, he did something that any swim fan would recognise, the double-arm swing and slap behind the back, his signature move. Phelps executes the final part of his routine. Enter blue head.

10:30: The starter gun fires and Michael launches from the blocks; nothing else exists. However, the second he meets the water, he realises his goggles are leaking. He anticipates the leak not to be too bad. But, by the second lap, everything starts to blur, and by the third he can't see anything, the lines of the pool, the marks on the walls, the distance left, all swallowed up by a big blue blur.

Notice: Phelps knew it would take him 21 strokes to complete that final lap. Everything else had gone perfectly for him through the day, he had accumulated small win after small win, from breakfast until the starter gun fired, and the goggle situation was just a small deviation. He remained firmly locked into blue head.

10:31: Phelps erupted, swimming at maximum output, as he classically does on his final lap. At the eighteenth stroke he started to anticipate the wall, he went for the nineteenth and then twentieth. He could hear the crowd cheer, but without vision, he had no idea who they were cheering for. But, as the videotape in his head played twenty-one, he automatically went for one more. With a last long stroke, arms stretched, he touched the wall.[59]

10:31:52:03: He turned around to look at the scoreboard, taking off his goggles, the water dripping down his eyes. It said 'WR'—(world record--1:52.03) next to his name, just as he had visualised. He had timed it perfectly, winning another gold.

> ***Note:*** We know that when things go wrong in training, we must deal with them, as we would be forced to in competition. One day in training, Bob Bowman accidentally stepped on and broke Michaels goggles. Bowman made Phelps wear the broken goggles during the session. The aim was to prepare Phelps for future challenges that could unfold, even if the likelihood was low. An example of high quality skill acquisition can enhance our performance for the realities of elite performance.

> ***Michael Phelps:*** 'It's just a routine. My routine. It's the routine I've gone through my whole life.'[58]

Michael Phelps's personalised routine helped move him from green head to blue when it mattered most, and kept him there, inoculating him from the type of scenario that would throw most performers into red head, where they would capitulate, concede defeat and blame their goggles.

Off-Switch: Blue to green

Jason Henderson is a US Navy SEAL who has been given one week's notice. He and his troop (team) will deploy as part of a standby task group to an extremely hostile part of the world. He has been instructed to execute initial reconnaissance to prepare future operations for a three-month tour, but he knows better. Three months can very quickly become six and, in the worst-case, he might not come back. Due to the operation being classified top secret, the only information he is permitted to share with his wife is that he is going away and doesn't know when he'll be back. He can't confirm where, for how long, or when she will next hear from him.

Jason will be leading a team of 23. Some have only just joined the unit and have never deployed before with the Troop, while others have more than ten years' experience. None have deployed to this part of the world before. The team will be operating in a new theatre, in a new role, on a new task, against a new enemy. There are a lot of unknowns.

Henderson's responsibility is to successfully manage the mission and the team. The primary deliverable is mission success, as well as the team's safe return. But perhaps the biggest pressure is to uphold the standards that make his unit one of the most revered the world over. If the team were to be compromised, or captured, the unit's established reputation (over generations) as one of the world's premier fighting forces is at stake. There is also reputational risk within the international community.

The role requires intricate communication with multi-government agencies, foreign partner forces, and the wider military. This brings with it all the challenges that arise when working in any team of teams; conflicting information, priorities, and methods of action. Jason has to diplomatically manage of all of these respectfully but assertively. He maintains strong eye contact and decisive, firm communication throughout. Jason smiles at nervous government stakeholders to alleviate their worries, citing data and experiences to back up his convictions in the unit's planned actions.

Henderson is highly concordant with his role. His wide grin, the bounce in his step, and his friendly show me, do it, let's go commands say it all. Deploying on this type of task is one of the most exciting parts of the job to him; just thinking about it sends him into blue head. He is confident his troop will exceed expectations and deliver success for the unit. He feels light, at ease and has a gleam in his eye. Too much blue, without systematically disengaging, can quickly turn to red. Luckily Jason knows this.

Jason must periodically detach from his blue head high, to sharpen his axe (in green head), so he can passionately re-engage to capitalise on this opportunity to excel. Plus, Jason must maximise his limited time left at home with his wife Kristine and their baby daughter Lily. This is where his off switch comes in. Jason needs to flick the switch and transition from steely-eyed SEAL Team operator (blue head) to husband and dad (green head), not just for the sake of his performance at work, but for the sake of his family.

> ***Jason Henderson:*** 'I can be sat at home with my family and my head can just start spinning [with excitement], I start thinking about the operation, how I could optimise my preparation. I've spent all my enthusiasm too early in previous deployments and ended up burning out. Its something I have to manage.'

Notice: The first thing Jason needs to do is congratulate himself for noticing. Most don't. Remember, all routines begin with awareness. As soon as we become aware of our emotions, we have the opportunity of controlling them. The objective for Henderson is to flick the switch and access green head.

As soon as we become aware of our emotions, we have the opportunity of controlling them'

> ***Jason Henderson:*** '[Before heading home] I make sure I wash my hands and arms properly to get any weapon oil off me, I also make a point to avoid leaving for home hungry or thirsty, "hangry" is sub-optimal for me.'

Notice: Jason removes the state-changing smell of weapon oil that he associates with blue zone. He also pays attention to his feelings of thirst and hunger. Low blood sugar and dehydration triggers the stress hormones associated with red head. Recognising these cues and attending to them is a great example of getting in front of our problems. After all, prevention always beats cure.

> ***Jason Henderson:*** 'I enjoy podcasts on the way into work [green to blue]. On the way home I avoid them, I enjoy them, but they can amp me up, which is not my aim on my way home [green head is], I really like big band music, there's a few I tend to listen to over and over again, Frank Sinatra, or Dean Martin, I can just float in and let it take me away.'

Notice: More awareness from Henderson on how his environment affects his position on the barometer. By switching from podcasts to relaxing big band music, he is able to facilitate the decompression from blue head to green.

> ***Jason Henderson:*** '[upon leaving work] I take off my pass, and leave it in the car, that's me de-servicing as an operator. And I re-surface to "Dad".'

Notice: Using a physical object as an anchor is a tried and tested technique to help you switch between heads.

> ***Jason Henderson:*** 'I started off doing this on the drive [his routine], but the dogs would start barking when they heard the car pull up. I tried to do it [the routine] at work before I left but the reality is that someone would knock on the door, the phone would ring, or if I did manage to switch off I'd get grabbed between my office and the car and get dragged back into blue or red head. Now I pull over just short of home to avoid all that.'

Notice: Jason's experience shows us how important it is to pick the right environment to flick our switch. By optimising his environment, Jason can remove triggers that disrupt his ability to execute his routine. Pulling into a forest car park on the way home achieved this for him.

> ***Jason Henderson:*** 'I pull over just short of home and run through my routine. I countdown 10-1 and then I'm straight into three big sighs with nice long exhales, and from here I roll into a grounding exercise, this plugs me in to the fact I'm home now. I know Kristine's first question is going to be "how was your day?" I have a think and make sure I have

> something more meaningful than "fine" to say. I try to be positive, but always honest.'

Notice: A frowning Jason lets out an impatient huff, clears his throat and goes straight into a distraction countdown to block any thoughts, eliminate any distractions, and prime his body to flick the off switch. By the time he's completed the routine he's leaning back, with loose muscles, slack limbs and softened features that imply calm. The routine brings Jason into green head, his focus moves into the present, tension eases, and his energy output slows, which all has a feel-good effect culminating with Jason setting off for home unhurried, satisfied and stoic.

> ***Jason Henderson:*** 'I make an effort to get out the car with calm enthusiasm, I might not always feel like going in Mr happy but the "fake it till you make it" eases me into family mode, within a couple of minutes of seeing them I am Mr Happy'

Notice: Through controlling his behaviour and putting on a smile, Jason's body leads his mind into green head and before he knows it, everything else fades away and he melts into the moment as Isla smiles back at him. He starts telling Lily jokes, expressing sincere interest in her day, which makes her feel cared for, considered and appreciated, which she is.

> ***Jason Henderson:*** 'I make the first fifteen minutes all about Kristine and Lily, the hugs, how was your day stuff, if one of us have had a tough day the other just hits the mute button and just listens. A lot of the time, one of us, just needs a vent, we tend to talk ourselves out of it as long as the other doesn't interrupt. This definitely sets the rest of the evening up on the right foot, that first

15 minutes for us is crucial.'

Notice: Jason focuses on the one thing that has a disproportionate impact on the quality of the rest of his evening; his family's mood. Our mood is the lens through which we look at the world, so by making sure his family's is optimised, he maximises the likelihood of having an enjoyable evening together.

> ***Jason Henderson:*** 'Then I continue to work through the gears, to really switch off, I shower, getting rid of any work-related triggers to the job, then I make sure I change my clothing'

Notice: Jason is now in the green zone, but he amplifies his state of relaxation and detachment by continuing to remove any triggers he associates with work. Fingers laced behind his head, half-closed eyes and humming suggest that he is getting there.

> ***Jason Henderson:*** 'The mobile [phone] goes into a drawer out of sight. I leave VIP mode on so, if it does go, I know it's urgent, this rarely happens. I check it around 19:00 and deal with anything important that might have come up, and put it away again for the evening, I use my iPad for social media, browsing online etc… my email and phone aren't linked to it.'

Notice: Once Jason is in green zone, he wants to make sure he stays there, guarding against non-urgent interruptions that can disrupt this peaceful state. A phone pinging all evening with banal questions and issues he can't do anything about until the next day anyway is a great example of this.

> ***Jason Henderson:*** 'It's not part of my routine but forward planning helps me get in, and stay in, green zone. The IDP capture most of the things that would have sent me into blue or red head. Seeing as there are outcomes, targets and plans in place, this reduces the flashes of blue and red I tend to experience. Now, if something new pops up I note it down on my phone and then add it to my plan the next day.'

Notice: Individual Development planning (Chapter 15) enabled Jason to maximise the quality of his preparation. When we feel prepared and have a plan in place, our perception of the demands imposed upon us reduces, and our perception of our capacity increases, reducing the likelihood of red head creeping in. Journalling and catching thoughts means we don't have to hold them in our head. It's always good to keep a notepad at arms length, be it physical or digital.

> ***Jason Henderson:*** 'I spend a good hour playing with Lily before we put her to bed. The rest of the evening is spent with Kristine, we eat together and then we go over the next days plan.'

Notice: Relationships, television, play or reading are great ways to pass time, relax and disengage from our craft. The trick is to make sure we find people, shows, games and books we sincerely enjoy. Deciding what to watch, or worse, being forced to watch something awful can be a red zone activity in itself. Plan ahead, and have a contingency.

> ***Jason Henderson:*** If I'm feeling any blue head before bed I'll do some breathing exercises in bed, which usually sends me

off. If I'm really awake I use a paperback, reading redirects my attention and I usually end up drifting off.'

Notice: Henderson's use of a contingency routine, parasympathetic breathing, when his sleep is interrupted is a great way to get back on track when things inevitably don't go to plan.

Jason Henderson's off switch helped him descend into green zone, enabling him to recoil fully charged into blue head, when it was time to compete. Henderson and his team deployed for five months, their achievements over that time frame ended up playing a key role in setting the units partner forces up for future operational success. Everyone came back safe.

Control-Switch: Red to blue

Owen Farrell has established himself as one of the best fly-halves in modern rugby. Having a reputation for being a hothead early in his career, Owen has gone on to become captain of England's national team and is now referred to as Ice Man, homage to his cold, calculating style.

Since before the Battle of Waterloo in 1815, England and France have been at each other's throats. In any sport this match causes emotions to run high for players and fans alike. It had been 13 long years since England's team had been victorious against the French. Since then the England team had gone through six different head coaches and debuted over 125 players. But finally England were Six Nations champions again, and travelling to Paris hoping for a victory that would give them a grand slam.[59] (This is achieved when one team wins 100% of their games, the ultimate achievement in European rugby.) For England this was a chance for redemption.

With the game coming to an end and England marginally leading, the French forward Paul Jedrasiak was penalised for a high tackle. Penalty to England. Owen Farrell was required to step up to secure an historic victory.

Farrell set the ball down for an attempt at goal, even though he was only just inside the French half, and had just missed his previous attempt. Only seconds earlier he was tackled by a 125kg opponent who runs 100m in 11 seconds and whose sole purpose in life is to put fly-halves like Owen on their backs. The rules state that Farrell had 60 seconds to prepare for his kick. That's 60 seconds to switch from red head to blue head. Let's break down how Farrell used a well-honed performance routine he has rehearsed thousands of times to help put England back on top of European rugby.

05 Seconds: Owen is aware, he's feeling the pressure, and doesn't want to let his teammates, country, or family, down.

Notice: The initial focus is to accept the emotion rather than overcome it. The emotional brain is more powerful and reacts faster than the frontal and unconscious brains. This is precisely why Farrell needs a rapid pattern of actions that can prevent him from starting to over-think and let his emotional brain run riot.

10 Seconds: Owen gets hold of the ball, he locates the valve and centres it on the tee before taking a big deep sigh.

Notice: When we don't respond to a challenge, our bodies will naturally release adrenaline. When adrenaline is coupled with negative thoughts we can end up anxious. Anxiety is nature's way of prompting us to take action. As soon as we act, anxiety will begin to recede.

> ***Owen Farrell:*** 'It doesn't matter what's just happened... [the missed kick, the tackle]. You've got a job to do straight away, so I'll always back myself and switch on to the next thing.'[60]

Notice: Farrell uses self-talk to reflect using logic and reasoning to drive positivity. The objective is to keep shifting the blood supply to the frontal lobes and unconscious brain, where Farrell has the capacity to overcome the challenge ahead.

25 Seconds: Owen starts to release some tension; he lightly stamps his feet or wiggles his fingers letting go of any nervous energy. What might look like some form of random movement, such as a shake of the hands, hips, or head, is actually an intentional effort to expend nervous energy. If it increases comfort and stability, do it. A bent neck, slight rocking, and fidgety movements are soon replaced with a with a sharp breath, high chin, and an unwavering gaze.

Notice: Once Farrell has neutralised his arousal and his unconscious brain is back in the driving seat, he needs to switch his focus to exploiting the opportunity ahead of him. His unconscious will naturally start acquiring data and facts like the angle, distance and trajectory he will need to kick. One significant challenge is muting the soundtrack of tens of thousands of whistles and jeers. The French crowd was riotous, baying for English blood. 'Please respect the kicker,' has always been a futile request when England plays in Paris.

> ***Owen Farrell:*** '[At the setup] I go through my steps, which is one back and three to the side... I'll pick something

> far behind on the post to focus on and narrow that target down… You try and block everything out, it's just you and the posts.'[61]

Notice: This activation phase of the routine enables him to shut out distractions, he continues narrowing his attention on the task at hand, letting everything else melt away. This ensures he doesn't leak ability as he summons all his focus and energy for the challenge at hand.

50 Seconds: His posture suddenly changes, Owen takes a deep breath in and lifts his chest, bringing his arms back to stabilise his centre of gravity. Farrell adopts a powerful postural stance. His thrusted chest, wide stance, and exposed neck say it all. Adopting a power pose initiates the super six hormones, the good chemicals, to fill his brain. While power-posing primes us for peak performance, it also sends a message of confidence, calm and control to our teammates and opponents.

> ***Owen Farrell:*** 'The weird, eye thing that you see?…I'm drawing a line from the ball to where I want to kick it …I'll keep drawing a line …Then I'll kick the ball along that line.'[62]

Notice: Farrell is purposely narrowing his attention by repeatedly looking down at the ball and up at the target, driving his focus until this is all that exists to him. His manic stare, as he stalks the imaginary ball through the posts, displays his single-minded focus. Then he thrusts his chest out even more as he explodes with action.

59 Seconds: WHACK! Three Points. Kickers like Owen know that, as long as everything is in place, the ball will go exactly

where they want it to.

Notice: Finally, Farrell personalises his routine with something that inspires him. Turning away before the ball had reached the posts, he humbly signals the initials JJ with his two fingers in honour of eleven-year-old Jack Johnson who was diagnosed with Duchenne Muscular Dystrophy, a cause close to his heart.[63]

Another penalty followed, from closer range. Farrell used the exact routine to stroke the ball between the posts to bring his own total to 21. England could celebrate the end of a long and painful thirteen-year wait. They were once again Grand Slam champions.

Now we have outlined what great routines look like, it's time to delve deeper into the techniques they are built from. The following chapter is dedicated to analysing techniques, such as those Michael Phelps, Jason Henderson and Owen Farrell employ to construct their routines, so that we can build our very own switches to flick when performance requires.

CHAPTER SUMMARY

- Routines are punctuated by a very deliberate set of actions with a clear purpose: to give us control over our emotions.
- Our *on, off* and *control* switches comprise a series of actions that generate a desired emotional state that optimises our performance.
- Each step in our routine acts as a series of small wins that give us a sense of building victory.
- As soon as we become aware of our emotions, we have the opportunity of controlling them.
- We must congratulate ourselves for noticing we're in the wrong zone. Most don't. This gives us the option of getting in front of our problems. Prevention always beats cure.
- When we don't respond to a challenge, our bodies will naturally release adrenaline. As soon as we act, by flicking our switch, anxiety will begin to recede.
- The consistent flow of the routine leaves no time for us to get caught up in the moment, we just flow with the slipstream of our routine.
- We need to execute each step systematically, checking them off one by one, small win after small win. This ensures we avoid leaking performance, or recovery.

20

BUILDING PERFORMANCE ROUTINES

> You can never solve a problem on the level on which it was created
>
> Albert Einstein

Owen Farrell and Michael Phelps use visualisation, Jason Henderson didn't. Jason Henderson and Michael Phelps use Progressive Muscular Relaxation, Owen Farrell didn't. Jason Henderson and Michael Phelps use music and audio books, Owen Farrell couldn't. And that's fine. Excellence is highly personal and so are our performance routines. Great routines are always unique to the individual's challenges, experiences, and environments.

Now it's time to unpack the techniques our outliers use to build their performance routines. This enables us to build our own bespoke versions so we can flick the switch when the moment requires. This chapter is where we delve deeper into the why and, most importantly, how of these techniques. As we do so, consider what resonates with your unique nature, challenges and environment. Remember, yet again, that you are the expert on you.

Distraction countdowns
(Great for red to blue, blue to green)

Jeff Bezos:
'I find as soon as I identify it, and make the first phone call, or send off the first email… It dramatically reduces any stress.'[64]

As soon as we act by initiating the first step, we take ownership of the situation. We move from prey to predator. The distraction countdown is a simple way to achieve this. If we're thinking about the future or thinking about the past, then we're not thinking about what we're doing right now in the present. Countdowns keep us in the now.

'If we're thinking about the future or thinking about the past, then we're not thinking about what we're doing right now'

We know that allowing our emotional brains to think is unhelpful. The familiar childhood admonition to count to or from ten works to halt this because of two key aspects: the time to pause, and distraction from the event. The immediate dialogue of the emotional brain looks like: 'I can't get up,' or 'this is so unfair,' or 'I'm going to kill him.' The distraction countdown counters with: 'Get up on the count of three, two, one, UP!'

The aim is to override the emotional brain before it can gain any momentum. When we occupy our minds with the countdown, we create time to diffuse the emotional reaction before we speak or act. While counting, we avoid fuelling the fire by mulling over whatever has happened. Doing so can prevent us from saying or doing something we'll regret, like sending an emotionally charged email, posting something regrettable on social media, or lashing out verbally. Sometimes just counting to ten allows the storm to pass.

Break it down with logic
(Great for: red to blue, and blue to green)

If the emotional brain doesn't have answers or can't make sense of a situation, it will act on impulsive feelings. Red head is stubborn and will not hand over control to blue head until it feels safe. The emotional brain will eventually accept reason. Using logic can therefore assist in transitioning the power supply from the emotional brain to the frontal brain. Here are three examples of how we can achieve this.

Option one: Rationalise the emotion

If a professional athlete such as footballer Cristiano Ronaldo were distracted by what he perceived to be a poor decision by the referee, then he might ask:

> ***Question One:*** 'How many times have you argued with referees in your career so far?'
>
> ***Cristiano Ronaldo:*** 'Several hundred.'
>
> ***Question Two:*** 'How many times in your career have the officials changed their decisions in your favour?'

Cristiano Ronaldo: 'Maybe three or four?'

The hope is that he starts to unravel the futility of his current approach, which helps his emotional brain to accept the logic and let the issue go.

Option two: Predict the future

Fast-forwarding to the end of a film may ruin it, but when it comes to emotional control, predicting the potential consequences of our actions can help us to save face. After we have paused to step back for a second, we can fast-forward into the future and imagine both short- and long-term impacts, which can help temper our feelings, see the bigger picture and make better decisions.

- Ask yourself: How will this decision affect me in a month?

  A year? Five years?

Option three: Putting things into perspective

Point One: Is it really that catastrophic?
Maybe you're losing, you messed something up, and you're behind schedule. It's not totally unexpected that we will mess up from time to time. Remember, excellence is volatile and there are no straight lines to the top.

Point Two: Failure is potential for improvement
For the most part, mistakes help us make crucial corrections that lead us to excellence, if we learn from them. This mind-set enables us to capitalise on failure as a way to help identify and overcome chinks in our armour.

Point Three: Give yourself the permission to be human[65]
It is totally normal to feel emotional. Accepting this fact is like a release valve that reduces our perception of the demands imposed on us, which takes the load off our shoulders.

Venting

(Great for: Red to blue)

We have to listen to the emotional brain before it will listen to us. Sometimes letting the emotional brain tire itself out before attempting to domesticate it is the most sensible option. Expressing the emotion acts like a release valve that allows the emotional brain to enter a state where it will listen to reason or switch off entirely. So, if we're muttering the same words over and over, verbally denying an event and recognising the loss of control, but we can't rein it in then, cry, vent, let it out. Don't pretend the negative emotions don't exist. This could be sixty-minute download to a friend, a five-minute riff to a colleague in the office, or a scream or slap on the thigh (your own) on the pitch, during a time-constrained performance situation.

'Sometimes letting the emotional brain tire itself out before attempting to domesticate it is the most sensible option'

We should do our venting in private with people we trust, ideally who recognise that this is just our emotional brain at work. Once initiated we need to make sure we let it all out, no matter how irrational, for as long as it takes. If interrupted mid-vent, the likelihood is more agitation. Let the vent run its course.

Occasionally it may require a second round.

Do not judge or care about the content. The rambling will get more and more stupid but less and less powerful. Eventually, we'll no longer feel the need to fill the silence; we'll relax our shoulders, tip our head back and take a big sigh. The venting will wither out and the frontal brain will kick back in, letting you know: 'I've had enough of this moaning, I'm taking charge now'.

When the emotional brain has unloaded, we'll feel better and it will start to concede power to the frontal brain. The emotional brain can make totally valid points that need to be taken forward. The taking forward, answers and solutions always lie in the frontal brain though. Here, we can extract the valid points and discard the nonsense.

This is not an excuse to stomp the ground, shout profanities, act out, or beat ourselves up. All of these add internal pressure and further increase the likelihood of a subsequent mistake. They also frustrate officials, teammates, bosses, friends, and fans while handing the competitive advantage to our opponents.

> ***Note:*** Collateral Damage- Take care of outbursts if you have them. Apologise if you have unduly affected others, or forgive yourself if you feel you have let yourself down. Guilt, shame, frustration and other emotions are signals to help you avoid future errors, if you are willing to learn from them.

> ***Tip:*** Never vent on social media.

Narrow the problem

(Great for: Red to blue)

Our level of stress can be attributed to the complexity of our problems. By breaking a complex problem down, solutions become easier to find. Here are four options how.

Option one: Naming the challenge

As the old adage goes, 'you've got to name it to tame it.' Take the challenge at hand and define it. Acquiring a detailed understanding of what it is that's causing the rigid posture, dry mouth and quiver in your stomach means we can cut it down to size, and thus confine it.

One of the problems with anxiety is that it's not fun to speak about the thing that's causing it. The problem is that not speaking about the stressor gives it more power over us which amplifies the racing pulse, berating thoughts, and thudding in our chests.

Generally, when we speak about our fears, we realise they aren't as bad as we assume, and also that we're braver and more capable than we thought. We can only realise this bravery if we speak about, and confront, the problem. This lightens the load and provides a sense of calm.

> 'When we speak about our fears, we realise they aren't as bad as we thought, and also that we're braver and more capable than we thought'

Option two: Break it down

Deconstruct the challenge into smaller and smaller challenges.

From one big mess, to a smaller mess, to a series of even smaller messes. As we do this, our perceptions of the battle we face will gradually shrink. This means we can start to lean in, commit, and that glint in our eye returns. We are back in control.

Option three: Reducing the demands

When our demands exceed our capacity the product is stress. Therefore, one way to reduce stress is to reduce our demands. Sometimes when our expectations are too high, we freeze and end up procrastinating. When something feels too stressful, terrifying, or we're blocked and the answers aren't flowing, we need to temporarily reduce our criteria for success. When we lower our standards to a threshold that we can confidently deal with, our frontal and unconscious brains can take the reigns. This increases the odds of us getting a win. Small wins can spiral us back on track fast growing our appetite for the next challenge.

Option four: Shortening the time frame

If we can't think about tomorrow because right now it's just too overwhelming, then don't. One of the best things we can do when we're faced with crisis is to shorten our time frame. Michael Phelps broke his race day down into a series of simple steps, or small wins, which enabled him to build victory focusing on just one small thing at a time. Narrowing the focus down to whatever we feel we can cope with, even if it is the next breath, reduces the load. Focus on taking that next breath, then the next one, then maybe we can focus on the next ten seconds, perhaps then the next minute, then the next five minutes, and so on. We will begin to build victory, like Michael Phelps did.

Hit mute

(Great for: Red to blue)

If interacting with another person whilst in red head, and leaving the situation is not an option, we might need to put ourselves on mute. In other words, stop speaking. If the people we communicate with are also in red head, remember that much of what we all say at this point may be extreme or exaggerated; resist the urge to respond at all. Both our mood and that of the person with whom we're conversing is temporary. Sometimes the best thing we can do is let the other person express their feelings.

Find the flip

(Great for: Red to blue)

Chaos usually elicits a negative image for most of us. It used to for me. The Chinese word for crisis, 危机 (*wéijī*), is composed of two different words: 'danger' and 'opportunity'. In every crisis, there are always opportunities to counter, innovate, and overcome.

As on the battlefield, there's a time to hold our position, a time to fall back and reassess, and times when we should attack. Those calls must be based on pragmatism (frontal brain), not impulse (emotional brain). When chaos strikes, our initial aim is always to control our arousal. The eye of the storm is the place to be.

Once we have controlled our arousal we need to engage our offensive spirit, switch to attack mode and exploit the opportunity within it. It is all very well avoiding or deflecting an opponent's punches, but to excel we must be ready to strike back too. This is called countering. In boxing, the counter-punch immediately follows an attack launched by an opponent that exploits the opening created in their guard.

'It is all very well avoiding or deflecting an opponent's punches, but to excel we must be ready to strike back too'

The art of counter-attack rests on the ability to negate or thwart the advantage sought by the enemy during attack, and then immediately press any opportunity that presents itself. To perform a successful counter-attack, we must strike the enemy decisively. The objective is inflicting shock and surprise. With the counter-attack front and centre, triggering our predatory blue head, we unleash the psychological fire-power that always finds a way forward.

Re-Frame the challenge

In red head we create narrow frames for our experiences, and this limits the way we think. We zero in on the problem, or the first solution that comes to mind, which may not be the best.

Emotional Brain: (Asks questions like) 'What is the sum of five plus five?'

Notice: This type of question leads us to conclude that our options are binary, when the reality is that they lie on a spectrum.

Frontal Brain: (Asks questions like) 'What two numbers add up to ten?'

Notice: The first question has only one right answer. The second question has infinite solutions, including negative numbers and fractions. These problems, which rely on simple addition, differ only in the way they are framed. By changing the frame, we dramatically change the range of possible solutions.

Re-framing is about switching perspectives. This is where we can take time to consider more options and assess alternatives. We can re-frame through observing, listening, and interviewing, putting ourselves in others' shoes and pulling their insights together to paint a detailed picture of the situation

▶ Exercise: Here are a few good questions to ask:

- What would this look like if the solution were simple?
- What is the last thing the opposition would expect you to do?
- If you only had a day to deliver the result, how would you do it?
- Could money, networks, effort fix this problem?
- To whom could you delegate it?
- Who could you ask for help?
- How could you eliminate parts of the problem?
- Who has solved this problem before?

Cue words

(Great for: Red to blue)

'Dominate the ball!' 'Quick feet, strong arms!' 'Ready-Set-Fire!' Cue words are signals to act. One word, phrase, or acronym that can optimise our emotional state and activate our advanced mental structures.

We can use them to guide the technical or tactical aspects of performance; Owen Farrell might use a cue like, 'dominate the ball' before executing his conversion. Then there are cues that remind us to use a particular skill or tendency, like 'Quick feet, strong arms.' Cues can be timing or rhythm-related, such as 'Ready-Set-Fire!' or energy-related action words like 'explode.' Some are spiritual, 'For the glory of God'. They can also be motivational, like 'just do it' or three words that relate to our concordant values. The only rule is that the words evoke personal meaning and emotion.

Visualisation

(Great for: Red to blue, blue, to green, and green to blue)

Throughout his career Michael Phelps would watch videotape in bed, before he fell asleep and when he woke up. The videotape actually referred to visualising the perfect race. Phelps would lie in bed with his eyes shut and visualise the perfect race, launching from the blocks in slow motion and swimming flawlessly. Likewise, Owen Farrell visualises an imaginary line from the ball to between the posts and stalks the ball travelling along it until he gets it just right.

Visualisation works by mentally simulating the steps required to achieve a goal. The reason it is so powerful is that our brain can't distinguish between the actual event and the vivid image of that event. Whether we experience something for real or visualise it, we activate the same parts of our mental structures. This is why visualisation enhances our mental structures, activates our psychological fire-power, and triggers hormonal changes like the super six, the combination of which maximises the technical ability we bring to the table. There are two key characteristics of great visualisation:

'Our brain can't distinguish between the actual event and the vivid image of that event'

Key Point One: Visualise the race, not just the finish line

Visualising winning a race is not as effective as visualising doing the hard work that enables us to win the race. We must focus on the process of getting to the goal, not just the outcomes of achieving it. Michael Phelps focused on the process required to achieve his goal, like the perfect entry to the water, things that could go wrong, and each stroke executed with technical precision. Not the medals, podiums and adoration associated with victory.

'Visualising winning a race is not as effective as visualising doing the hard work that enables us to win the race'

Key Point Two: The more senses involved, the better

We must make visualisation as real as possible. The senses of sight, sound, smell, touch, and taste combine to create high-definition mental movies. Michael Phelps sees the stillness of the water at the start position. He hears the roar of the crowd intensifying as the race progresses. He can smell the chlorine. He feels his hands carve through the water without a splash. He even evokes emotions such as apprehension, nervous energy and tension; and he visualises himself successfully managing all this. This sensory activation magnifies the potency of the technique.

Visualisation can be performed by anyone, anywhere, anytime. Phelps would watch his mental tape in bed before he went to sleep, when he woke up, before and even during a race. You can too.

- ▶ Exercise:
  What will you see, how will you feel, what will you hear, and what might you smell? The more senses you can involve the more effective your visualisation will be.

Behave to become

(Great for: Red to blue, blue to green and green to blue)

As the old slogan goes, 'just do it' is very often the best approach. If you want to feel more confident, smile, look others in the eye and ask questions. If you want to get more work done, sit down and do some. If you want to work hard, ignore distractions, actively listen and go the extra mile. The message is that when we don't have confidence, resilience or motivation, it's actually easier to behave ourselves into these states; rather than think our way.

> 'If you want to feel more confident, smile, look others in the eye and ask questions. If you want to get more work done, sit down and do some. If you want to work hard, ignore distractions, actively listen and go the extra mile'

In physics, activation energy is the initial spark needed to catalyse a reaction. The same activation energy, both physical and psychological, is needed for us to overcome our inertia and kick-start us into action. This is about changing our behaviour first and trusting that the feelings will follow. Also known as fake it 'til you make it.' Starting is the hardest part; we gain momentum as we go. It might feel like action follows feeling, but really action and feeling go together. By regulating the action, which is under our direct control, we can indirectly regulate the feeling, which is not.

> ▶ Exercise: Set a goal of behaving the emotion the moment requires from you. The rule is that you have the option to stop after two minutes if the emotion hasn't taken over. Chances are your feelings will have caught up with your actions and the emotion will have taken hold. Two minutes is hardly overwhelming, consequently we are more likely to initiate this technique.

Music, prayer, story or conversation
(Great for: Red to blue, blue to green and green to blue)

Music that conjures energy. Prayer that summons strength. Story that inspires positivity. Conversations that rouse confidence. They all have the power to make the hair on the backs of our necks stand up.

Music for energy

Music can perform the functions of a time machine. A single song, the lyrics, tempo, mood can take us back to a time, a place, or set of emotions like nothing else can. To switch on, Michael Phelps would listen to Lil Wayne, Young Jeezy, and Jay Z This increased his heart rate, blood pressure and triggered the secretion of the super six hormones we associate with blue head as he transitioned from green to blue head.

Music for focus

An effective way to block out red zone distractions is to listen to the same song on repeat. Doing so is thought to help maintain focus by helping us dissolve into the song, which restricts our minds from wandering.

Music for relaxation

Classical music can de-activate the stress hormones we associate with red head. The intricate patterns and gradually unfolding textures can be the perfect soundtrack for green head.

Story for decompression

Jason Henderson (Chapter 19) used podcasts to 'amp up' while transitioning from green head to blue on his journey to work. To decompress to green head on the way home he would listen to big band music.

Prayer for positivity

The 'fittest man on earth' CrossFit games champion between 2011 and 2014, Rich Froning, engages in prayer before competition. Prayer is another act that can bring us into the present moment, bringing hope, showing gratitude, and narrowing our focus to the moment.

Conversations for inspiration

Powerful Ted talks, scintillating YouTube clips from expert performers can evoke a variety of emotions that help us transition into blue or green states. Whether we're having a rough day, are struggling to get up for it, or just can't switch off, finding inspirational or poignant talks that we can resonate with can be effective ways to flick the switch.

> ▶ Exercise: The key thing is that your connection with the material is meaningful and bespoke to you. Why not create your own *on*, *off* and *control* switch playlists on Spotify, YouTube, Audible, or a notebook for prayer.

Pick a focal point

(Great for: Red to blue, blue to green and green to blue)

If our attention is on the crowd, the referee, or our families, it's not on the task at hand and we are leaking ability. Owen Farrell would narrow his attention by repeatedly looking down at the ball and up at the target. In baseball, pitchers may check the bases, regardless of whether any players are on them, before a pitch. A day trader might click through each piece of software on their screen.

'If our attention is on the crowd, the referee, or our families, it's not on the task at hand and we are leaking ability'

Focusing on our performance environment constricts our attention and can bring us into the moment. The aim is a laser-like focus on the task at hand. Scanning the technical environment brings our attention to the task at hand, away from the jeering crowd, trash talk, and any other form of distraction.

> ***Note:*** Peripheral vision- If our objective is to switch off, then a blurred expansive gaze, widens our attention reducing arousal.

Adopt an alter ego

(Great for: Red to blue, green to blue and blue to green)

> ***Beyoncé Knowles-Carter:*** 'She [Sasha Fierce] doesn't do interviews, ... she only performs.'[66]

Singer, songwriter, producer, dancer and actress Beyoncé Knowles-Carter is also known as Sasha Fierce, a confident, dominant, and powerful woman who struts her stuff in concert and music videos. When it's time to switch on, Beyoncé conjures her alter ego, Sasha Fierce, to get the job done. Beyoncé imitates the behaviour of this fictional character who excels in the type of sassy, confident, assertive behaviour she aims to exhibit on stage. Sasha Fierce customarily appears right before Beyoncé is about to take the stage.

> ***Beyoncé Knowles-Carter:*** 'Usually when I hear the chords, when I put on my stilettos. Like the moment right before when you're nervous,' she says. 'then Sasha Fierce appears, and my posture and the way I speak and everything is different.'[66]

When you adopt an alter ego, you access parts of you that allow you to complete difficult tasks, like handling conflict, projecting confidence, or strutting your stuff on stage like Beyoncé.

> ***Beyoncé Knowles-Carter:*** 'It's kind of like doing a movie. When you put on the wig and put on the clothes, you walk different,' she says. 'It's no different from anyone else. I feel like we all kind of have that thing that takes over.' She continues, 'Sasha Fierce is the fun, more sensual, more aggressive, more outspoken side and more glamorous side that comes out when I'm working and when I'm on the stage,' explains Beyoncé. 'I have someone else that takes over when it's time for me to work and when I'm onstage, this alter ego that I've created kind of protects me and who I really am.'[66]

We know what we need to achieve, and we know the behaviour needed to achieve it, but sometimes we just feel conflicted or insecure about exhibiting certain behaviours. Enter the alter ego. An alter ego can be defined as another version of oneself. Essentially it's putting someone else in charge. This causes us to feel less insecure and more empowered to engage in the behaviour. Our alter ego provides us with some interpersonal distance that makes us feel comfortable. Maybe it's to assert yourself, compete in extreme sports, or to disengage entirely.

For Beyoncé it's putting on her stilettos, for Jason Henderson it's putting away his ID pass that enabled him to transition between 'super-soldier' and 'dad'.

▶ Exercise: What roles do you have? Find a piece of clothing, accessory, or trigger you can identify with to access an alter ego that could optimise your emotions and behaviour for your craft.

Self-Talk
(Great for: Red to blue, blue to green and green to blue)

Owen Farrell:
'It doesn't matter what's just happened [missed the last kick] you've got a job to do.'

Our words prime our thoughts, emotions and mood. Self-talk is the script we use to frame the situation. It's something we all do. The pertinent question is, how do the words we use affect our energy and attention? By checking the quality of our self-talk, we can identify and eliminate destructive internal chat that detracts our attention and energy. Here are four ways we can optimise:

One: Change 'I am' to, 'This is.'
Example: 'This is tense', instead of 'I am tense.'

Note: The latter insinuates our mistakes or failures are our identities. The former insinuates reality, which is that our mistakes or failures are temporary.

Two: Swap 'I can't' to, 'I don't know how yet.'

Note: The unconscious message of the latter is that there is a solution out there and our focus is to find it. Because if we 'can't,' why bother trying?

Three: Replace: 'You need to stop looking down, you look so nervous,' with 'You need to look up, lift your chin, and make eye contact.'

Note: This draws our energy and attention to the solution and opportunity, which is to display confident behaviour and get back on top. Instead we might focus on the threat, which can cause us to dwell, whine, become the victim and even trigger more red head.

Four: We can even talk to ourselves in the third person, using 'he', 'she,' or 'they,' or refer to ourselves by name. I might say to myself: 'James, you need to stay focused and execute your process, the results will come.'

Note: Using the third person in self-talk can help us step back and think more objectively about our responses and emotions, whether we're thinking about a past event or looking into the future.

▶ Exercise: Take some time to reflect on how you speak to yourself. How do those words affect your emotions and your attention? Would you be comfortable speaking to a teammate, colleague or friend that way?

Grounding

(Great for: Red to blue, blue to green and green to blue)

Like an anchor in choppy waters grounding is about reconnecting to the present by bringing attention to a specific point. This strategy is really helpful in situations where we find ourselves becoming caught up in strong emotions like anxiety, anger, or sadness; or if we catch ourselves engaging in frustrating or spiralling thoughts.

Note: The word grounding obviously means to connect with the earth, and by earth we mean, the moment.

▶ Exercise One: Simply notice five things we can see, four things we can hear, three things we can feel, two we can smell and one we can taste. Using our senses: sight, hearing, smell, taste, touch, we can very quickly reconnect our brains and bodies in the present. Focusing on our basic human senses brings our attention away from the past or future and into the moment.

Exercise Two: Grounding can also help us find our centres of gravity, literally. Imagine a spot that exists two inches below your navel and two inches below the surface of your belly, this is your centre. Now imagine roots sprouting from your feet into the ground that keep you steady, secure and safe. This is what athletes like Owen Farrell attempt to achieve when they talk about finding their centre of gravity.

▶ Exercise Three: Another grounding exercise is to remind yourself of who you are: Say your name. 'My name is James King.' Say your age. 'I am 35 years old.' Say where you are now. 'I am at home in the New Forest, United Kingdom.' Say what you have done today. 'I am writing about grounding.' Say what you will do next. 'I will write about Progressive Muscular Relaxation.'

Try these exercises for yourself and notice how your attention narrows and your focus switches into the present.

Progressive Muscular Relaxation (PMR)

(Great for: Red to blue, blue to green)

Bob Bowman (Michael Phelps's coach) first met Michael as a seven-year-old, and could see Phelps was highly concordant with swimming, but he also saw a child prone to stress. As a child Phelps struggled with calm before a race. The first technique he was introduced to was a PMR script Bowman encouraged Phelps's mother to read him each night.

PMR Script: 'Tighten your right hand into a fist and release it. Imagine the tension melting away.

Note: Michael would repeat this process, tensing and releasing each part of his body before he fell asleep each night.

Many of us experience stress and anxiety as physical tension in our bodies, and Progressive Muscular Relaxation helps alleviate this tension through tensing and relaxing a sequence of muscle groups. The process consists of tensing and then relaxing one muscle group at a time throughout the entire body. It can be performed anywhere, anytime; lying in bed, seated in a meeting, or on the pitch.

Mindfulness

(Great for: Red to blue, blue to green)

Mindfulness is like training a puppy to sit. In this case, your mind is the puppy. Believe it or not, stillness is the mind's natural state.

'Mindfulness is like training a puppy to sit. In this case, your mind is the puppy'

The basic steps of mindfulness are as follows:

Step One: Close your eyes, bring your full attention to the feeling of your breath. You're not thinking about your breath, just focusing on the raw physical sensations.

Step Two: This is where all the benefits come from.

As soon as you start trying to focus on that breath, you're going to start thinking about what you what you had for breakfast, that article on LinkedIn and the text message you forgot to reply to. When these thoughts inevitably kick in, your job is to notice. Notice the thought as a feather, acknowledge it, and let it float away. Noticing is the key moment, noticing is victory.

Noticing is the key moment,
noticing is victory.

Ironically, this moment of distraction is when most people think they have failed. 'I just can't clear my mind' is the biggest misconception about meditation. We don't need to clear our minds, that's impossible, unless you're enlightened, a psychopath, or dead.

The only goal is to notice when we become distracted and bring our attention back to our breathing, our bodies, or the moment, for what might feel the millionth time. Noticing each thought and letting it go is like is like a bicep curl but for our brain. Over time our minds become obedient and sit on cue. This enables us to sustain deeper focus, a lower stress response, and quieten our internal chatter.

'Noticing each thought and
letting it go is like doing a bicep
curl for our brain'

Change your internal representations
(Great for: Red to blue, blue to green and green to blue)

Internal Representation: How we represent an idea of reality in our minds

Our brains create internal representations that impact our emotional state. These representations can consist of pictures, sounds, feelings, tastes, smells and thoughts, and are based on how we perceive the situation. The good news is that changing the pictures in our heads, changes the emotions they generate.

Imagine you have a touch-screen smart board in your head, and you can use your mind to change the picture; swiping things away, changing the contrast, increasing the definition, zooming in or out, changing the colours and even deleting things completely.

Owen Farrell used this technique to fade out the jeering crowd by shrinking everything out except the ball, the posts and himself. The way athletes like Owen flick nervous energy out of their fingers or through their feet through lightly stamping the ground are examples of how we can change the pictures in our heads to change the way we feel.

If we're feeling red head, we can disconnect by stepping out of the image so we are now looking at the situation from a bird's-eye view. We could imagine ourselves changing colour, perhaps we start to turn blue. We can fade the picture, make the image black and white, make the looks on teammates' faces fuzzy, switch the sound off, move it far away, or shrink the picture into a tiny square. By making the emotions less bright, less colourful, and further away, we weaken their power.

If the picture has positive connotations we might decide to view the event through our minds' eye to amplify those emotions associated with it. By making the internal representation bigger, brighter, and higher definition, we can further activate the emotions we associate with it.

Physical reset

(Great for: Red to blue, blue to green and green to blue)

A thudding heartbeat. A racing mind. Sweat streaming down our brow. This is not necessarily anxiety. However, when we experience these symptoms, our emotional brains start to search for predictions to explain these physical sensations. A lot of the time the causes are physical rather than psychological. Maybe we haven't taken a deep breath for an hour, or we're dehydrated, our blood sugar is low, we didn't sleep well last night, or haven't moved from our desks all morning? Perhaps all of the above.

I recommend a physical check-in whenever we notice red head sensations set in. If it's 15:00 and something kicks off and our only source of fuel for the day so far is the four americanos we consumed (at 150mg of caffeine per hit) because we skipped breakfast and missed lunch, and now we're jogging on the spot with steam coming from our ears, we probably don't need to question our existential dilemmas. Instead, we probably need to take a deep breath, hydrate, eat, and go to the bathroom, move our body and maybe even take sixty seconds of silence.

- Prioritise the check-in based on what would kill us first in nature should we fail to address it:

One: Are you breathing properly? This will be the next technique we explore.

Two: How thirsty are you on a scale of 1-10? If you are below 7 you are possibly up to 2% of your bodyweight dehydrated, which can reduce cognitive function by up to 20%.

Three: Do you need to go to the toilet? Restricting the urge to go spikes blood pressure and stress hormones.

Four: On a scale of 1-10, how hungry are you? If it's above a 6, your blood sugar is most likely at the lower range of normal.

Five: Are you putting away too much caffeine? Caffeine is a stimulant; its jittery effects are the same as those you experience in a frightening event.

Six: Do you need a moment of quiet? Take a time-out. Even sixty seconds of silence can give you the space to think.

We must listen to our brains and bodies. They can trigger hunger, thirst, or that we need the bathroom, or quiet time, but we have to act on what they are telling us.

'We must listen to our brains and bodies. They can trigger hunger, thirst, or that we need the bathroom, or quiet time, but we have to act on what they are telling us'

Breathe

(Great for: Red to blue, blue to green and green to blue)

Michael Phelps engaged in meditative breath work. Jason Henderson took three deep sighs. Owen Farrell took three sharp breaths. We need to control our breathing, or our breathing will control us.

'We need to control our breathing, or our breathing will control us'

How we breathe is the perfect barometer for our emotions. When our breath is short, shallow, and irregular our minds are all over the place. When our breath is deep, and stable so is our mind.

The purpose of breathing is to get oxygen into our lungs and remove carbon dioxide from them. There are two parts to the breath, the inhalation, and the exhalation. Our diaphragms act like large pistons regulating our breathing and drawing air into the lungs. Our blood then delivers that oxygen to every single cell in the body.

We take breathing for granted because it's largely automatic. The following techniques give us a unique opportunity to spark significant changes in our emotional states within seconds. Here are four exercises we can put to work.

One: Parasympathetic breathing

Start with the inhale, the active part of the breath. The diaphragm has to work, to contract as we do so. At the top of the breath we're going to hold, pause for a second, before exhaling slowly, for at least double the time of the inhale. This is what induces that parasympathetic recovery, we want to enjoy that smooth, gentle exhale, and then as we empty our lungs, we pause again at the bottom before we repeat that cycle.

Note: This produces a calming influence that lowers our heart rate, our blood pressure, promotes digestion and the uptake of nutrients. It restores, recovers, and regenerates us. Our green head runs on our parasympathetic nervous system. When conducting parasympathetic breathing, the vagus nerve signals the brain to relax. We can literally take a power rest in a room full of people using this technique.

Great for: Red to blue, blue to green.

Two: The sigh

All you need to do is (close your eyes if you want) take in a deep breath, pause and then exhale slowly with an audible satisfying sigh. You'll feel comfortable and it might even make you yawn.

Note: This is another great option that can activate rest, recovery and rejuvenation (green head) in just a few seconds. Notice that you usually sigh unconsciously at times of red head. The sigh fills your lungs more than your normal breath would, which helps oxygenate your brain and body, giving a relieving effect.

Great for: Red to blue, blue to green

Three breath breather

This is where you take three deep, parasympathetic breaths (as described above) and add the sigh to the exhale. In just 45 seconds you can activate your parasympathetic nervous system, release tension, expel carbon dioxide and oxygenate your brain.

Great for: Red to blue, blue to green

Four: The activation breath:

The activation breath starts with a short and sharp inhale

through the nose, followed by a pause, that precedes a short, sharp exhale through your nose, before pausing and the cycle repeats. One second in, one-second pause, one-second out, one-second pause and repeat is about right.

Note: This can also be used to summon energy and focus. Four to five of the activation breaths will flood your brain and body with oxygen and leave you primed for action.

Great for: green to blue

These techniques can be used anywhere, at any time, by anyone. At work, on the pitch, before a big meeting, during a speech, on the commute, before bed, when you wake up.

Power posing

Owen Farrell would take a deep breath in and lift his chest. Michael Phelps would conduct the double-arm swing and back slap. Jason Henderson sat back with his hands clasped behind his head. In as little as sixty seconds, through adopting an alpha pose, we can change the way we think, feel and perform.

'In as little as sixty seconds, through adopting an alpha pose, we can change the way we think, feel and perform'

We humans, like other animals, express power through open, expansive postures and also express powerlessness through closed, contractive postures. Power poses such as the wonder woman or superman stance, where your shoulders are back, chest is out and chin is held high, cause positive changes that stimulate the production of the blue-head hormones (the super six), green-head hormones (the feel-good hormones) and, simultaneously, lower the red-head stress hormones. Low power poses such as the slouched back, tucked chin, and bent neck elicit the reverse effect on our hormones.

Power Poses: These are characterised by expansive open postures, spread arms, legs out and a generous occupation of space. Chin exposed, walking with wide steps, and arms loose at your sides swinging, using exaggerated movements, and sitting with your hands interlocked behind your head.

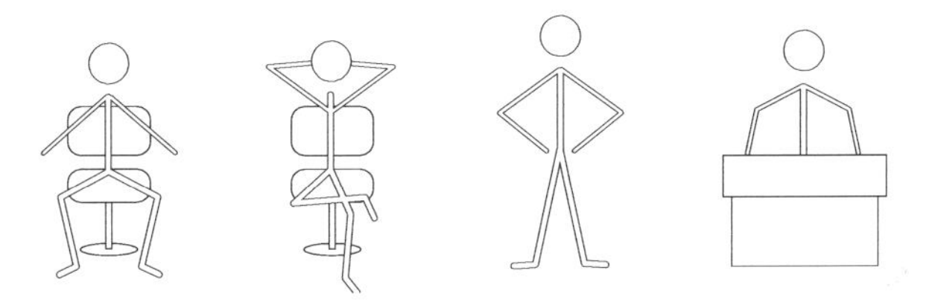

Note: Even our facial displays can affect our emotional states. Using our 'smile muscle' increases enjoyment, tilting our head upwards induces pride, and hunched postures can elicit depressed feelings. By simply shifting posture, we can prepare our physical and psychological systems to enhance the way we think, feel and perform.

Contractive Poses: These poses are expressed through minimising occupied space, including crossed arms and legs, a narrow stance, a hunched back, hands covering face, and a tucked chin.

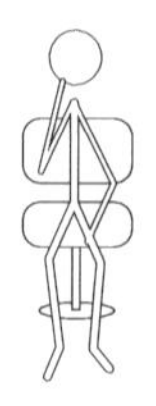

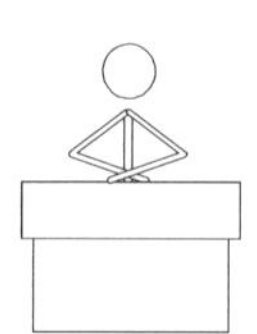

Emotional control routines can be utilised before, during, and after performance. They can last a split second or hours. Some are cerebral and contemplative, others are overt and expressive. They can be elaborate or really simple; structured or loose. If our preference is flexibility, then we can build the routine with this in mind.

The most critical feature of a great routine is individualisation. It's our routine, for our performance. Routines should be built upon our own unique personalities, challenge points, demands, resources, environment, time, and location. We must have resonance with the techniques we employ and develop comfort in using them.

Make sure to build your routines around things that are always available, not a lucky pair of pants. A routine becomes a superstition when a particular action is given magical significance. Adversaries can prey on superstitions, and lucky objects can be lost or stolen, leaving you routineless when you need it most.

The routine drowns everything else out, whatever the stakes, whether it's the winning point, sailing ahead or snatching a victory from the jaws of defeat. Investing the time and effort to get this right and allows us to become the master of our emotions and formidable opponents.

> ***Note:*** Make sure you get your routine right. If you notice that you have missed part of your routine, added a random behaviour, completed the routine in the wrong order, or been interrupted by a competitor. Stop!

> Start again. If you notice your competition executing routines, do everything you can to interrupt them.

We have our concordant goals, have engaged in three-dimensional training, and have mastered our emotions so that we can deliver all our technical ability on demand and under pressure when it counts. The product will be success. We have worked so hard to achieve success, we had better make sure we sustain it. No one wants to be the one-hit wonder.

CHAPTER SUMMARY

- Excellence is highly personal and so are our emotions.
- The objective is to build our own highly effective routines that work for us.
- Our routines will be unique to our individual challenges.
- Routines should be built upon our own unique personality, demands, time, and location.
- Emotional control routines can be utilised before, during, and after performance, and can last a split second or hours.
- Some routines are cerebral and contemplative, others are overt and expressive.
- They can be elaborate or really simple; structured or loose.
- We must have resonance with the techniques we employ and develop comfort in using them.
- If a technique doesn't resonate, don't use it.
- If you notice that you have missed part of your routine, added a random behaviour, completed the routine in the wrong order, or been interrupted by a competitor. Stop! Start again.

PART 5

CONTINUOUS IMPROVEMENT

21

POST SUMMIT PERIL

The time to repair the roof is when the sun is shining
John F. Kennedy

Serena Williams is arguably the most dominant player to ever step on court. At nineteen years old, Williams burst onto the scene to win the US Open. Her powerful style of play has led her to 23 Grand Slam singles titles (and four Olympic gold medals), the most in the history of tennis. In 2020, the 39-year-old is still competing as hard as ever.[67]

Bill Gates, the founder of Microsoft, became the youngest billionaire in the world in 1987. His achievements include inspiring the era of the home computer and commercialising the operating system Windows, which is used by almost 90% of the world's computers. He had a 24-year run as the richest man in the world, to this day Bill sits comfortably in third place.[68]

Sir Alex Ferguson is revered across the globe as one of the greatest football managers of all time. The former Manchester United manager has won more trophies than any other manager in the history of football. Between 1986 and 2013 he won 38 trophies, including thirteen English Premier League titles (EPL), five Football Association (FA) cups, and two UEFA (Union of European Football Associations) Champions League titles. His 26-year spell with Manchester United makes him the longest-serving manager in the Premier League's history where the current average life span of a manager is less than two-and-a-half years.[69]

Twenty years … thirty years … lifetimes. There are those who experience success and those who sustain it. Serena Williams, Bill Gates, and Sir Alex certainly weren't one-hit wonders. They embedded themselves at the top of a galaxy of stars, sustaining elite performance at the pinnacle of their crafts for decades.

If we don't continue to accelerate, what happens? We regress. Money depreciates unless invested; fitness diminishes if we stop training, and hard-earned skills fade unless they are honed. That is because where we are isn't where we stay. Progress is not something we capture and retain. We only get to keep our progress if we keep making progress. Only those who continuously improve get to stay at the top.

'Progress is not something we capture and retain. We only get to keep our progress if we keep making progress'

For most, the effect of success can be compared to what mountaineers call the post-summit peril. When it comes to death rates on Mount Everest, the vast majority occur on the way down. By the time we summit we're exhausted. The temptation is to bask in glory and take in the view from the top. The risk is that we switch off mentally, start to take short cuts, cut corners and, as a consequence, more people die coming down than going up.

Success, to many, is perceived as a permanent state. But once successful isn't the same as continuing to be successful. History is full of humans who blindly assumed that because they achieved success, they would continue to be successful in the future. Individuals like Mike Tyson, Tiger Woods or Macaulay Culkin burst onto the scene only to fall back and regress. At the organisational level, the movie industry has Blockbuster. Banking has Lehman Brothers. For every Apple, there are plenty more Ataris.

There are countless successful individuals and organisations that stood still or slipped back, while the rest of the world continued to accelerate and eventually overtake. The next Tiger Woods, Mike Tyson or Macaulay Culkin could be anyone. No individual or organisation is more than a few months from failure. We should never feel safe to rest on our laurels.

'No individual or organisation is more than a few months from failure'

Outliers like Serena, Bill and Sir Alex know that, unless we maintain our alignment with the principles that got us to the top in the first place, we will stop accelerating, come to a standstill and eventually fall backwards. In fact, recognising we can lose success helps develop the mentality we need to stay successful.

'Unless we maintain our alignment with the principles that got us to the top in the first place, we will stop accelerating, come to a standstill and eventually fall backwards'

The challenge success brings

When we become successful our enemy is no longer the competition. We become our own worst enemies. Buster Douglas didn't end Mike Tyson. Rory McIlroy didn't kill Tiger Woods. Apple didn't kill Atari. Mike Tyson killed Mike Tyson. Tiger Woods killed Tiger Woods. And Atari killed Atari.

Success changes the perspective from which we see the world, bringing with it a series of dangerous biases that can prevent future success.

Bias One- The illusion of continuity

Continuity bias: Our propensity to assume that the future will resemble the present.

This psychological illusion convinces us that we have experienced significant personal growth to get to the top of the mountain and that is precisely where we'll stay. This destructive bias causes many to turn a blind eye to any information that suggests otherwise. We hit cruise control and expect things to stay as they are.

When we feel like we've made it, it can be hard to imagine pushing our current achievements further. We believe we've peaked and forget that our potential is always expandable. We start to act as if that potential were already reached, which can kill our hunger to improve. The urgency, adversity, and pressure that got us to the top has gone. Who cares? We're already number one.

The illusion of continuity also downplays the real risks we face. This is often referred to as the ostrich effect, where we put our heads in the sand and pretend threats don't exist. Consequently, we underestimate the likelihood of making mistakes, when they might strike, and how significant their effects can be. The result is poor preparation, weak back-up plans, and paralysis when the inevitable threats do strike.

> 'The urgency, adversity, and pressure that got us to the top has gone. Who cares? We're already number one'

The illusion of continuity also downplays the real risks we face. This is often referred to as the ostrich effect, where we put our heads in the sand and pretend threats don't exist. Consequently, we underestimate the likelihood of making mistakes, when they might strike, and how significant their effects can be. The result is poor preparation, weak back-up plans, and paralysis when the inevitable threats do strike.

The reality is that we only ever reach the peak of our current ability, never our potential. There is always a way to get better. Our job is to find it. If we don't, someone else will.

> 'There is always a way to get better. Our job is to find it. If we don't, someone else will'

Performers who are hired directly into organisations like SEAL Team Six, Goldman Sachs and Manchester United and who have only ever seen success are most vulnerable to this risk. Inheriting success is no different from inheriting wealth, the risk is taking that success for granted and complacency creeping in. The second that these performers start to believe they are successful just for being in these culturally elite organisations is the second they are ripe for the taking.

'Inheriting success is no different from inheriting wealth, the risk is taking that success for granted and complacency creeping in'

Note: Did NASA predict SpaceX? Did Obama predict Trump? Did the EU predict Brexit? Did any of us predict the COVID 19 pandemic? These are all examples of the illusion of continuity we take for granted in times of success.

Bias Two- The illusion of personal control

The illusion of personal control: The propensity to over-estimate our own role and downplay the role of randomness in our success

When we succeed, the media, friends and the public will be full of admiration for our achievements and will tell us how talented we are. The biggest risk is that we believe the hype and allow the feeling that we've seen it, done it, know it, and completed it to set in.

Headline metrics like company stock price, position in a sporting league, or number of followers on Instagram mean it is easy to acquire a distorted perception of our own genius. The danger is that we overestimate the contribution of our skill and downplay the role of randomness in our success. The more successful we become, the more powerful this effect. The alarming thing is that this illusion is strengthened by stressful and competitive situations.

> 'Headline metrics like company stock price, position in a sporting league, or number of followers on Instagram mean it is easy to acquire a distorted perception of our own genius'

We end up thinking that we are successful because of our own genius rather than our ability to align with the principles we've discussed so far in this book is what stacked the probability of success so high in our favour.

The illusions of continuity and of personal control combine to give us a false sense of permanence. Which can lead to comfort. And comfort can lead to complacency.

When complacency sets in

When we're complacent, we're vulnerable. The risk is that we start adopting bad habits. It starts with the small things; like going through the motions in training sessions, skipping a feedback session and missing a few Individual Development Plan (IDP) meetings. This is often the beginning of the end. In second place it's obvious to go the extra mile, arrive early and stay late. It's easy to work harder, show humility and respect the competition.

> 'In second place it's obvious to go the extra mile, arrive early, stay late and go hard. It's easy to work harder, show humility and respect the competition'

The dangerous thing about complacency is that the damage is slow and silent. The descent occurs the same way the colourless, tasteless, and odourless drop of arsenic, taken over a long stretch of time, ultimately brings death to the victim.

The decline is invisible which is why so many individuals and organisations wait for the shit to hit the fan before making a special effort to improve. This is too late. The exponential breakthroughs that got us to the top work both ways, and can spit us out the bottom just as exponentially.

'The exponential breakthroughs that got us to the top work both ways, and can spit us out the bottom just as exponentially'

When this happens we assume the cause to be poor planning, lack of discipline, or bad luck. Then we rush to come up with an improvement plan, by default to working harder for longer, or maybe someone's head rolls (coach, manager, or yours). This is the crash diet approach to improvement. Crash-diets don't sustain excellence.

The demand capacity deficit*

The final reason sustaining success is challenging is that the responsibilities, pressures and expectations of performance tend to advance in parallel with our success. This means that, as we progress towards our goals, the demands imposed on us gradually increase. We tend to acquire extra-curricular demands as we navigate life; maybe we get married, have children, take on financial responsibilities and

*This idea was conceptualised by Loehr and Schwartz in their best-selling book: *The Power of Full Engagement*.[70]

Post Summit Peril

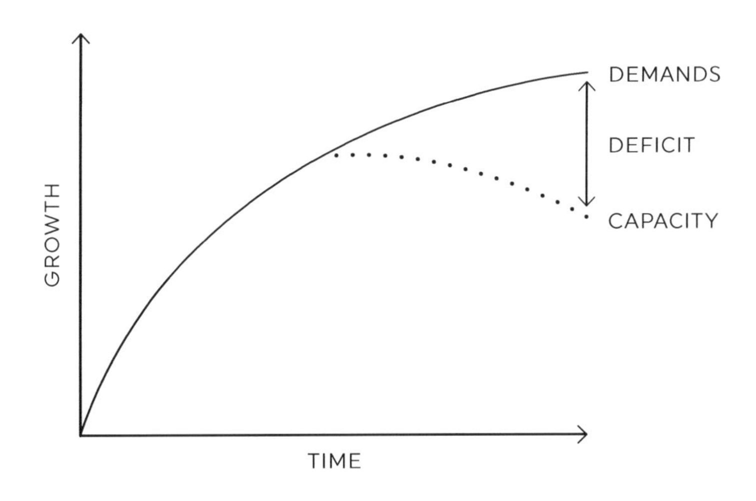

personal obligations. Simultaneously we experience the progressive loss of capacity that comes naturally with the ageing process.

'When we spend more units of effort than we can recover, the eventual consequence is that we create a gap between our capacity and the demands imposed on us'

When this happens, we borrow physiological and psychological effort, on credit. We summon the stress hormones cortisol, nor-adrenaline and adrenaline to over-ride our need for rest and recovery.

Chronic energy expenditure with insufficient recovery leads to red head where our performance suffers and eventually we begin to break down and eventually burn-out. Something has to give. This could be alignment with the principles that got us to the top in the first place, our relationships with loved ones or our physical and mental health. Failing to master recovery has de-railed many would-be elite performers.

Illustration adapted from: Tony Schwartz- Talks at Google.[71]

> ***Note:*** We must not wait to get sick to get better. To win the war on complacency, we must start by confronting the need for change before it's breathing fire and staring deep into our eyes.

In the next section we will explain the principles that negate the threat the illusion of continuity, the illusion of personal control and demand capacity deficit have on our ability to sustain elite performance- starting with the demand capacity deficit. In Part Four we discussed how to manage our emotions in the moment, but how do we keep it all together for longer periods of time -- over tournaments, across seasons, and throughout a career like Serena Williams, Bill Gates and Sir Alex Ferguson did? In the next chapter we outline the things to do today to make sure we continue to win tomorrow.

CHAPTER SUMMARY

- Where we are isn't where we stay. We only get to keep our progress if we continue making progress.
- Recognising we can lose success helps develop the mentality we need to stay successful.
- We only ever reach the peak of our current ability, never our potential. We are forever a work in progress that mistakenly likes to think we're complete.
- Continuity bias causes us to assume that the future will resemble the present; downplaying the real risks we face, when they might strike, and how significant their effects can be.
- The illusion of personal control has us downplay the role of randomness in our success and end up thinking our own genius is the true cause.
- These biases can make us complacent, when we're complacent, we're vulnerable. The risk is we start adopting bad habits.
- The damage is slow and silent but the exponential breakthroughs that got us to the top can spit us out the bottom just as exponentially.
- The demands of performance advance in parallel with our success simultaneously we experience a progressive loss of capacity with the ageing process.
- Without conscious intervention a gap develops between our capacity and the demands imposed on us that degrades our performance.

- We can't wait to get sick to get better. We must confront the need for change before it's breathing fire and staring deep into our eyes.

22

WIN THE DAY

Nothing is worth more than this day
Johann Wolfgang von Goethe

Joe Rogan is an American comedian and podcast host. *The Joe Rogan Experience* is one of the world's largest and most influential podcasts with monthly downloads estimated to be north of 200million. Guests have included Elon Musk, Mike Tyson and Bernie Sanders. In May 2020 he agreed the world's biggest podcast licensing deal with Spotify worth an estimated $100million.[72]

At 53, Rogan looks more like a professional athlete than a comedian. This is the product of his dedication to sustaining the success he has worked so hard to achieve. His impeccable daily routine keeps him performing at the highest level.

James Montgomery (*Rolling Stone* magazine): 'From his early morning workouts to his late-night comedy sets, Rogan makes use of every minute of the day, and then finds a way to squeeze even more out of each moment.'[73]

He starts his day with water and Himalayan pink salt followed by a Kale shake. Then he engages in meditation but not in the conventional manner. Rogan has found that total isolation in his sensory deprivation tank is the perfect way to help polish the finishing touches of a breakthrough idea.

He insists on at least 30 minutes of exercise each day which he prefers to blowing his body to pieces with maximal training a few times a week.

Joe Rogan:

'I don't go to failure. I don't believe in going to failure. What I think you're best off doing is less repetitions but more often. So, instead of doing one day where you blow your whole fucking system out and you do 'one more bro, come on. One more!!' And then the next day you can barely walk.'[74]

When he's not working, he is walking his golden retriever, Marshall, spending time with his wife and daughters, practising Mixed Martial Arts, playing pool, hanging out at the comedy club, or letting his mind wander in his sauna or floatation tank.

At the end of a day Joe prioritises getting at least seven hours of quality sleep. It's so important to him that he even measures the quality and quantity of his shut-eye using his Whoop band.

Joe Rogan:

'My Whoop tells me every night how much I sleep. It made

> me accountable. Because I was like ahhhh, I get seven or eight hours every night. I was getting four or five. And I was like, oh you lying bitch. It made me concentrate more on getting more sleep.'[74]

Joe's daily routine helps maximise his performance, quality of life and recovery so he can win his days and sustain the success he has worked so hard to build.

Master the day and the years will take care of themselves. Outliers who sustain excellence all adhere to specific, but unique, daily routines. In order to maximise continued growth, we need structure so that we can win our days, instead of wing our days.

> 'In order to maximise continued growth, we need structure so that we can win our days instead of wing our days'

When we break down tournaments, seasons and careers, they are all just a series of days that repeat. To excel we must win each day, one after the other. Over time, these winning days compound into winning months, winning years and winning careers.

Whether it's our morning routine, how we prepare for sleep, or our eating habits. Winning the day is about progress, fun and building in recovery so we can go again tomorrow.

Our body is designed to run like a Swiss watch. It has a clock which tells us when to sleep, wake and eat. We call this circadian rhythm. To stay on the 24-hour cycle our brain needs predictability and routine. Conflict between our lifestyles and our clocks impairs our emotional control, immune systems and ultimately our performance.

When there is chaos in our days, there is chaos in our minds. Routine gives us the predictability we need to thrive psychologically. When we're in control of our days, we're in control of our emotions and this means we can access all our technical abilities, stick to our principles and conserve our energy and attention for high-value activity.

Circadian Rhythm: A natural, internal process that regulates the sleep-wake cycle and repeats on each rotation of the Earth

Through establishing a pattern of actions that repeat and become the symphony of our daily lives, we can maximise our most limited resources; time and effort.

Units of effort: A finite amount of energy and attention (willpower and discipline) we can invest each day

Energy can be considered as our capacity to do work. Imagine that we have a limit of 100 units of effort to spend each day. Every time we think, decide or act, we exert units of effort, withdrawing from our balance. To maximise our progress, we must invest them as effectively as possible. Choosing what time to set our alarm takes out a little bit, deciding what to wear to work a uses a little more, bigger decisions such as deciding whether to take out a multi-million dollar position in Apple, or whether to take the critical shot, all empty our account faster. If we over draw our units of effort with trivial decisions, we have less energy and attention to invest in high-value activities, where we maximise our progress.

The good news is that, whilst time is finite, it passes by and is gone for ever, our energy is not. Yes, when we initiate any action, we draw down our units of effort. But, when we access green head and recover, we fill those reserves back up.[75]

'Whilst time is finite, it passes by and is gone for ever, our energy is not'

The challenge now is to plan one winning day that switches us between green head and blue head that we can repeat. We need to make sure we are pushing hard on the right things at the right times, and then recovering our energy so we can maximise our effort and our chances of sustaining success.

'We need to make sure we push hard on the right things at the right times, and then systematically replenish our energy'

The winning day

Winning the day requires us to master 5 interconnected areas:

The things we do every day are often the most important things we do. Activities like waking up, getting dressed, travelling to work,

lunch, and sleep combine to make up more than 66% of our lives. If we're not optimising them, then there is no way we're going to be optimising our performance, quality of life or health.

'The things we do every day are often the most important things we do'

Note: It's your winning day. If you don't like waking up at 04:30, don't. If you don't like green juice, don't drink it, and if you don't like exercise first thing in the morning, then don't do it. Be concordant with your unique biology and psychology, not those of the people you admire. The winning day is not a one-size-fits-all routine; it is about reflecting on what works for you and then automating that. The order of all the components described can be customised to what works best for you.

Morning routine

Win the morning, and the odds are we'll win the day. Mastering a morning routine is the lead domino that sets the trajectory for the rest of the day, so we need to get it right.

'Win the morning, and the odds are we'll win the day'

The objective is a calm and controlled morning, where we're in charge. So, the question is, do we hop out of bed and attack with clear purposeful action? Or do wake up exhausted, then trawl through social media, before initiating a red-headed race to get to work on time?

Note: Smart-Phones- Are you on your phone like a laboratory rat at a cocaine pellet dispenser? Is checking your phone the first thing you do in the morning and the last thing you do at night? If so, you can consider it an addiction. You need to own your phone, or it will own you. Using your phone and the applications on it should be a strategic decision, not involuntary. Try leaving your phone on flight mode or out of arm's reach to avoid becoming a smart-phone junkie.

Wake Time

The time we wake up is the anchor point for our biological clocks. A fixed wake time keeps us in sync with it, which has two key benefits.

Benefit One - First, we will begin to wake up naturally, in green head, as opposed to the cacophony of doom that represents our alarm clocks priming us for red head.

Benefit Two - Our body's sleep time is based on our wake time. So consistent wake times lead to us to consistent sleep times. That two-hour lie-in feels great at the time, but it pushes our sleep time to later that evening which is not so great.

Sunlight

The hands of our body clocks are powered by sunlight and movement, not coffee and wine. As soon as we're up, we need daylight. Throwing open our curtains as soon as we wake up, getting ready in daylight, and going outside as soon as appropriate is optimal. When our eyes detect sunlight, our brains stimulate the production of cortisol, which activates our energy and attention and leaves us feeling alert for the day ahead. Just two minutes of sun hitting our retinas is all we need to kick-start this process. Even if it's cloudy, ten minutes outside will still activate the cortisol we need to win the day in front of us.

Personal administration

Before the bullet dodging and fire-fighting that is work-related emails, voicemails, and checking our daily planner begins, we must take care of our personal administration. I recommend the physical check-in (chapter 19); breathe, hydrate, go to the bathroom, eat, and move. Suppressing these biological needs summons the stress hormones that prime us for red head and immediately starts burning through our precious units of effort.

Accumulate small wins

Admiral William McRaven:

> 'If you make your bed every morning, you will have accomplished the first task of the day. It will give you a small sense of pride, and it will encourage you to do another task, and another, and another. And by the end of the day that one task completed will have turned into many tasks completed.' The Admiral adds, 'If by chance you have a miserable day, you will come home to a bed that is made - that you made. And a made bed gives you encouragement that tomorrow will be better.'[76]

Many outlier performers advocate accumulating small wins first thing in the morning, to give us that sense of building victory Michael Phelps talked about his pre-race routine. A small win could be as simple as making our beds, exercising, meditating, or leaving our homes in order. The powerful unconscious messages we reinforce here is that we are the sort of person that has standards and does what is required to maintains those standards.

Hydrate

Most of us wake up with 1% bodyweight dehydration. This can cause headaches, irritability, and decreased mental performance (by up to 20%). The first thing we need to put into our bodies is water. Not coffee. For our brains, waking the body up with a coffee is like using a fire alarm as an alarm clock, it stimulates the release of stress hormones, which make us susceptible to red head should a trigger arise.

The message here is not to eliminate coffee, I love coffee, but hydrating with water first is optimal. Coffee is a powerful performance enhancing drug; a neuro-stimulant with psychoactive properties that fight fatigue and increase alertness, reaction time, concentration, and endurance. So, let's use it as a strategic performance enhancer for when we need to actuate these benefits.

Fuel

Food affects our hormones; hormones affect how we feel, and how we feel affects our performance. Plus, the brain needs a steady supply of high-quality fuel to optimise its performance. Umming and aahing over what to have for breakfast expends effort we need to preserve for high-value activity. I recommend creating what lifestyle design experts call a capsule diet. This includes breakfast options that:

1. we enjoy,
2. are nutritious, and
3. can be prepared easily with the time and resources we have available.

Each morning we can just cycle through the same few options. We can obviously upgrade those options as time, resources, and tastes change.

Getting dressed

Steve Jobs wore a black turtle-neck and New Balance sneakers every day. Mark Zuckerberg has ten identical t-shirts in his closet. Hedge Fund manager Ray Dalio wears the same suit every day. Why? Because when we automate our 'what am I going to wear today part of the day,' we never have to spend any units of effort thinking about it.

Mark Zuckerberg:

'I really want to clear my life to make it so that I have to make as few decisions as possible about anything except how to best serve this community.'[77]

Outliers automate the decisions they can, and we can do the same. Avoiding making daily decisions about what to wear when no one cares whether our outfit is awesome or not conserves units of effort that we can deploy to our high-value activities. Obviously, we can still have some unique outfits for special events and formal occasions.

▶ Morning Routine Reflection Questions

Take two minutes; reflect on your current morning routine:

1. Do you wake feeling rested, before your alarm, at a consistent time?
2. Do you get at least a few minutes of daylight within an hour of waking?

3. Do you hydrate with water?
4. Do you conduct a physical check-in?
5. Do you accumulate your first small win?
6. Do you fuel with an enjoyable, nutritious breakfast?
7. Do you dress without thinking?

Pre-Performance transition

This is all about the slow transition from green to blue. Its how we leave home, our commute, and the first twenty minutes or so at work. Or, if we're working from home, it's about flicking the switch each morning from green to blue head. This transition is one of those things we do every day, which makes it important to get right.

We can use this time for:

One - Flicking the switch: Initiate our blue-head routine
Two - Emotional Control Techniques: Mediating, visualisation, breath-work, or PMR
Three - Learning: Listening to a podcast, TED talk, audiobook, comedy, blue-zone playlist, or reading.
Four - Work-tasks: Dealing with emails, making some calls mentally rehearsing the day ahead, conducting some preparation.
Five - Pursuing a goal: Learning a language, exercising (walking, running, cycling) to work, engaging in professional development.

Note: This is the perfect time for that coffee.

Performance

Prioritise high-value activity

> Things that matter most should never be at
> the mercy of those that matter least
>
> Johann Wolfgang von Goethe

The phone hasn't rung all day. No one has messaged. No alerts. But as soon as we need to focus, everyone will start calling, texting, and emailing. We know that to excel we need to plug into blue head, dissolve into our craft, and lose ourselves in the high-value activities that maximise progress.

'To excel we need to plug into blue head, dissolve into our craft, and lose ourselves in the high-value activities that maximise progress'

The objective is to get into blue head and channel all that energy and attention into the task at hand. I recommend setting some large, uninterrupted blocks of deep work for high-quality thinking while our energy, willpower and discipline are at their highest. Block out calendars as if for a critical meeting. Accumulating progress early in the day generates the momentum we need to build victory. Protect this time fiercely.

Deep Work: To focus without distraction on high-value activity

Every time we switch our attention from one task to another and then back again, there's a huge cost in terms of units of effort.

Task switching includes that quick chat with a colleague, a glance at our phone, or eyeballing an email. For a deep work session to occur there must be zero distraction; the phone goes into flight mode, Outlook is closed, and instant message alerts are turned off.

For a deep work session to occur there must be zero distraction; the phone goes into flight mode, Outlook is closed, and instant message alerts are turned off. Accumulating progress early in the day generates the momentum we need to build victory. Protect this time fiercely.

> ***Note:*** Eating the frog, slaying the dragon, or the worst-first principle, all provide alternative approaches where we attack the work we enjoy the least first, while our mental resources are highest.

Schedule green head

Deep work in blue head is demanding and can also be addictive; the super-six blue head hormones can lock us into an enthralling high. Somewhere between approximately 60 and 180 minutes and we'll start to experience lapses in concentration, irritability or daydreaming. This is an indication its time to flick the switch.

Benefit one - recovery

Switching off periodically renews psychological fire-power for our next burst of activity. Going harder for longer is often perceived as the route to success, and the need for recovery is often viewed as evidence of weakness. This is a misconception that must be dispelled in organisations that want to sustain and retain their performers. When we override these signals by summoning the life-or-death stress hormones we impair our ability to think, our health and burn through our units of effort fast. This is a short-term solution with long-term implications that should be leveraged in genuine emergencies, not as part of a daily routine.

Benefit two- creativity

Creativity involves cycling between different parts of our brain. Switching between blue and green head is the perfect stimulus to prompt novel performance breakthroughs. The creative process can be broken down into four stages:[78]

Preparation	the intellectual investigation of the idea (blue head)
Incubation	unconscious processing and rumination on the idea (green head)
Illumination	a flash of insight as a breakthrough reveals itself (green head)
Verification	testing and codifying the validity of the creative breakthrough (blue head)

The Preparation and verification stages rely on blue-head thinking in the frontal brain, such as deep work. However, incubation and illumination all occur in green head, when we are not actively seeking answers but just in the moment, feeling good, and not thinking about much at all. Green head switches off the frontal brain, allowing space for our supercomputer, the unconscious brain, to emerge with that flash of insight. This is why so many of us have breakthrough moments in the shower, the gym, or laughing and joking with friends.

'Green head disengages the frontal brain, allowing space for our supercomputer, the unconscious brain, to emerge with novel solutions'

Benefit Three- Anticipation

Just thinking about green-head activities can raise our levels of feel-good endorphins by almost 30%. Anticipating watching our favourite movies, seeing a loved one, or going out for a meal can light up the pleasure centres in our brains as much as the reward itself. In fact, most of the pleasure we experience is from anticipating an event, not the event itself.

'Most of the pleasure we experience is from anticipating an event, not the event itself'

This is why I like to end my working day with a strength and conditioning session. The anticipation fills my brain with the feel-good hormones linked to the super six. Anticipating that training session makes my whole day a more positive experience.

> ***Note:*** We don't have to sit cross-legged, humming to ancient Tibetan chants, while banging a tambourine to get into green zone. Recovery can be as simple as taking a stroll, grabbing a hot drink, or sitting in the sun for fifteen minutes. The options are unlimited. The key thing is that, whatever green head is for us, we must schedule it.

Optimising Workspace

Our workspace can prime us to think, feel and act in certain ways and has the potential to drive our performance. What we are sensing in our environment at any moment changes our biochemistry. The brain, and the nervous, endocrine, and immune systems are constantly interacting. We need to reflect on what thoughts and feelings our environments summon, and then look for opportunities to optimise. The following passive characteristics can significantly affect our performance:

Colours - Colours subliminally prime our emotions as follows:

- Blue and green improve efficiency and focus.
- Grey, beige, and white induce feelings of sadness.
- Yellow creates a sense of happiness and creativity.
- Red increases heart rate and boosts energy.

Lighting - Rooms with bright light, both natural and artificial, can enhance positive emotions, energy and attention. Whereas dimly lit rooms can induce depression, anxiety and fatigue.

Mess - Mess primes us to be messy. Order primes us to be orderly. When our workspace is strewn with documents we are more likely to engage in messy behaviour. On the other hand, a clear storage system primes us to keep it that way.

Quiet space - Relaxation and prayer rooms, or private space for making personal calls, can all promote green zone activities that facilitate recovery.

Resources - Every time our wi-fi cuts out, phone signal drops, or the printer plays up, we receive a splash of those red head stress hormones into our bloodstream. The resources we require to win each day must be fit for purpose. The message is: if it can drag us into red zone and it needs fixing, we need to fix it.

Design - The art that hangs on the walls, the floor plan, perks such as catered meals, an on-site gym, or a lounge to unwind in are all design features that can energise. Simple ways to optimise include pictures or quotes that prime and inspire the winning behaviours and concordant values of our organisation.

Note: Please don't throw in some beanbags, a ping-pong table, and abstract art just for the sake of it. Any optimisations should be strategic.

Cultural protocols - Deep work between 08:00 and 11:00, uplifting music between 12:00 and 13:00, and clear guidelines for communication are all examples of how to reinforce natural oscillation between deep work and recovery; blue and green head.

Communication guidelines:

Instant message - for short, simple questions that require binary or one-word answers

Email - for documenting ideas that need an electronic record and require full attention from the recipient

Call - for important information that requires more complex, non-binary answers

In-Person - for urgent and important matters only

Senses - We are primed through our senses, by what we see, smell, hear, taste and even feel in the environment. Adjustments might include: opening windows, using mirrors for natural light, requesting better lighting, using noise-cancelling headphones, optimising the temperature, getting a comfortable chair, a bigger desk, or more workspace, better storage and some plants. Prioritise what needs fixing and fix it.

Identify value and eliminate waste

At any point in time there are two types of activity we can engage in, only one is optimal. First are the activities that add to our performance, which we call value. Then there are those activities we engage in that don't, which we call waste. Every ounce of effort should be evaluated by the extent to which it adds value to our performance. There are seven types of waste we need to identify and eliminate:

Low quality work – Training in our comfort zone, a poor report, or unprepared colleagues is wasted work that must be disregarded or fixed.

Excessive work – An athlete over-training, an analyst researching into excessive detail, or a salesperson pitching to a client who doesn't qualify to purchase the product is waste.

Waiting – People failing to meet deadlines, teammates delaying the start of a training session, or restrictions in accessing vital resources mean that we can't proceed to the next action.

Under-utilised talent – Not using everyone available in the performance environment to solve challenges, or even worse, not consulting them at all.

Movement – Having to walk through three different offices to access the scanner, driving three hours (there and back) to conduct training, excessive time spent setting up and taking down training simulations, all spend precious units of effort.

Resources – The video, case studies, and exercises we need to become the gym rat must be accessible when we need them.

Work that's not our own – Too many quick chats, questions or helping hands can swallow up our units of effort fast with no value added to performance. Say No.

Lunch

We should be as strategic about lunch hour as we are about deep work. There are three reasons:

One- We need to fuel our brains and bodies to function at their best
Two- We need time to recharge our energy and attention
Three- Lunch is a great opportunity to create positive anticipation

When it comes to optimising this part of the day there are two key questions:

Question one: What are you eating?

Are you spending valuable units of effort force-feeding yourself dry chicken and salad that leaves you feeling hungry? Are you digesting greasy pizza slices that leave you fighting the urge not to fall into that carb coma for the rest of the afternoon? I recommend creating another capsule diet. The same rules apply as breakfast: that it's enjoyable, nutritious, and can be prepared with the time and resources we have available.

Question two: How is the experience?

Do we chomp down a sandwich at the closest café with our eyes glued to our phones? Do we devour a salad at our desks with one hand on our keyboards? Or do we skip lunch altogether because we have too much on our plates? Equally, starving yourself to check off one more item on your to-do lists does not make you a hero. We inevitably pay the price in terms of our most valuable currency, performance, when we can't concentrate or make that creative breakthrough later in the day.

'Starving yourself to check off one more item on your to-do lists does not make you a hero'

Take a real break. We can invigorate our afternoons by spending time doing what we enjoy. Eating with a friend, watching something inspiring or grabbing a dose of sunlight and fresh air. This way lunch becomes a positive experience we anticipate. In a win agenda there will be periods where lunch might be sacrificed for the greater good. Just make sure this doesn't become the norm.

▶ Reflection questions:

- Who do you eat with?
- What conversations do you have?
- In what environment?
- What effect does that have on you?
- Where does that place you on the barometer?
- Could it be optimised?

Note: Where possible, don't check your e-mail, bring work with you or talk about work during lunch.

The afternoon performance

Its 14:00 and we have things to do, but the only thing we want to do is take a nap. For some, the afternoon drop in energy and attention can lead to inefficient expenditure of energy, careless mistakes and lost productivity, so avoid scheduling high-value activity around this time if possible. This sluggish time of day is great for completing simple, less demanding work like filing, checking emails and printing.

Should you be so lucky, go an take that nap, if possible between 13:00 and 15:00. If napping between 16:00 and 19:00, limit it to

20 minutes to avoid disrupting the evening's sleep.

> ***Note:*** If you are sensitive to the post-lunch dip try limiting carbohydrates. The tasty pick-me-up causes a sudden spike in blood sugar, which is usually followed by a crash that leaves us tired and hungry again.

Batching

Imagine putting the washing machines on every time we had a new pair of dirty socks. The set-up cost would make this ridiculous: carrying the socks downstairs, getting the washing machine tablet out of the box, adjusting the controls, opening the washing machine, closing the machine, switching it on, waiting, then emptying the machine, getting the clothes rail out, hanging up the socks. This task takes the same time whether washing one or twenty pairs of socks, which is why we wait for a critical mass of laundry to accumulate and then initiate the wash.

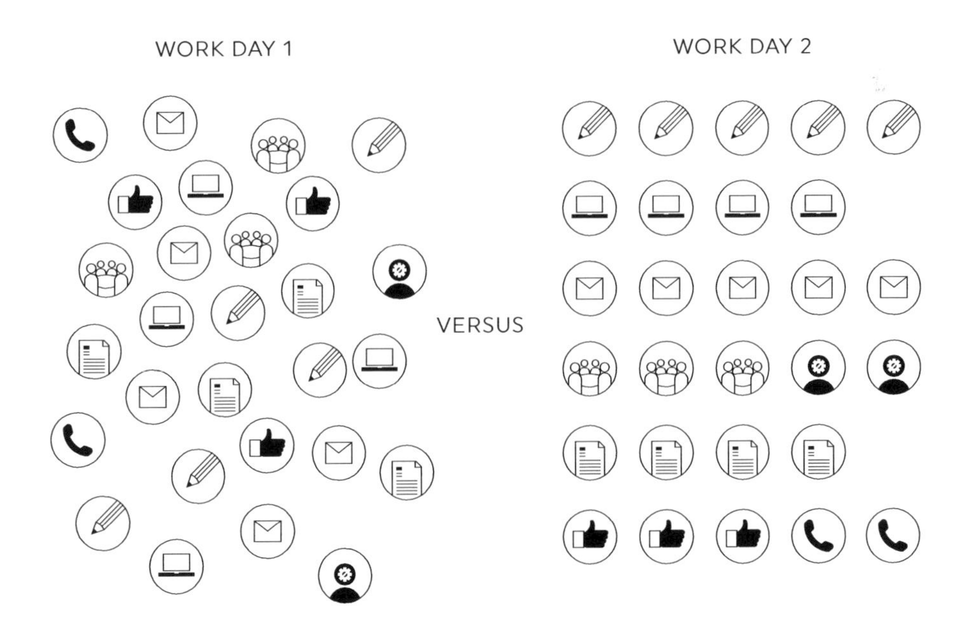

The same principle applies for mental work. Activities like administrative tasks, phone calls, photocopying, managing our calendars, and scheduling meetings. When we have all these tasks scattered across the day, it's almost impossible to engage in deep work.

> ***Note:*** Think about what you could batch on a daily, weekly, monthly, or even an annual basis. We can create administrative weeks; win agenda deep-work months, and annual slots for professional development.

Physical exercise

> John Ratey
> (Harvard University, Professor of Psychiatry):
> 'In a way, exercise can be thought of as a psychiatrist's dream treatment. It works on anxiety, on panic disorder, on stress in general, which has a lot to do with depression. And it generates the release of neurotransmitters – norepinephrine, serotonin, and dopamine – that are very similar to our most important psychiatric medicines [super-six hormones]. Having a bout of exercise is like taking a little bit of Prozac and a little bit of Ritalin, right where it is supposed to go.'[79]

We need exercise. If we want to maximise our performance, exercise is mandatory. It is scientifically proven to enhance both mood and health. From a psychological standpoint, exercise is like a miracle drug. It releases the pleasure-inducing hormones called endorphins, which shift the baseline of our positive emotions.

Exercise has enormous health benefits too. When we enter red head and receive that jolt of stress hormones, they circulate as toxins in our body until they are metabolised for energy. Exercise accelerates this process by burning off all these stress by-products, detoxifying us and removing the associated health risks.

The best type of exercise is the exercise we enjoy and consistently do. Whatever that is, schedule it. We're not talking about gruesome CrossFit sessions, triathlons or marathon running. Exercise can range from gardening, to twenty-minute strolls, five-minute HIIT sessions, two-hour runs and everything in between. Work within the constraints of time, resources, and interests.

'The best type of exercise is the exercise we enjoy and consistently do. Whatever that is, schedule it'

Reflection

Reflection: Serious thought or consideration

Reflection is proven to accelerate skill acquisition and retention, boost positive emotion and improve our health. Great reflection involves two components; the first is to capitalise on personal feedback, and the second is to reap the benefits that gratitude brings.

Component One- Personal Feedback

We know that feedback begins and ends with us. This means we have to schedule time to do it. Reflecting on our own thoughts and feelings about our performance enhances our mental structures for our craft. Whether it's running through the feedback scripts in chapter 14, or just considering whether we're on target, and if not, thinking about where we're going wrong, and how we might modify our future efforts accordingly.

Note: no matter how good the outcomes are, there are always opportunities for improvement.

Component Two- Gratitude

That chat with a colleague at lunch, the enlightening podcast episode on the way to work, the warmth of the sun on our face, are great to begin with but without a conscious search and the acknowledgement that these are positive experiences, we eventually stop appreciating those moments and over time they lose their power. This is due to a process called hedonic adaptation.

Hedonic Adaptation - The tendency to quickly return to a stable mood despite a spike in positive or negative events

The benefit of hedonic adaptation is that we recover from negative events. The downside is we stop appreciating all the good things. Expressing gratitude for the good things, trains our brains to focus on the positives counteracting the inherent negativity bias primed into us by nature, and drilled into us environmentally by the media who bombard us with sensationalised negativity that has us subordinating our attention to their platforms.

The deliberate search for, and recognition that, we have experienced something positive, keeps these positive emotions around for longer, and amplifies their intensity. This prompts a surge in the feel-good chemicals such as dopamine, serotonin and oxytocin. These all contribute to feelings of positivity, connection and contentment.

'Expressing gratitude for the good things, trains our brains to focus on the positives counteracting the inherent negativity bias primed into us by nature'

Gratitude activates the parts of our brains involved in feelings of reward. The more we exercise this part of the brain, the better we get at tuning into the positive things we experience. In the midst of negative events this helps us not to lose sight of the good. Through reflecting on, and appreciating, the positive things we experience, no matter how fleeting, we begin to perceive our reality with a more optimistic outlook.

- Exercise One: Visualise your day so far, as you replay the day from waking up until now, notice the positive emotions you experienced, reflecting on what happened in those moments
- Exercise Two: Spend sixty seconds thinking about three positive experiences you have had today. You can make a mental note, write them down, store them digitally, or share them with a colleague or friend.

Note: A key to experiencing more time in green zone is not only to look for new opportunities, but also to make the most of the ones we already have. We need to make sure we acknowledge and appreciate the laughter at lunch, the learning breakthrough, or kindness from a teammate. No matter how small, try to find something new each day.

Post-Performance transition

Our aim here is to transition from blue head to green head.

Options include:

One- Flicking the switch: Initiate our off switch routine
Two- Green Zone Techniques: Mediating, visualisation, breath-work, or PMR
Three- Learning: Listening to a podcast, TED talk, audiobook, comedy, blue-zone playlist, or reading.
Four- Work-tasks: Work out any knotty sections of our work, respond to email, and complete digital administration
Five- Pursuing a goal: Learning a language, exercising (walking, running, cycling) to work, engaging in professional development.

▶ Reflection Questions: Start by reflecting on your transition. What do you do? How do you feel? Could it be optimised?

Evening routine

To optimise the evening there are four key considerations:

Arriving home

Do you arrive home to smiles, hugs and an orderly environment, or a whiney, chaotic mess? Repeat the latter for enough days in a row and we are sure to spiral into negative equity in terms of our units of effort. Some like their friends or family to bounce up and greet them with ear-to-ear smiles; others prefer some space to decompress. Either way, there will likely be some give and take. Considered compromise of needs usually benefits all involved.

> ***Note:*** Do whatever it takes to structure your time with family and friends so that it becomes a source of joy and renewal, rather than one more demand in an already highly demanding life.

Scheduling green-head activities

Joe Rogan makes time for his family and his golden retriever, Marshall, he hits the comedy club with close friends and engages in Mixed Martial Arts training. The objective is to access green head. Whatever that is for you, structure it.

Defaulting to the path of least resistance and binging on Netflix for hours, just because it's the easiest thing to do is an example of what we call junk recovery. Binging Netflix if that is exactly what you need is high quality conscious intervention.

> Junk Recovery: Unconscious low quality recovery
>
> Quality Recovery: Consciously structured intentional restoration

There are three areas we might need to structure recovery: physically, emotionally or mentally. The type of activity we engage in might be different for each.

> *Physical*
>
> We might structure some time for: meditation, sleep, screen-time (box-sets, home-movies, cinema), relaxing with family/friends or arrange a spa day/ massage.

Emotional
We might have a few drinks with a friend, some feel-good food, mindless TV and film, or a good old scroll through social-media.

Mental
We might decide to exercise, go fishing, play golf, engage in outdoor activities, practise yoga, reading, conversation, cinema, or socialise with loved ones.

Like all things, recovery is highly personal, and one person's green head can be another's red. The take-home message is that the things we do for the sake of pure enjoyment, whatever they are, must be scheduled.

Fuel

In the evening our willpower is at its lowest, one risk is defaulting to eating whatever is quickest and easiest, which tends to be the least nutritious. Unless it's a special occasion, we have excess time or enjoy cooking I recommend the same capsule principle we applied at breakfast and lunch. Cycling through four or five nutritious, sustainable, and tasty meals allows us to shop and cook on autopilot. As before, when you get tired of one of the recipes, or the seasons and your taste buds change, spice things up with something new.

Sleep

When we get sleep right magical things happen to our brains and bodies. Capturing and retaining all the progress we make throughout the day is directly linked to the quality of our sleep. This makes sleep a significant piece of the performance puzzle.

There are three key benefits of great sleep.

Benefit one: Capturing progress

Ever heard the saying, 'a mind like a sponge'? Sleep creates what called the dry-sponge effect, which is what enables our brains to soak up the learning opportunities we are exposed to. With insufficient sleep we end up with the opposite, a wet-sponge effect, meaning our brains can't absorb new opportunities for progress.

Benefit two: Retaining progress

During deep sleep powerful brainwaves act like a file transfer mechanism shifting what we have learned from a short-term fragile storage bay to a robust long-term memory bank locking in changes to our mental structures, ensuring that learning sticks. When we're deprived of sleep, the hippocampus, the part of the brain which acts as our memory storage system, shuts down. On just five hours' sleep, incoming files are effectively bounced and we end up with a 40% deficit in memory and learning. [80]

Benefit three: Superior health

Our immune systems comprise natural killer cells responsible for identifying and eliminating threats to our health. They are like the Navy SEALs of the immune system mercilessly obliterating cancerous tumour masses and other pathogens. We want these immune assassins maximally active at all times. Just one night of four hours' sleep and natural killer cell activity is reduced by 70%[79]. This increases the likelihood of illness and accelerated ageing.

> ***Note:*** For men, sleeping five hours a night will cause your testosterone levels to drop to the levels of someone ten years your senior.

It's quite clear that sleep is no optional extra but a non-negotiable necessity. There are twelve actions we can take to optimise:

Remove Stigma: First things first, we need to prioritise sleep. Any stigma of laziness associated with it must be eradicated.

Lighting: When night falls, the reduction in light prompts the release of the sleep hormone melatonin, which triggers the brain to enter sleep mode. The blue glow from our smart phones, tablets, computer screens, and televisions suppresses the production of melatonin, which means we miss out on its wonderful tranquillising effect. Light from televisions, laptops, tablets and phones isn't bad light, it's badly timed light. During the day, blue light is good and can help activate our energy levels.

> ***Note:*** We have evolved to sleep with the yellows and red ambers of the fire, so swapping blue bulbs for red, using blue light filtering glasses, or switching our devices to night mode can mitigate this effect. Pitch black is best for deep sleep, so blackout curtains and blinds are highly recommended.

Regular sleep times: This keep our body running like the Swiss watch it wants to be, so regular wake and sleep times are important. Always standardise where possible.

Avoid caffeine: Avoid after 15:00. It can take up to 6 hours for the total amount of caffeine ingested to reduce by half, which impairs our ability to fall, and stay, asleep.

Re-brand the bedroom: It is not a home office, playroom or wardrobe, it is a relaxation and recovery room. A chaotic environment creates a chaotic mind. Get a comfortable bed in which you feel safe and secure. De-clutter and make sure the bedroom is a haven.

Keep cool: To enter into high-quality deep sleep you need to drop your core temperature by 2–3 degrees. Room temperature of 17–19°C is optimal for most.

Sync with your natural rhythm: Morning larks favour waking up and going to bed early, and tend to peak early in the day. On the other hand, night owls prefer to sleep and stay up later, and perform best in the afternoon and evening.

Tossing and turning: Tossing and turning: Inevitably there will be nights on which we just don't drift off. To ensure we associate bed as the place where we sleep, and not somewhere we toss and turn, bored and anxious, if we find ourselves tossing and turning, leave the bedroom. Also, if we are waking up through the night, there is no need to panic. Sleep is poly-phasic, so, instead of clocking hours, we clock cycles that are approximately 90-minutes long. Waking up for a pee, or short periods of wakefulness, are nothing to worry about.

Note: Waking up through the night is no need to panic. Sleep is poly-phasic, so, instead of clocking hours, we clock cycles that are approximately 90-minutes long. Waking up for a pee, or short periods of wakefulness, are nothing to worry about.

If you have busy thoughts, download them: Perform a brain dump of all the thoughts in your head in a journal before going to bed. Journal on a notepad, capture the essential points, knowing we can deal with those issues the next day.

Shut down technology: Sixty minutes before designated bedtime switch it all off. A popular way to switch focus from work-related activity is through some light reading (preferably fiction). Watching a pleasant or comforting and familiar television show can also help us to shut down.

Green zone techniques: Green zone techniques: To really wind down and assist sleep, parasympathetic breathing exercises, meditation, PMR, or visualisation can all prompt a calming effect and signal to our brains and bodies that it's time to switch off and recover.

Gentle exercise: A 20-minute walk, or some restorative yoga, burns off the by-products of stress accumulated throughout the day, and simultaneously boosts melatonin production, activating the parasympathetic (restorative) nervous system.

Hopefully by now we have an idea of what a winning day looks like. Through optimising our very own daily routines we bring the structure and renewal we need to mitigate the natural decline the ageing process brings. The predictability of our winning day maximises the development, recovery and fun we can squeeze out of it, super-charging the quality of life we experience alongside and after all of our achievement.

Designing a winning day is the easy bit. The challenge now is to stick to it consistently. We don't have to remind ourselves to brush our teeth, in fact, it feels wrong not brushing our teeth. Why? Because we've automated that part of our winning day brushing our teeth is something which we feel consistently drawn to do. In the penultimate chapter of this book we explore how to convert our winning days into a system of functional habits that act as a catalyst for continuous improvement. We will focus on how to automate the behaviours that win our days, and break the ones that don't.

CHAPTER SUMMARY

- Excellence is a series of days. To excel we must win each day, one after the other. These winning days compound into winning months, winning years, and winning careers.
- We need structure so that we can win our days, instead of wing our days. We are designed to run like a Swiss watch. To stay on the 24-hour cycle our brain needs predictability and routine.
- The things we do every day are often the most important things we do. They combine to make up more than 66% of our lives. To thrive we must optimise.
- Imagine that we have a finite 100 units of effort to spend each day. To maximise our units of progress, we must invest them as effectively as possible.
- Whilst the number of hours in each day is fixed, the energy available to us is not. Through systematic disengagement we are renewing our capacity so we can re-engage harder.
- Switching off periodically renews our psychological fire-power for our next burst of activity. We must get the balance right between expending energy and renewing it.
- Our daily routine must be concordant with our unique biology and psychology, not those of the people we admire.
- Winning the day mitigates the demands of elite performance, as well as the natural decline the ageing process brings by providing structure and renewal.
- Master the day and the years will take care of themselves.

Recommended Reading

Loehr and Schwartz - *The Power of Full Engagement*
Matthew Walker - *Why We Sleep*

23

AUTOMATING EXCELLENCE

We are what we repeatedly do. Excellence, then,
is not an act, but a habit

Aristotle

Mat Fraser is the most dominant athlete in the history of CrossFit. He has won five consecutive CrossFit games Championships between 2016 and 2020. For the last five years Fraser has decimated his peers on the competition floor earning him the title, the 'Fittest Man on Earth'. The 5'7" and 190 pounds powerhouse can back squat 220kg; snatch 142kg, and breeze through 75 pull-ups in one set.

> ***Mat Fraser:*** "If I had won in 2015 while carrying those bad habits, I would have kept those bad habits. I would have thought "I can do this while eating terribly. I can do this while training sporadically," but now I realise, with three years in a row of breaking my own record of margin of victory, that would have never of happened without that incredibly disappointing loss.'[81]

Total domination hasn't always been the way. In the 2015 CrossFit games we saw a 26-year-old Fraser clinch a podium finish in a not-so-insignificant second place, finishing behind another CrossFit deity, Rich Froning (see Chapter 16). It was a finish that would be etched into Fraser's mind forever.

> ***Mat Fraser:*** I hated my 2015 medal, you know, I got second place. And that second place to me just represented the cut corners, the slacking off, the thinking that I could out-train a bad diet. Simple stuff like that.' [81]

Mat Fraser had a problem, and losing the 2015 CrossFit Games was the impetus he needed to solve it. He switched out the half a litre of ice-cream every other night, inconsistent sleep times and other unhealthy lifestyle choices. Fraser set consistent wake times, outsourced his entire nutrition and moved to Tennessee to train with the four-time champion Rich Froning. He didn't just plan the perfect day, he automated it.

What appears as a more focused and disciplined Mat Fraser is the same man with a more robust set of habits. Since that life-changing loss at the 2015 Games, Fraser has not lost a competition at any level. Each of his four consecutive gold medals at the CrossFit Games have enjoyed a greater margin of victory than the last. Automating his habits transitioned him from 'elite CrossFitter' to 'five-time undisputed champion' who has sustained his success and continues to accelerate away from the rest.

Outliers do ordinary things, but they do them without thinking, consistently well, and for a long time, which is what gets them to the top and keeps them there. We too are capable of doing hard things but the problem is some days we just don't feel like doing them.

'Outliers do ordinary things, but they do them without thinking, consistently, and for a long time, which is what gets them to the top and keeps them there'

Habit: An unconscious automatic reaction to a situation

Sometimes, sustaining all it takes to excel can feel impossible. This feeling is driven by the thinking that executing all these habits is a case of sheer discipline. If we miss a training session, procrastinate, or sleep in, we assume it's because we lack discipline, or are mentally weak. We can choose to overpower temptation through forcing discipline, but this burns through our units of effort fast and, in the long-term, it's a losing strategy.

Discipline is important. No one with a right mind would argue otherwise. But elite performers like Mat Fraser who appear to have tremendous discipline are ironically the ones who need it the least. Outliers have an internal compulsion to act on the right thing at the right time, and it strikes them without thinking. They have structured their lives in ways that do not require spartan willpower to help them win their day. They have formed great habits. Yet again, we are going to have to work smarter, not harder, if we really want to win our days.

'Outliers have an internal compulsion to act on the right thing at the right time, and it strikes them without thinking'

Nothing consolidates our development trajectories like a set of functional habits. They are like algorithms operating in the background that power our lives. Once formed, it's easier to execute a habit than to override it. Plus, executing habits is automatic and effortless, which means they sustain us whether we're inspired, motivated, determined, or not even in red head.

'Executing habits is automatic and effortless, which means they sustain us whether we're inspired, motivated, determined, or not'

We all have sub-optimal habits like eating junk food, spending too much time on social media, or procrastinating on development work. Especially when we're doing well. We also all have positive habits we know we need to engage in more frequently, like reviewing our concordant goals, designing three-dimensional training, or optimising our performance routines.

Before we can optimise our habits, we need to understand how they work. Habits arise in a three-step cycle. The basic process is that we: (1) sense a cue (2) execute a routine and (3) get our reward.

Step one- Cue: A trigger that sparks a precise set of automatic reactions

The cue could range from:

Cue	Example
Sound	Favourite song
Sight	Cookies on the table-top
Smell	Fresh bread from the bakery
Feeling	Boredom, frustration, or excitement

Time	Waking up, lunchtime, leaving work
Person	Friend, colleague, or family member
Location	Home, work, gym

Step two- Routine: The specific series of actions we undertake when the cue is triggered

A routine could include collections of actions such as:

Cue	Example
Boredom	Grab a coke, eat chocolate and browse social media
Wakeup	Cold shower, meditate, visualisation, stretch
See colleague	Coffee, muffin, moan

Step three- Reward: The benefit we receive from executing our routine

These could include:

Cue	Routine	Reward
Boredom	Grab a coke, eat chocolate and browse social media	Escape from boredom, feel content.
Wakeup	Cold shower, meditate, visualisation, stretch	Endorphin rush, feel motivated, feel in control

See colleague	Coffee, muffin, moan	Vent, laughter, social acceptance, praise

When we repeat the cue, routine and reward cycle enough, the reward will eventually create a craving- the catalyst behind every habit.

Craving: the desire to execute a behaviour

Cravings are driven by the pleasure hormone dopamine, which is way more powerful than our discipline, motivation, and resilience. The first time we do something, the dopamine comes after we complete the behaviour. We drink coffee and then feel good. But the more we repeat the habit, the earlier the dopamine is released. Eventually just thinking about that coffee makes us feel good. The dopamine makes us desire it.

'Cravings are driven by the pleasure hormone dopamine, which is way more powerful than our discipline, motivation, and resilience'

The problem is that our brain doesn't function well with extreme highs of dopamine, so to reduce the intensity, a shut-off valve kicks in and de-sensitises our brains to the dopamine. This decreases the pleasure we experience until eventually we no longer get that high. This is why some struggle to get going without their morning coffee. Now they require that coffee just to feel normal. At this point a habit is born.

Understanding the three-step habit cycle means that we can design, build and reshape the component parts to eliminate negative habits and fortify positive habits. That will be our focus now, starting with cues.

Cues

The first things that dictate behaviour are the cues in front of us. Through keeping the cues for desirable behaviour front and centre, we can trigger the cravings that compel us to take action. Through making the cues for our undesirable behaviour invisible, very often the entire habit disintegrates. We must become the architects of our environment, filling it with productive cues and eliminating the negative ones.

Building positive habits

We must plant the cues that trigger the behaviours that win our days. If we want to practise the guitar, then don't tuck it away in the closet. If we want to drink more water, keep filled water bottles stored in the locations we will find ourselves that day. If we want to read more, leave our book in the same visible spot we usually keep our phone.

> 'We must plant the cues that trigger the behaviours that win our days'

Note: When we establish habits at a new coffee shop, gym, or part of our office or home, it means that we don't have to contend with pre-existing cues, and thus we allow new habits to form without contending with pre-existing cues. If new isn't possible then we can redefine the characteristics within our current environment. This room/ lighting/ music/ clothing (cues) triggers work-mode; that room/ lighting/ music/ clothing (cues) triggers relaxation time. The same principle applies to our digital space. Our laptops are for work, our tablets, for browsing the internet, social media, and other recreational activities.

Eliminating negative habits

No cue, No craving. The cue is what creates the craving behind every habit. Without the craving, we avoid the anticipatory dopamine squirt and there is no desire to engage in the bad habit. Removing things from plain sight is one way to do this. If we're interrupted by calls, emails and texts, then leave the phone in another room. If we're wasting too much time on Netflix, move the television out of the bedroom. If we're playing too much Fifa or Fortnite, unplug the console and store it out of sight. If we're feeling insecure, stop following social media accounts that trigger feelings of inadequacy.

'No cue, No craving'

Routines

Path of Least Resistance: The easiest course of action becomes the default

When deciding between two similar options, we will naturally gravitate towards the path of least resistance. There is an energy cost to engage in any behaviour. The less energy it takes to enact the behaviour the more likely it is to occur. The key is to reduce the effort required to enact our good habits, and increase the effort associated with our bad ones.

'The key is to reduce the effort required to enact our good habits, and increase the effort associated with our bad ones'

Building Positive Habits

Do not make new habits challenging. If we want to make a habit stick, we need to make it easy to do. Remember, starting is the hardest part; we gain momentum as we go. Meditate for one minute instead of twenty. Sit down and read one page of a novel, instead of three chapters. Eat one piece of fruit instead of five a day. Performing the habit is much more important than doing the perfect amount required to excel.

By starting out small, we are less likely to say no. This way we'll do it even when we don't feel like it; this way we create habits that last and will grow. Chances are we will end up meditating for more than a minute, reading more than one page, and eating more than one piece of fruit.

'If we want to make a habit stick, we need to make it easy to do'

Note: Habit Stacking: We can use existing habits to build in new ones through adding them to an existing routine. For example, after I pour my cup of coffee each morning, I stretch for one minute. After stretching for a minute, I visualise executing my winning day.

Eliminating negative habits

If you want to do something less, make it hard. If a routine requires more effort than we're prepared to expend, then we just won't execute it. Any behaviour that is easy to get addicted to like trawling through social media, binging series after series, and ordering junk food can be performed with negligible effort.

'If a routine requires more effort than we're prepared to expend, then we just won't execute it'

Storing unhealthy food in the garage, forcing us to exert inconvenient effort to get it. Deleting social media apps on our phones, so we are forced to log into a web browser each time. Removing our credit card information from e-commerce sites so we can't buy with one click. Setting the alarm and leaving it in another room to force ourselves to get up when it goes off. These are all examples of how we can make our bad habits harder to execute.

> ***Note:*** We can even make the habit impossible to execute. This way we can take advantage of our good intentions before we fall victim to temptation. For example, applications like Offtime, breakfree, or Flipd allow us to set custom lockouts; be it social media, email or games. We can literally block our work email between Friday and Monday, or over the weekend.

Rewards

Whenever we perceive that something will be rewarding, our levels of dopamine spike in anticipation, and whenever dopamine rises, so does our motivation to act. If we remove the reward, we remove the motivation. If we increase the reward, we increase the motivation.

'If we remove the reward, we remove the motivation. If we increase the reward, we increase the motivation'

Building positive habits

There are three ways we can use rewards to build positive habits:

One: Establish a clear reward

We can make new habits way more appealing by linking the activities we already do, like drinking wine, having a bath or watching Netflix, with those we want to establish like reading, meditating or going to bed early. We call this temptation bundling[82]. If trying to read more, do so with a glass of wine. We can meditate in a perfectly drawn bath. Or we can exercise while we watch Netflix. The reward for engaging in our new habits is getting to savour the things we already like to do.

Two: Habit tracking

There is nothing more motivating than victory. With habit tracking, all we need is a calendar and a pen. Every day that we execute our routine, we can mark the calendar with a big green tick. Marking that tick becomes a reward itself, verifying our effort and achievement. We forget about the long-term outcomes

1 ✓	2 ✓	3 ✓	4 ✓	5 ✓	6 ✓	7 ✓
8 ✓	9 ✓	10 ✓	11	12	13	14
15	16	17	18	19	20	21

and instead lock in our focus on the process as we chase down daily victory. Plus, if we do slip up we receive immediate visual confrontation.

Three: Social circle

It is easy to put in the extra hours, if everyone else does. It's easier to get to sleep an hour earlier if everyone else does. It's easier to be active if everyone else is. We are social-beings who want to fit in. Popular habits amongst our peer groups automatically become attractive to us. Spending time with those who have established the habits we seek increases the probability of sticking to the change. Not only that, it's also a great source of information, encouragement, feedback and praise.

'It is easy to put in the extra hours, if everyone else does. It's easier to get to sleep an hour earlier if everyone else does. It's easier to be active if everyone else is'

> ***Note:*** This is why Mat Fraser moved all the way to Tennessee so he could train with former champion Rich Froning and women's champion Tia-Clair Toomey.

Eliminating bad habits

First, we need to figure out what the reward is. It isn't always that obvious. But, there is always a benefit in there somewhere, even if objectively the habit appears to be a really stupid one. The reward we crave is not the routine we execute, but the change we feel from executing it. We need to switch our thinking from 'Why did I do that?' to 'what did I get out of it?' The question then becomes whether there are more functional ways to feel different?

Once we've determined which reward is driving the behaviour, we can search for more functional ways to achieve the same reward. If we're craving sugar, it is not necessarily chocolate we need. Try an orange, kiwi fruit, or apple. Chances are that the sugar in the fruit will satisfy the craving. By substituting a new routine (orange for chocolate) we can optimise the habit. Here, we work with the same cues and rewards, but adapt the routine.

> 'Once we've determined which reward is driving the behaviour, we can search for more functional ways to achieve the same reward'

> ***Note*** - When it comes to snacking the question is whether the reward we're seeking is to satisfy hunger or overcome boredom? Most of the time snacking is a symptom of boredom and can be substituted with another routine. This can range from engaging your mind in a game (board, electronic, or physical), stimulating conversation (digital or in-person), or simply eating something less unhealthy. It doesn't have to be perfect- better is better.

Planning

Written plans can double the rate at which we acquire habits. Specifically writing about where we perceive temptation to be strongest, when it is likely to occur and what strategy could overcome it, increases the probability of staying on track. The process primes our minds to exhibit the adaptive response if and when challenges arise.

- Exercise:

  What will happen if you change this habit?

  What will happen if you don't change this habit?

  What is the cue?

  What is the routine?

  What is the reward?

  How will you avoid any negative cues? How will you respond if you do encounter them?

  Or... How will you plant positive cues? How will you respond when you encounter them?

  How will you feel if you make the right choices?

  How will you feel if you make the wrong choices?

  What will forming this habit mean for you?

Making it stick

As we become the architects of our environment and manipulate the habit cycle to optimise habits and automate our winning days, there are four key points we must take into consideration:

One - Better not perfect

As the saying goes perfection is the enemy of progress. We will end up experiencing paralysis by analysis as we attempt to find the optimal training plan, diet or gym. When it comes to forming great habits, the key is to just start with repeating what we know is better. Better will grow.

Two - Consistency beats quantity

The other potential problem is thinking that, if we can't do the whole thing, then we shouldn't do it at all. If we don't have enough time to do a full workout, we can do ten minutes. If we don't have enough time to write an article, we can write a paragraph. If we don't have enough time to do yoga, we can take three deep breaths. We don't have to do it all. Individually, these less than perfect behaviours seem insignificant. But the cumulative impact of sticking to our schedules is what forms robust habits that stick.

Three - One thing at a time

Start with one habit. When we've got that one under control, add another. Get that under control, and add another. And so on. When it comes to the cost of forming habits, maintenance is much cheaper than creation. Focus on one habit at a time, and soon enough, we'll be ready for the circus.

> 'When it comes to the cost of forming habits, maintenance is much cheaper than creation'

Four- Avoid consecutive errors

We avoid social media all day, then by 15:00 we can't help ourselves and log in. We get up on time all week, then on Friday, hit the snooze button. We follow our new eating plan religiously for a week and then break it with a Saturday binge. Slip-ups don't make us a failure, they make us human. Slip ups aren't the problem, failing to get back on track is. That is why we must do all we can to avoid consecutive errors.

Through leveraging these principles the natural compulsion to engage in the right behaviours at the right times will strike us without thinking. Sticking to the principles that sent us to the top in the first place means we maximise our chances of staying there. A powerful set of functional habits enables us to conserve our energy, willpower and effort so we can sustain elite performance across seasons, decades and careers and continue accelerating away from the rest of the competition. In the final chapter of this book we turn our attention to the future.

CHAPTER SUMMARY

- Discipline is important. But those who appear to have tremendous discipline are the ones who need it the least. They have structured their lives in ways that do not require spartan willpower to win the day.
- Outliers have an internal compulsion to act on the right thing at the right time, and it strikes them without thinking.
- Executing habits is automatic and effortless, which means they sustain us whether we're inspired, motivated, determined, or not- even in red zone. They are way more powerful than discipline, motivation, and resilience.
- Understanding the three-step habit cycle means that we can design, build and reshape the component parts to eliminate negative habits and fortify positive habits.
- Cues: We must plant the cues that trigger the behaviours that win our days. When it comes to our negative habits it's a case of no cue, no craving.
- Routines: When deciding between two similar options, we will naturally gravitate towards the path of least resistance. The key is to reduce the effort required to enact our good habits; make them easy. And increase the effort associated with our bad ones; make them hard.
- Rewards: The reward we crave is not the habit itself, but the change in state it delivers. Once we've determined which reward is driving the behaviour, we can search for more functional ways to achieve the same reward.

- When it comes to forming a powerful set of habits better beats perfect and consistency beats quantity. Start with one habit at a time and remember, slip-ups don't make us a failure, they make us human, just try to avoid consecutive errors.

Recommended reading

James Clear - *Atomic habits*
Charles Duhigg - *The Power of Habit*

24

INNOVATION

It is not the strongest of the species that survive, not the most intelligent, but the one most responsive to change
Charles Darwin

MI5 is the United Kingdom's domestic counter-terrorist security agency that works alongside the Secret Intelligence Service (MI6). Its role is to keep the United Kingdom safe from the threat of terrorism and to identify and prosecute networks of foreign spies.

Andrew Parker [Director General, MI5]:
'We have a long tradition of innovation, and of responding successfully to the changing threats we face.' He continues, 'This evening I want to talk about a modern MI5. About how MI5 is changing, just as the world around us is changing. And about what we need to do if we are to continue to protect the UK against those who wish us all harm.' He adds, 'Today we face a three-dimensional threat: at home, overseas, and online.' He expands, commenting; 'The threat we are facing today is

on a scale and at a tempo that I have not seen before in my career. We have thwarted six attempts at terrorist attacks in the UK in the last year [2019], and several plots overseas… Innovation is critical if the modern the MI5 can continue to succeed in protecting this country in changing times.'[83]

During his thirty-seven years with the organisation, seven at the pinnacle as Director General, Andrew Parker has dealt with the IRA, Islamist terror plots, Russian and Chinese espionage and the rise of far-right and hard-left extremist groups.

Andrew Parker:

'The skills we need today, and the way we work, are very different to the organisation I joined in 1983.' He says 'Certainly we need to retain and evolve our traditional strengths in gathering and assessing intelligence, and recruiting and running agents. But just as important today are the ways in which we harness technology, our data analysis skills, and the quality of our partnerships.'[83]

The capabilities of MI5 and its intelligence officers must constantly adapt. Rising to the challenge; they are revolutionising spy craft with artificial intelligence, new live media interviews, apps that track terror suspects and using machine learning to maximise the extraction of effective intelligence. They have even developed an investment fund to nurture start-ups developing the tools they require. Ultimately, individuals like Andrew Parker and organisations like MI5 have no option. For them it really is innovate or (people will) die.

Andrew Parker:
'It is the quality of our people and our partnerships – and that ability to adapt and to innovate – that gives me greatest confidence about the future.'[83]

Nothing is permanent. Everything exists in a cycle of creation, transformation and destruction. Change is constant and without exception.

The dangerous thing is that much of this is invisible. The highest mountains are slowly wearing away, every species is morphing into something new, and our own abilities and the demands imposed on us are all part of this imperceptible slide towards something new. What does this mean for us? Innovate or die.

Innovation: Providing solutions to meet emerging demands

When most of us think about innovation, we think about the late Steve Jobs at Apple, Elon Musk at Tesla or Jeff Bezos at Amazon, individuals who have transformed markets. We pay less attention to others such as Bill Gates at Microsoft, Lloyd Blankfein, senior Chairman of Goldman Sachs, and Sir Alex Ferguson at Manchester United, who managed to stay on top for decades, even as competitors rose up to challenge them. The question is how?

Although we tend to think of innovation as a single brilliant flash of insight, the truth is there is something much more profound than just a concordant, skilful performer, keeping it together and driving excellence. Those who sustain excellence align with the same set of principles that drive their ability to innovate. A blueprint for innovation enables us to maximise the rate we emerge with solutions to the challenges that changing conditions bring. This means that innovation can be engineered, which means it can be learned, and taught.

In this chapter we uncover four key principles that enable us to systematically pursue innovation. These principles enable us to operationalise the unrelenting pursuit of excellence, stop complacency in its tracks, and give us the confidence to attack challenges head-on with full conviction. Each one channels our human capabilities by converting the raw materials of innovation; talent, ambition and effort, to generate both incremental evolution, and breakthrough solutions that cause disruptive revolution.

Principle one	In consideration of our *vision*
Principle two	*Understand* the current reality
Principle three	Establish a *target* to direct action
Principle four	*Experiment* through obstacles to test and expand knowledge

Principle One: Establish Your vision

Vision: A broad description of the ultimate condition we want to move towards

A vision acts as our North Star that holds still while the rest of the sky moves around it. The closer we get to it, the higher the star looks in the sky. As we move forward, our vision reminds us that there is always further to go. Although we must strive to be number one, we must never let ourselves get there. A defining characteristic of a great vision is that it keeps us in second place. This is how it stimulates the urgency, adversity and pressure we need to drive progress.

Make the boat go faster
GB Rowing

For Team GB, five simple words, Make the boat go faster, succinctly describe the problem the team aims to solve, giving everyone a clear purpose in solving it. It is tangible and easy to visualise, which means each performer can internalise the collective vision and make it their own. Every single action is made with the intention of realising this vision.

Ben Hunt-Davis:

> 'We have one very, very simple question we were always asking ourselves and each other. Before we did any training session, before we before we did pretty well anything. And that very simple question was, will it make the boat go faster.'[84] He adds 'It [the vision] wasn't "will it help us win?" because we couldn't control that. The "will it make the boat go faster?" question was what we had to do; we can control how fast our boat went. So the idea was, everything we did was staking us in that direction.' He goes on to comment, 'Whether it be before we sat on the rowing machine for 70 minutes, will it make the boat go faster, unfortunately yes, so that's what we would do. Before going out to the pub, will it make the boat go faster, unfortunately no, so we didn't.'[85]

The vision is not a finite, achievable end-state like winning gold, being world-champion or attaining a world-record. These are all achievable targets that should be celebrated on the path to making the boat go faster. But, after all these achievements, when we look up at the vision, the guiding force remains, forcing us to rethink our potential. This way, celebrating success is never the end of the improvement cycle; but the transitional period to the next improvement plan.

'Celebrating success is not the end of the improvement cycle; it's the transitional period to the next improvement plan'

Mars and Beyond
SpaceX

Garrett Reisman [Senior SpaceX Engineer]:
'[Elon] measures pretty much every major decision by whether or not it brings the day when we have a self-sustainable colony on Mars sooner or later... Every single decision he makes, he makes through that prism'[86]

A great vision also inspires. All of Elon Musk's companies are founded upon inspirational goals. The earth is quite literally the burning platform that has sparked his drive for electric vehicles (Tesla), renewable energy (Solar City), and life on Mars (SpaceX). Saving the planet and the human race are pretty compelling calls to action. This creates a sense of great urgency and ludicrously high expectations.

Organise the world's information
Google

A great vision also expands our awareness to both threats and opportunities along with our ability to act on them. This awareness distinguishes the likes of Google who were alert and open-minded enough to seize the opportunity to acquire companies like Instagram and YouTube as they continue to accelerate away from the competition. We can only imagine a world where John Antioco, former CEO of Blockbuster, had a vision to 'entertain all'. He might have perceived the likes of Netflix as an opportunity instead of something to sweep under the carpet. Likewise, imagine if Stephen Elop, while CEO of Nokia, had the vision of 'bringing the best user experience to customers,' perhaps they too would have more carefully considered the infamous iPhone and tablet that would end up annihilating Nokia.

> ***Note:*** My vision is to accelerate excellence. It gave me a constructive dissatisfaction with the status quo in human performance re-framing how I looked at my own development. Expanding my options for progress, it prompted me to study courses in clinical psychology, positive psychology and neuroscience. It has also led me to train in domains outside of the status quo within performance psychology, like Lean, NLP and hypnotherapy.

Principle Two: Understand reality

Sir David Brailsford:

> 'Ultimately the starting point is to truly analyse the demands of the event. You sit down and you try to figure it out: what does winning look like, what are the components, what does it take to win, what are all the different aspects which you need to accomplish in order to win. The more work you do on that, the more accuracy it gives you in terms of knowing where

> you have got to go… We would go to the nth degree in terms of truly understanding what winning looked like… We spent more time than any other team in the world doing that particular work.'[87]

Sir David Brailsford led British cyclists to win 59 World Championships across different disciplines from 2003 to 2013. He led the British cycling team, Team Sky (now General Manager of Ineos Grenadiers) to win the 2012, 2013, 2015, 2016, 2017 and 2018 Tours de France. This success was built upon a methodical understanding of reality and knowing what it would take to win. While their competitors jumped to solutions, acted on assumptions and copied each other, Brailsford and his team worked smarter. They stepped back and focused on reducing winning in cycling to its most fundamental truths.

> ***Note:*** To many reason by analogy, attempting to innovate by coping the recipes of others, falling for sales pitches or leaning on best practices approved by the majority. Instead we should reason by first principles, breaking our problems down into their basic elements and then reassembling them from the ground up. This allows us to cut through the fog of careless reasoning and inadequate analogies to emerge with opportunities that others miss.

A significant step early on was the use of power meters, along with other technologies like video analysis and aerodynamic testing, that allowed the team to create a systematic analysis of the numbers that the riders could produce, including lap times, cadences, power outputs and drag factors. This allowed them to conduct in-depth analysis of what it took to win and where they needed to innovate. They even developed a blueprint for it. A thick document titled 'What It'll Take to Win' with a checklist for each rider outlining the 74 factors, qualitative and quantitative, that encapsulate the team's understanding of what it takes to win. The aim was to focus on the areas that offer the greatest contribution to the most crucial variable: power output.

> ***Note:*** An expert knows when it's time to call in an Expert. Team Sky eliminated blind spots by calling in staff from outside cycling, including performance analysts, physiologists, psychologists, biomechanists and logistics experts.

Solutions Should Fall In Our Laps

We need to understand our current reality so well that the problems and their solutions fall in our laps. This ensures we channel the urgency, adversity and pressure activated by our vision to solve to right problems.

> 'We need to understand our current reality so well that the problems and their solutions fall in our laps'

Coming up with ideas is easy. There are endless ways we could attempt to innovate. This is why it's so easy to fool ourselves that we know what will lead to superior performance. Identifying the right problems and solving them is the real challenge. Without an intimate understanding of what it takes to win and where we are now in relation to that, it's impossible to understand which actions will make the boat go fastest. If what we need to innovate isn't obvious, then we don't understand the problem well enough. 'I don't know' is a completely acceptable answer and far better than just assuming we do know, when really we don't.

'If what we need to innovate isn't obvious, then we don't understand the problem well enough'

To establish the actual situation, not what we think it is or wish it were, we must start with actively questioning every assumption we think we know, and generating an accurate knowledge base that is grounded in data and facts. Starting with: What are we absolutely sure is true? What are our assumptions? What has been proven? This process should be stripped of emotion and rooted in detailed rational analysis:

Opinions like: 'things are going well'

Need to be replaced with facts like: 'sales are increasing by 2.5% each week'

Generalisations like: 'We were world-class last week'
Need to be replaced with specificity like: 'Our possession was 85%, we created 10 goal-scoring opportunities, and converted 5'

This can help us break out of herd mentality, encourage us to think outside the box and generate unique solutions to our own bespoke problems.

Note: When you can't extract exact data for your craft, start with using the 1–10 scoring mechanism discussed in Chapter [15]. A calibrated IDP will eliminate blind spots, elicit objective outcomes and reduce susceptibility to bias.

Track Trajectory

Ben Hunt-Davis:

If you pick up on what the commentators were saying about us and our chances, our hopes, they hadn't really looked at what we were doing for the two years leading up to that race [trajectory], they were judging us on the seven years of previous results [snapshots].'[84]

This is how most of us assess our performance, based on a snapshot result at a single moment in time like: Profit, position in the league or number of followers. On the other hand we have trajectory. A trajectory is a series of positions over time like: Goal difference, rate of increase/ decrease in likes or price-to-earnings ratio.

Snapshot: a single moment in time

Trajectory: a series of positions over time

Once we know the metrics that matter most, we can track their trajectory over time to make better, more informed, strategic decisions maximising the effectiveness of our actions. This works in two ways:

Benefit One: Trajectory displays rate of progression

Trajectory shows us where we're heading and how fast we're heading there. If we have 10,000 customers, but lose more than we gain each month, then we're on a bad trajectory. Conversely, if we have 1,000 customers, but gain more than we lose every month, we're on the path towards success. This enables us to see if there are dark clouds or sunshine on the horizon.

'Trajectory shows us where we're heading and how fast we're heading there'

Benefit Two: Trajectory increases our sensitivity to change
If snapshots are like measuring in miles, then trajectory is like measuring in metres. If we're gaining unwanted weight, and notice it when we're one kilogram overweight, we can identify the causes and adjust accordingly. On the other hand, if we don't notice the gain until we're ten kilograms overweight, the situation is much more difficult to manage.

Outliers like Sir Dave Brailsford don't experience fewer problems, but they do spot problems much earlier than the rest, while the problems are still small. When we spot small problems early, it's much easier to understand, and do something about, them. This means we can get in front of potential challenges before the failure plays out or the opportunity disappears. A better understanding of the impact of our actions also helps us maximise the quality of our future actions.

'Outliers like Sir Dave Brailsford don't experience fewer problems, but they do spot problems much earlier than the rest, while the problems are still small'

Focusing on trajectory also enables us to avoid getting too excited or discouraged by a single positive or negative outcome along the way because now our performance is judged on a series of results as opposed to the latest snapshot.

> ***Note:*** Compare you to you- comparison should be against our own trajectories. Where are we improving most rapidly, and how can we do more of that? Simultaneously, ask, where is improvement slowing down, and how can we change what we're doing to improve the trajectory?

Never Trust Success

Team Sky didn't let the fact they won the race stop them from identifying an opportunity to improve. If they see a drop in power output, despite winning the race, then they will conduct a rigorous examination to find out why. We increase our chances of staying successful by treating our successes with the same scepticism as our failures. We need to ask sceptical questions, especially when we have glowing headline metrics, questions like: Why did we actually succeed? Did we truly outperform the rest? Did circumstance give us a 30% tailwind? It is so easy to confuse great strategy with great conditions, timing and luck.

We need to recognise that we cant see ourselves objectively. This is why sometimes we confuse what we wish were true with what is really true. This is why we need data. It requires an extra mental gear to judge our own processes and outcomes sceptically, rather than building a subjective story that serves our narrative. There needs to be amnesty for those who are radically transparent about our weaknesses, ask uncomfortable questions, and constructively criticise.

Principle Three: Have a clear target to aim at

Target: The aim of attack

Sir Dave Brailsford; 2010 [Team Sky Target]:
'To win the greatest bike race in the world, within five years, to do it with a British rider, and do it clean. And in doing so to inspire a million people to take up cycling.'[88]

Once we have a target, our mind-set switches to: What prevents us from achieving the target? This question forces us to uncover obstacles that establish a performance gap that moves us into the adaptive zone summoning more of the urgency, adversity and pressure we need to drive innovation.

It is the successive completion of targets that moves us closer and closer to our vision. The questions we are trying to answer are: Where do we want to be next?

Sir Dave Brailsford [2020]:
'We met all of our objectives - ahead of schedule. We won the Tour de France twice. We won 165 races in total. We won them clean. We played a big part in the revolution of cycling as a great participation and spectator sport, especially in the UK, Team Sky's home, but elsewhere too.'[88]

When it comes to innovation we need to replace: 'If it ain't broke, don't fix it' with: 'If it ain't broke, hit it with a sledgehammer.'

Sir Dave Brailsford [2020]:
'The fact that we did manage to meet all of our objectives, on one level, is great. But in a culture like Team Sky's, which is

> built on constantly asking if we could do better, success means never resting on our laurels. I am immensely proud of the team, but it is in our DNA always to think that we could have done more and pushed the boundaries further. Our 2020 mission is very simple - for Team Sky [Ineos] to be indisputably and consistently the best cycling team in the world – and to be viewed as one of the very best sports teams in the world.'[88]

Luckily, at the top, our vision reminds us that, despite our achievement, we must set the next target that moves us a step closer to our vision. Achievement is not the end of the improvement cycle, setting the next target is. This forces us to reflect hard, raise the bar and fight to find competition. This reveals the next set of obstacles that move us back into the adaptive zone before complacency gets a chance to slip in.

> 'We must reflect hard, raise the bar and fight to find competition'

Sir Dave Brailsford knows that the best form of defence is to attack. The battle for Team Sky was no longer Australia, Germany and the USA. Their new battlefield was global sport. This changes the game. Immediately they transition from the big fish in the small pond to a smaller fish in a bigger pond. Now they are competing with the likes of New Zealand rugby, Real Madrid and the LA Lakers. No longer number one, they are forced to reinvent, re-connect, and build on their success to date. This summons the urgency, adversity and pressure they needed to drive innovation.

Principle Four- Experimentation

> Knowing how to deal well with what you don't know is much more important than anything you know
>
> Ray Dalio

Experimenting is like shining a torch into the dark to help us see the way ahead. The process of experimentation is about demonstrating factually that we have discovered valuable truths we can apply to make our boat go faster. The good news is that experimentation and finding solutions is what we humans are programmed to be good at: applying creativity, resourcefulness and effort to solve problems.

> Experiment: a scientific procedure undertaken to create a discovery

Experimentation works contrary to traditional development, there is no whiteboard gamesmanship, excessive discussion and striving for perfection here. Talking through our problems is an important part of overcoming challenges. But after a certain point we begin to deceive ourselves in to thinking we're making progress. The reason we do so much talking is because it's easy. But talking doesn't count as work. In fact, it competes for the same units of effort as doing. Endless discussions, sharing opinions, or judging what might happen does not expand what we know. Testing does. The defining theme of experimentation is action. As soon as we hear ourselves say 'I believe,' or 'I think', stop and experiment as quickly as possible.

'As soon as we hear ourselves say 'I believe,' or 'I think', stop and experiment as quickly as possible'

The optimal pattern of experimentation has four stages (PDCA):

One: Plan - A proposal for achieving something
Two: Do - Execute the plan
Three: Check - Determine accuracy
Four: Adapt - Adjust to new conditions

Step one: Plan

Here we need to isolate and define the biggest problem and make a prediction on how to solve it. There are three key steps:

Step one- Define what action we need to take

Step two- Predict what we expect to happen

Step three- Set out a clear baseline metric so we can measure the result

The aim is to begin the learning process as soon as possible, so the rule here is that a good plan today is better than a perfect plan tomorrow.

'A good plan today is better than a perfect plan tomorrow'

Step two: Do it

As soon as we take action according to the plan learning begins. Action provides us with a reaction, which means we can stop telling people about our plans and start showing them our results.

'Action provides us with a reaction, which means we can stop telling people about our plans and start showing them our results'

Note: Experiments can be run on the smallest scale to ensure they don't interrupt the rest of our process or operation.

Step three: Check

Now we compare the results of our experiment with our prediction. To continue to excel we need to kill the ideas that don't work fast and double down on the ones that do. If we're not improving our core performance metrics, then we need to know. Aspiring elite performers tend to be optimistic by nature. We want to believe in our ideas, even when the writing's on the wall. Without objectively checking results we risk living in our own subjective realities, using after-the-fact rationalisation to hide failure. This is about holding ourselves accountable. It allows us to confront one of the most difficult questions we face. To pivot or persevere?

'We need to kill the ideas that don't work fast and double down on the ones that do'

Pivot: Change course

A pivot is a radical course correction, going in a new direction, with a new prediction about our product, strategy or business model. We need to consider pivoting when the metrics indicate that we're not making enough progress. The misguided decision to persevere with ideas that just don't work can leave us stuck in the land of the living dead.

Persevere: Continue with our course of action

If we experience positive changes in metrics, then we have the quantitative validation that we are moving in the right direction and that we should persevere. This allows us to show coach, investors, employees, and ourselves, that we are making genuine progress, not deluding ourselves in terms of how much progress we're getting for our efforts.

Step four: Adapt

Those eureka moments where, in a flash, everything suddenly clicks are often the product of eliminating what doesn't work first. With innovation we are always working with issues we don't yet know how to respond to, fix or create. This will mean failing. Think of failure as the inevitable cost we must pay to eventually to be right.

> 'With innovation we are always working with issues we don't yet know how to respond to, fix or create. This will mean failing'

A failure is not good or bad. It is simply another data point that helps guide innovation. It's ok to fail, but it is unacceptable not to identify, analyse, and learn from failure. Plus, we'll only repeat errors until we learn from them. The learnings in this phase become the starting point for the next PDCA cycle.

> 'A failure is not good or bad. It is simply another data point that helps guide innovation'

Note: If the experiment is a success, then great! We can celebrate. For a moment. After all, achievement is the gateway to our next improvement plan, not the end.

Iteration

Iteration: the plan, do, check, adapt process repeated over and over

The faster we iterate, the faster we innovate. The aim is small, rapid steps, with learning and adjustments occurring as we go. All innovation should be geared to accelerate this process. Due to the fact races can be won by a tenth of a second, Team Sky use different iterations of their skin suits and Protone helmets at every race. Likewise, comedians like Joe Rogan will make multiple iterations of the same sketch behind the scenes in smaller comedy clubs to optimise it before releasing a Netflix special. At Tesla, a product traditionally considered to be finished and complete, is now open-ended and continuously iterating. Elon Musk is challenging the status quo by releasing frequent software updates to improve and change the functionality of Tesla cars after the point of sale.

'The faster we iterate, the faster we innovate'

Innovation is without end. The constancy of change guarantees the need for adapting what currently constitutes excellence. Without it we slowly but surely let complacency set in and we will slip back. There is no single point where learning ends and we are left with just excellence. Progress is a fluid, continual process with no finish line.

'There is no single point where learning ends and we are left with just excellence. Progress is a fluid, continual process with no finish line'

CHAPTER SUMMARY

- Nothing is permanent. Everything exists in a cycle of creation, transformation and destruction. The dangerous thing is that much of this is invisible.
- Our own abilities and the demands imposed on us are all part of this imperceptible slide towards something new. This means it's innovate or die.
- Vision: It acts as our North Star. As we move forward, it always reminds us that there is further to go. Keeping us in second place, stimulating the urgency, adversity and pressure we need to drive progress.
- Understanding reality: We need to understand what it takes to win and know where we are in relation to that. This ensures we channel the urgency, adversity and pressure to innovate the right things.
- Target: The successive completion of targets moves us closer and closer to our vision. Each target uncovers obstacles, establishing a performance gap moving us into the adaptive zone, and activating the psychological fire-power that drives innovation.
- Experiment: Knowing how to deal well with what we don't know is much more important than anything we know.
- As soon as we hear ourselves say 'I think', stop and experiment as quickly as possible. Isolate and define the biggest problem, make a prediction and then test it.
- Celebrating success is never the end of the improvement cycle; but the transitional period to the next improvement plan.

- Iteration is the scientific process repeated over and over, each cycle accelerating us forwards. The faster we iterate, the faster we innovate.
- Innovation is without end. There is no single point where learning ends and we are left with just excellence. Progress is a fluid, continual process with no finish line'

CONCLUSION

Now this is not the end. It is not even the
beginning of the end. But it is, perhaps,
the end of the beginning
Winston Churchill

Cristiano Ronaldo did it. J.K. Rowling did it. Elon Musk did it. Now it's your turn. While I hope you've enjoyed reading this book, the magic happens when you lift the words off the pages and align with the principles they contain. Accelerating your pursuit of excellence is one of most thrilling and meaningful experiences you can know.

People who read books on revolutionary new ways to excel fall into one of two categories. The first experiences a high that fades, and before they know it, it's back to business as usual- nothing changes. The second group also feel the high, but they sustain it and go on to achieve significant change. What distinguishes the two? Putting these principles to work immediately. This book contains potentially game-changing information, but it can't change anything if you don't act on it.

Your job now is building the casino: finding your sweet spot, engaging in three-dimensional training, becoming the master of your emotions, winning your days and experimenting your way towards your vision. So what are you going to do first? I recommend starting with the principles that resonate most with you. None of the outlier performers or organisations that you heard about in this book followed an exact prescription.

The human body will do whatever it is trained to do. It is never too late. Wherever you are in life, or your career; if you align with these principles then all the evidence suggests that you will improve, adapt and achieve as you start uncovering and realising that potential everything you can be. Remember, this is not just for accelerating excellence; but also for maximising your quality of life. When you get that nagging feeling that things aren't going to plan, check in, and calibrate. You will find answers here.

My hope is that you have emerged from this book inspired about your ability to maximise the unique gifts you bring to the table, recognising the expandable nature of your potential, and understanding that, while accelerating excellence is challenging, it is not as complicated as you might have thought.

For me, this is just the beginning. This book introduces the fundamental principles you need to start accelerating your pursuit of excellence. There is plenty more to come. Until then good luck and enjoy

Note: I'd love to hear about your experiences,please send your stories and learnings to: results@jamesaking.com

ACKNOWLEDGEMENTS

It goes without saying that the information in this book is built upon a synthesis of great practical and academic work conducted by others, credit for that must be attributed to them.

Through a combination of luck and strategy I have been privileged to work with some incredible people. I want to express my gratitude to them for giving me an opportunity to put these principles to work.

I'm someone who needs discussion and conversation to get in my sweet spot, activate my psychological fire-power and access my technical ability. I depend on this. My ideas and thoughts have been shaped by the conversations, feedback and input from some very special people. Their feedback helped make this the book it is.

Editorial assistance: Thanks to Michele Mastriciani, Jasmin Naim, and Rebecca Wright for their skill and effort.

REFERENCES

PART ONE

Chapter One

1 BBC.co.uk (29 February 2016) Oscars 2016: Leonardo DiCaprio finally wins Academy Award https://www.bbc.co.uk/news/entertainment-arts-35670715. Accessed 27 November 2020.

2 YouTube (2 February 2017) Women's final 2017 Australian Open Tennis Live 7HD Melbourne 28 January 2017 - Serena and Venus Williams. https://www.youtube.com/watch?v=pKEpeAYTZio Accessed 27 November 2020.

3 Malik, T. (6 February 2018) Success! SpaceX Launches Falcon Heavy Rocket on Historic Maiden Voyage. https://www.space.com/39607-spacex-falcon-heavy-first-test-flight-launch.html. Accessed 27 November 2020

Chapter Two

4 Singularity hub (06 April 2016) Alison E Berman, Jason Dorrier and David J. Hill. *How to think exponentially and better predict the future.* https://singularityhub.com/2016/04/05/how-to-think-exponentially-and-better-predict-the-future/ Accessed 27 November 2020.

PART TWO

Chapter Three

5 BBC.co.uk (1 September 2013) Gareth Bale joins Real Madrid from Spurs in £85m world record deal https://www.bbc.co.uk/sport/football/23538218. Accessed 27 November 2020.

6 YouTube (26 May 2018) Gareth Bale scores BEST GOAL EVER in a Champions League final with overhead kick vs Liverpool. https://www.youtube.com/watch?v=7JbOoJ_dge4&list=PLubVgegS36EPg_Cmh__WBPcD6v5L5CuXV&index=11&t=0s&app=desktop. Accessed 27 November 2020.

7 Sheldon, K.M. (2002). The self-concordance model of healthy goal striving: When personal goals correctly represent the person. In *Handbook of Self-determination Research*, pp.65-86. edited by Edward L. Deci, Richard M. Ryan. University of Rochester Press.

8 October 31st 2011. Harvard University 12 Positive Psychology. https://www.youtube.com/watch?v=Lu0nUPELsHM&t=0s. Last accessed 27 November 2020.

Chapter Four

9 New York Post (13 December 2015) Conor McGregor Destroys Aldo with One Stunning Punch. https://nypost.com/2015/12/13/conor-mcgregor-stunningly-destroys-aldo-with-one-punch/. Accessed 27 November 2020.

10 YouTube (13 December 2015) Conor McGregor KO's Jose Aldo In 13 Seconds at UFC 194. https://www.youtube.com/watch?v=CI2N1-7tmYc. Accessed November 2020.

11 YouTube (28 December 2015) Conor McGregor: I am not Talented, I am Obsessed. https://www.youtube.com/watch?v=t89RVPNnv4U. Accessed 27 November 2020.

12 Ferriss, T. (2010) *The 4-Hour Body: An incredible guide to rapid fat-loss, incredible sex and becoming superhuman.* Harmony.

13 Bolt, U. (2013) *Faster Than Lightning: My autobiography.* HarperSport.

14 Star Talk Radio Show (22 March 2015) *The Future of Humanity with Elon Musk* https://www.startalkradio.net/tag/elon-musk/

15 YouTube (5 November 2017) Elon Musk Master Programmer. Wrote his first program when he was 12! https://www.youtube.com/watch?v=QcBeqDwp49k. (Accessed 27 November 2020.

16 McDonald, D. (2014) *Last Man Standing: The ascent of Jamie Dimon and JP Morgan Chase.* New York. Simon & Schuster.

17 JPmorganchase.com (4 May 2017) *What High School Students Learn From Jamie Dimon* https://www.jpmorganchase.com/news-stories/what-high-school-students-learn-from-jamie-dimon. Accessed 27 November 2020.

18 Shamsian, J. (31 July 2018) How J.K. Rowling went from struggling single mom to the world's most successful author. *Insider.com.* https://www.insider.com/jk-rowling-harry-potter-author-biography-2017-7. Accessed 27 November 2020.

19 CBBC Newsround (18 July 2005) Read the Full JK Rowling Interview. http://news.bbc.co.uk/cbbcnews/hi/newsid_4690000/newsid_4690800/4690885.stm Accessed 27 November 2020.

Chapter Five

20 Nagelhout, R. (2017) *Elon Musk: Space entrepreneur.* New York, Ny. Lucent Books.

21 Hedegaard, E. (June 2019). Kevin Costner: A Hollywood Gunslinger Looks Back. https://www.rollingstone.com/tv/tv-features/kevin-costner-yellowstone-interview-847773/. Last Accessed November 2020.

22 Meredith, F. (9 July 2005) Simply Wizard. *The Irish Times.* https://www.irishtimes.com/news/simply-wizard-1.466451 Accessed 27 November 2020

23 http://www.accio-quote.org/articles/2002/1102-aebiography.htm

24 Schruers, F. (December 2014) Kevin Costner Keeps Calm and Takes Action. AARP The Magazine. https://www.aarp.org/entertainment/style-trends/info-2014/kevin-costner-aarp-interview.html. Accessed 27 November 2020.

25 Nme.com (14 June 2015) *Ed Sheeran says rapping to Eminem got rid of his childhood stutter* https://www.nme.com/news/music/ed-sheeran-42-1207521. Accessed 27 November 2020.

26 GQ Australia (9 March 2017) Eminem helped Ed Sheeran overcome his stammer. https://www.gq.com.au/entertainment/celebrity/eminem-helped-ed-sheeran-overcome-his-stammer/news-story/28f775fbbe017a5b077d24f4c82135b7#:~:text=He%20credits%20an%20unlikely%20mentor,to%20improve%20his%20vocal%20fluency. Accessed 27 November 2020.

27 Gary Vaynerchuck (13 December 2019) Game Changers Summit Keynote 2019. https://www.youtube.com/watch?v=-bG82D4bPWc. Accessed 27 November 2020.

28 Rowling, J.K. (2015) *Very Good Lives: The fringe benefits of failure and the importance of imagination.* Sphere.

29 9SportPro (7 August 2018) Douglas Costa: Its impossible to follow Cristiano Ronaldo in training! https://www.9sportpro.com/40495/ Accessed 27 November 2020.

30 Katwala, A. (9 August 2018) What's driving Elon Musk? Wired. https://www.wired.co.uk/article/whats-driving-elon-musk. Accessed 27 November 2020.

Chapter Six

31 Balague, G (2015) *Cristiano Ronaldo: The biography.* Orion.

32 Bolt, U. (2013) *Faster Than Lightning: My autobiography.* HarperSport.

33 Kahlow, A (1 March 2017) Patagonia's CEO says Conscious leaders need to stand for something. SocapDigital. https://socapglobal.com/2017/03/patagonias-ceo-says-conscious-leaders-need-stand-something/ Accessed 27 November 2020.

34 Condon, C. (11 November 2019) JPMorgan's Dimon laments income inequality, won't assail CEO pay. https://www.bloomberg.com/news/articles/2019-11-11/jpmorgan-s-dimon-laments-income-inequality-won-t-assail-ceo-pay Accessed 27 November 2020.

35 Kahlow, A (1 March 2017) Patagonia's CEO says Conscious leaders need to stand for something. SocapDigital. https://socapglobal.com/2017/03/patagonias-ceo-says-conscious-leaders-need-stand-something/ Accessed 27 November 2020.

36 Katwala, A. (9 August 2018) What's driving Elon Musk? *Wired.* https://www.wired.co.uk/article/whats-driving-elon-musk. Accessed 27 November 2020.

37 Beer, J. (28 November 2018) Patagonia is giving its $10 million tax cut back to the planet. *Fast Company.* https://www.fastcompany.com/90273496/patagonia-is-giving-its-10-million-tax-cut-back-to-the-planet. Accessed 27 November 2020.

Chapter Nine

38 Miller, Bennett (2011) Moneyball. Columbia Pictures.

PART THREE

Chapter Ten

39 NBANetwork (14 June 2020) #OTD in 1998, the Chicago Bulls won their 6th NBA title , beating the Utah Jazz in Game 6 of the '98 Finals. https://nbanetwork.org/post/620909003178999808/otd-in-1998-the-chicago-bulls-won-their-6th-nba . Accessed 27 November 2020.

Chapter Eleven

40 University of Oxford: Introduction and History. https://www.ox.ac.uk/about/organisation/history#:~:text=As%20the%20oldest%20university%20in,attending%20the%20University%20of%20Paris. Accessed 27 November 2020.

Chapter Twelve

41 Royal Air Force: F-35 Lightning. https://www.raf.mod.uk/aircraft/lightning-f35b/ Accessed 27 November 2020.

Chapter Thirteen

42 Navy Seals.com (31 October 2016) Navy SEALS History. https://web.archive.org/web/20161031225738/http://navyseals.com/nsw/navy-seal-history/ Accessed 27 November 2020

Chapter Fourteen

43 Shamrock, Frank. Uncaged: My life as a champion MMA fighter. Chicago: Chicago Review Press, 2012.

44 Moore, Richard. (2013) *Mastermind: How Dave Brailsford Reinvented the Wheel.* BackPage Press.

Chapter Fifteen

45 Dizik, A. (26 December 2016) Why your New Year's resolutions often fail. BBC.com. https://www.bbc.com/worklife/article/20161220-why-your-new-years-resolutions-often-fail Accessed 27 November 2020.

46 TennisX: Roger Federer's Grand Slam Titles, Finals, Records. https://www.tennis-x.com/grand-slam-finals/roger-federer.php Accessed 27 November 2020.

Chapter Sixteen

47 YouTube (22 November 2019) 'Tesla armor glass' shatters during new electric Cybertruck demo. https://www.youtube.com/watch?v=Ka_khhOd8YI Accessed 27 November 2020

48 Weitering, H. (May 2020) Elon Musk 'overcome with emotion' after SpaceX's 1st astronaut launch. https://www.space.com/elon-musk-emotional-spacex-astronaut-launch.html. Accessed 27 November 2020.

52 Dweck, C. S. 2006. *Mindset: the new psychology of success.*New York, Random House.)

50 Ben-Shahar, T. 2009 *The pursuit of perfect.* HighBridge Company.

51 Collins, D.J., Abbott, A. and Richards, H. (2011) *Performance Psychology: A practitioner's guide.* Churchill Livingstone.

PART FOUR

Chapter Seventeen

52 Kansas City Chiefs: Patrick Mahomes wins MVP of Superbowl LIV. Chiefs.com. https://www.chiefs.com/video/patrick-mahomes-wins-mvp-of-super-bowl-liv. Accessed 27 November 2020.

53 BBC News (19 April 2018) Tammie Jo Shults: Southwest pilot praised for safe landing. https://www.bbc.co.uk/news/world-us-canada-43804253 Accessed 27 November 2020

Chapter Eighteen

54 Jackson, S.A. & Csikzsentmihalyi, M. (1999) *Flow in Sports: The keys to optimal experiences and performances.* Human Kinetics.

55 Russell, J.A. (1980) A circumplex model of affect. *Journal of personality and social psychology*, 39(6), p.1161-1178.

Chapter Nineteen

56 Venkat, R. (5 September 2020) Michael Phelps: The man who dominated the Olympic pool like no other. https://www.olympicchannel.com/en/stories/features/detail/michael-phelps-olympic-medals-record-how-many-gold-swimmer-world-record/ Accessed 27 November 2020.

57 Duhigg, C. (2014) The power of habit: why we do what we do in life and business. Random House.

58 Phelps, M. & Abrahamson, A. (2008) No limits: the will to succeed. London, Simon & Schuster.

59 Fordyce, T. (2016) Six Nations 2016: England win Grand Slam with France victory. https://www.bbc.co.uk/sport/rugby-union/35821697 Accessed 27 November 2020.

60 Wilkinson, C. (24 January 2014) FT Masterclass: Goal kicking with Owen Farrell. https://www.ft.com/content/751786d0-83c2-11e3-86c9-00144feab7de. Accessed 27 November 2020

61 YouTube (23 February 2015) Pitch Demo: Owen Farrell kicking masterclass: Rugby Tonight. https://www.youtube.com/watch?v=roYfwZ6sCXU Accessed 27 November 2020.

62 Wood, A. (2 February 2019) Owen Farrell: England Six Nations star's bizarre kicking style revealed. The Express. https://www.express.co.uk/sport/rugby-union/1081656/Owen-Farrell-England-Six-Nations-Ireland Accessed 27 November 2020

63 Joining Jack: Duchenne UK. https://www.duchenneuk.org/joining-jack Accessed 27 November 2020.

Chapter Twenty

67 Academy of Achievement (4 May 2001) Jeffrey P. Bezos: King of Cyber-Commerce. https://achievement.org/achiever/jeffrey-p-bezos/#interview Accessed 27 November 2020.

65 Ben-Shahar, T. (2009) *The pursuit of perfect: How to stop chasing perfection and start living a richer, happier life*. McGraw Hill Education

66 YouTube (17 August 2019) 2008 Beyonce interview with Oprah Winfrey. https://www.youtube.com/watch?v=4AA5G8vCl9w Accessed 27 November 2020.

PART FIVE

Chapter Twenty One

67 TennisX: Serena Williams' Grand Slams: titles, finals, records. https://www.tennis-x.com/grand-slam-finals/serena-williams.php Accessed 27 November 2020.

68 Berger, S. (25 February 2019) 28-year old Bill Gates wasn't worried about burning out young – here's why. Make it: CNBC.com. https://www.cnbc.com/2019/02/25/28-year-old-bill-gates-said-he-wouldnt-burn-out-by-the-time-he-was-30.html Accessed 27 November 2020.

69 League Managers Association (LMA): Sir Alex Ferguson CBE. http://www.leaguemanagers.com/managers/sir-alex-ferguson/ Accessed 27 November 2020.

70 SS- Loehr, J., & Schwartz, T. (2003) The power of full engagement: Managing energy, not time, is the key to high performance an*d personal renewal.* New York. Simon and Schuster.)

71 YouTube. 17 April 2008. The Energy Project | Tony Schwartz | Talks at Google. https://www.youtube.com/watch?v=tke6X2eME3c Last Accessed 27 November 2020.

Chapter Twenty Two

72 BBC.com (20 May 2020) Why Joe Rogan's exclusive Spotify deal matters. https://www.bbc.co.uk/news/entertainment-arts-52736364 Accessed 27 November 2020.

73 Montgomery, J. (22 October 2015) Joe Rogan: A day (or so) in the life of UFC's funniest guy. Rolling Stone. https://www.rollingstone.com/culture/culture-news/joe-rogan-a-day-or-so-in-the-life-of-ufcs-funniest-guy-175229/ Accessed 27 November 2020.

74 Youtube (15 June 2018) Joe Rogan- How to workout smarter https://www.youtube.com/watch?v=_fbCcWyYthQ. Accessed 27 November 2020.

75 Loehr, J., & Schwartz, T. (2003) The power of full engagement: Managing energy, not time, is the key to high performance and personal renewal. New York. Simon and Schuster.

76 YouTube (24 May 2017) "Make your bed" by US Navy Admiral William H McRaven. https://www.youtube.com/watch?v=GmFwRkl-TTc&trk=organization-update-content_share-video-embed_share-article_title Accessed 27 November 2020.

77 Kim, E. (7 November 2014) Here's the reason Mark Zuckerberg wears the same t-shirt every day. BusinessInsider. https://www.businessinsider.com/mark-zuckerberg-same-t-shirt-2014-11?r=US&IR=T Accessed 27 November 2020.

78 Wallas, G. (1926). The art of thought. J. Cape: London.

79 Ben-Shahar, T. (29 December 2007) Cheer up – here's how… The Guardian. https://www.theguardian.com/lifeandstyle/2007/dec/29/healthandwellbeing.mentalhealth Accessed 27 November 2020.

80 Walker, M., 2017. Why we sleep: The new science of sleep and dreams. Penguin UK.

Chapter Twenty Three

81 Cooper, E. (2019) Why Mat Fraser's 2016 second-place medal is still his most precious. *Men's Health* https://www.menshealth.com/uk/fitness/a28548685/mat-fraser-crossfit-games/ Accessed 27 November 2020.

82 Milkman, K.L., Minson, J.A. and Volpp, K.G., 2014. *Holding the Hunger Games hostage at the gym: An evaluation of temptation bundling.* Management science, 60(2), pp.283-299

Chapter Twenty Four

86 MI5 (28 October 2015) News and Speeches: A modern MI5. https://www.mi5.gov.uk/cy/news/a-modern-mi5 Accessed 27 November 2020

84 Ben Hunt-Davis YouTube (Sep 28 2015) Ben Hunt-Davis - Continuous Improvement. https://www.youtube.com/watch?v=Ih0thFPjvck

85 YouTube (October 15 2015) Will It Make the Boat Go faster- Ben Hunt-Davis. https://www.youtube.com/watch?v=VlTfbGemGcM

86 YouTube (7th Feb 2020) Joe Rogan Experience 1425 - Garrett Reisman. https://www.youtube.com/watch?v=3RG5pXTpLBI

87 Fotheringham, W. (5 July 2014) Sir Dave Brailsford focused on sustaining Sky's Tour de France success. https://www.theguardian.com/sport/2014/jul/05/dave-brailsford-team-sky-tour-de-france Accessed 27 November 2020.

88 Sky Sports (11 January 2015) Team Sky "2020 Vision" https://www.skysports.com/more-sports/cycling/news/17547/9641328/team-sky-2020-vision Accessed 27 November 2020.

BIBLIOGRAPHY

PART ONE

Chapter One

Draganski, B., Gaser, C., Kempermann, G., Kuhn, H.G., Winkler, J., Büchel, C. & May, A. (2006) Temporal and spatial dynamics of brain structure changes during extensive learning. *Journal of neuroscience*, *26*(23), pp.6314-6317.

Gage, F.H. (2002) Neurogenesis in the adult brain. *Journal of neuroscience*, *22*(3), pp.612-613.

Gaser, C. & Schlaug, G. (2003) Gray matter differences between musicians and nonmusicians. *Annals of the New York Academy of Sciences*, *999*(1), pp.514-517.

Kühn, S., Gleich, T., Lorenz, R.C., Lindenberger, U. & Gallinat, J. (2014) Playing Super Mario induces structural brain plasticity: gray matter changes resulting from training with a commercial video game. *Molecular psychiatry*, *19*(2), pp.265-271.

Maguire, E.A., Gadian, D.G., Johnsrude, I.S., Good, C.D., Ashburner, J., Frackowiak, R.S. & Frith, C.D. (2000) Navigation-related structural change in the hippocampi of taxi drivers. *Proceedings of the National Academy of Sciences*, *97*(8), pp.4398-4403.

Mechelli, A., Crinion, J.T., Noppeney, U., O'Doherty, J., Ashburner, J., Frackowiak, R.S. & Price, C.J. (2004) Structural plasticity in the bilingual brain: Proficiency in a second language and age at acquisition affect grey matter density. *Nature*, *431*(7010), pp.757-757.

Chapter Two

Collins, D.J., Abbott, A. and Richards, H. (2011) *Performance Psychology: A practitioner's guide.* Churchill Livingstone.

PART TWO

Chapter Three

Berridge, K.C. (2004) Motivation concepts in behavioral neuroscience. *Physiology & behavior*, *81*(2), pp.179-209.

Deci, E.L. & Ryan, R.M. (2000) The" what" and" why" of goal pursuits: Human needs and the self-determination of behavior. *Psychological inquiry*, *11*(4), pp.227-268.

Duckworth, A.L., Peterson, C., Matthews, M.D. & Kelly, D.R. (2007) Grit: perseverance and passion for long-term goals. *Journal of personality and social psychology*, *92*(6), pp.1087-1101.

Elliot, A.J. & Thrash, T.M. (2002) Approach-avoidance motivation in personality: approach and avoidance temperaments and goals. *Journal of personality and social psychology*, *82*(5), pp.804.-118

Festinger, L. (1957) *A theory of cognitive dissonance.* Stanford University Press.

Greguras, G.J. and Diefendorff, J.M. (2010) Why does proactive personality predict employee life satisfaction and work behaviors? A field investigation of the mediating role of the self-concordance model. *Personnel psychology*, *63*(3), pp.539-560.

Ikemoto, S. & Panksepp, J. (1996) Dissociations between appetitive and consummatory responses by pharmacological manipulations of reward-relevant brain regions. *Behavioral neuroscience*, *110*(2), pp.331-345.

Jennings, J.H., Ung, R.L., Resendez, S.L., Stamatakis, A.M., Taylor, J.G., Huang, J., Veleta, K., Kantak, P.A., Aita, M., Shilling-Scrivo, K., Ramakrishnan, C., Deisseroth, K., Otte, S., & Stuber, G.D. (2015) Visualizing hypothalamic network dynamics for appetitive and consummatory behaviors. *Cell, 160*(3), pp.516-527.

Judge, T. A., Bono, J. E., Erez, A., & Locke, E. A. (2005). Core self-evaluations and job and life satisfaction: The role of self-concordance and goal attainment. *Journal of applied psychology, 90*(2), pp.257–268.

Koestner, R., Lekes, N., Powers, T. A., & Chicoine, E. (2002). Attaining personal goals: Self-concordance plus implementation intentions equals success. *Journal of personality and social psychology, 83*(1), pp.231–244.

Oettingen, G. & Gollwitzer, P.M. (2004). Goal setting and goal striving. In Brewer, M. *Perspectives on social psychology: Emotion and motivation*. pp.165-183. Blackwell Publishing.

Roth, S. & Cohen, L.J. (1986). Approach, avoidance, and coping with stress. *American psychologist, 41*(7), p.813.-819

Sheldon, K.M. (2002). The self-concordance model of healthy goal striving: When personal goals correctly represent the person. In *Handbook of self-determination research*, pp.65-86. edited by Edward L. Deci, Richard M. Ryan. University of Rochester Press.

Sheldon, K.M., Elliot, A.J., Kim, Y. & Kasser, T. (2001). What is satisfying about satisfying events? Testing 10 candidate psychological needs. *Journal of personality and social psychology, 80,* pp.325–339.

Sheldon, K.M. & Kasser, T. (1998). Pursuing personal goals: Skills enable progress but not all progress is beneficial. *Personality and social psychology bulletin, 24*(12), pp.1319-1331.

Smith, A.L., Ntoumanis, N., Duda, J.L. & Vansteenkiste, M. (2011). Goal striving, coping, and well-being: A prospective investigation of the self-concordance model in sport. *Journal of sport and exercise psychology 33*(1) pp.124–145.

Smith, A., Ntoumanis, N. & Duda, J. (2007). Goal striving, goal attainment, and well-being: Adapting and testing the self-concordance model in sport. *Journal of sport and exercise psychology*, *29*(6), pp.763-782.

Vasalampi, K., Salmela-Aro, K. & Nurmi, J.E. (2009). Adolescents' self-concordance, school engagement, and burnout predict their educational trajectories. *European psychologist*, *14*(4), pp.332-341.

Werner, K.M., Milyavskaya, M., Foxen-Craft, E. & Koestner, R. (2016). Some goals just feel easier: Self-concordance leads to goal progress through subjective ease, not effort. *Personality and Individual Differences*, *96*, pp.237-242.

Chapter Four

Biswas-Diener, R. & Dean, B. (2007). *Positive psychology coaching: Putting the science of happiness to work for your clients.* Hoboken, NJ: Wiley.

Burke, D. & Linley, P.A. (2007). Enhancing goal self-concordance through coaching. *International coaching psychology review, 2*(1), pp.62–69.

Clifton, D.O. & Anderson, E. (2002). *StrengthsQuest: Discover and develop your strengths in academics, career, and beyond.* Washington, DC: The Gallup Organization.

Clifton, D. & Harter, J.K. (2003). Investing in strengths. In K. Cameron, J. Dutton & R. Quinn (Eds.), *Positive organisational scholarship: Foundations of a new discipline.* San Francisco: Berrett-Koehler Publishers.

Govindji, R. & Linley, P.A. (2007). Strengths use, self-concordance and well-being: Implications for strengths coaching and coaching psychologists. *International coaching psychology review, 2*(2), pp.143–153.

Linley, P.A. (2008). *Average to A+: Realising strengths in yourself and others.* Coventry, UK: CAPP Press.

Linley, P.A. & Harrington, S. (2006). Strengths coaching: A potential-guided approach to coaching psychology. *International coaching psychology review, 1*(1), pp.37–46.

Linley, P.A., Maltby, J., Wood, A.M., Harrington, S., Peterson, C., Park, N. & Seligman, M.E.P. (2007). Character strengths in the United Kingdom: The VIA Inventory of Strengths. *Personality and individual differences, 43*(2), pp.341–351.

Linley, P.A., Nielsen, K.M., Gillett, R. & Biswas-Diener, R. (2010) Using signature strengths in pursuit of goals: Effects on goal progress, need satisfaction, and well-being, and implications for coaching psychologists. *International coaching psychology review, 5*(1), pp.6-15.

Linley, P.A., Willars, J. & Biswas-Diener, R. (2010). *The strengths book: Be confident, be successful, and enjoy better relationships by realising the best of you.* Coventry, UK: CAPP Press.

Linley, P.A., Woolston, L. & Biswas-Diener, R. (2009). Strengths coaching with leaders. *International coaching psychology review, 4*(1), pp.37–48.

Lyons, L.S. & Linley, P.A. (2008). Situational strengths: A strategic approach linking personal capability to corporate success. *Organisations and people, 15*(2), pp.4–11.

MacKinnon, D.W. (1962) The nature and nurture of creative talent. *American psychologist, 17*(7), p.484-495.

Matthews, M.D., Eid, J., Kelly, D.R., Bailey, J.K.S. & Peterson, C. (2006). Character strengths and virtues of developing military leaders: An international comparison. *Military psychology, 18*(1), S57–S68.

Oishi, S. (2000). Goals as the cornerstones of subjective well-being: Linking individuals and cultures. In E. Diener & E.M. Suh (Eds.), *Culture and subjective well-being* (pp.87–112). Cambridge, MA: MIT Press.

Peterson, C., Park, N., Hall, N. & Seligman, M.E.P. (2009). Zest and work. *Journal of organizational behaviour, 30*(2), pp.161–172.
Peterson, C. & Seligman, M.E.P. (2004). *Character strengths and virtues: A handbook and classification.* New York: Oxford University Press.
Snyder, C.R. & Lopez, S. (2007). *Positive psychology: The scientific and practical explorations of human strengths.* Thousand Oaks, CA: Sage Publications.

Chapter Five

Deci, E.L. & Ryan, R.M. (2000) The" what" and" why" of goal pursuits: Human needs and the self-determination of behavior. *Psychological inquiry, 11*(4), pp.227-268.
Duckworth, A.L., Peterson, C., Matthews, M.D. & Kelly, D.R. (2007) Grit: perseverance and passion for long-term goals. *Journal of personality and social psychology, 92*(6), p.1087-1101.
Duckworth, A.L., Steen, T.A. & Seligman, M.E., 2005. Positive psychology in clinical practice. *Annual review of clinical psychology, 1*, pp.629-651.
Gottschalg, O. and Zollo, M. (2007) Interest alignment and competitive advantage. *Academy of management review, 32*(2), pp.418-437.
Koestner, R., Lekes, N., Powers, T. A., & Chicoine, E. (2002). Attaining personal goals: Self-concordance plus implementation intentions equals success. *Journal of personality and social psychology, 83*(1), pp.231–244.
Sheldon, K.M. & Houser-Marko, L. (2001). Self-concordance, goal attainment, and the pursuit of happiness: Can there be an upward spiral? *Journal of personality and social psychology, 80*, pp.152–165.

Chapter Six

Branson, C.M. (2008) Achieving organisational change through values alignment. *Journal of educational administration. 46*(3) pp.376-395.

Deci, E.L. & Ryan, R.M. (2000) The" what" and" why" of goal pursuits: Human needs and the self-determination of behavior. *Psychological inquiry*, *11*(4), pp.227-268.

Demartini, J.F. (2013) *The Values Factor: The secret to creating an inspired and fulfilling life*. Berkley Books.

Koestner, R., Lekes, N., Powers, T. A., & Chicoine, E. (2002). Attaining personal goals: Self-concordance plus implementation intentions equals success. *Journal of personality and social psychology*, *83*(1), pp.231–244.

Lee, M.A. and Kawachi, I. (2019) The keys to happiness: Associations between personal values regarding core life domains and happiness in South Korea. *PloS one*, *14*(1), p.e0209821.

Niculescu, D.C. (2014) The learning experience in a value-based leadership. *Business excellence and management*, *4*(4), pp.58-69.

Parks, L. and Guay, R.P. (2009) Personality, values, and motivation. *Personality and individual differences*, *47*(7), pp.675-684.

Sheldon, K.M. & Houser-Marko, L. (2001). Self-concordance, goal attainment, and the pursuit of happiness: Can there be an upward spiral? *Journal of personality and social psychology*, *80*, pp.152–165.

Sinek, S. (2009) *Start with why: How great leaders inspire everyone to take action*. New York. Portfolio.

Tomczyk, D., Lee, J. and Winslow, E. (2013) Entrepreneurs' personal values, compensation, and high growth firm performance. *Journal of small business management*, *51*(1), pp.66-82.

Vinson, D.E., Scott, J.E. and Lamont, L.M. (1977) The role of personal values in marketing and consumer behavior. *Journal of marketing*, *41*(2), pp.44-50.

Chapter Seven

Sheldon, K. M., & Elliot, A. J. (1999). Goal striving, need satisfaction, and longitudinal well-being: The self-concordance model. *Journal of personality and social psychology*, *76*(3), pp.482–497.

Sheldon, K.M. & Houser-Marko, L. (2001). Self-concordance, goal attainment, and the pursuit of happiness: Can there be an upward spiral? *Journal of personality and social psychology, 80*(1), pp.152–165.

Chapter Eight

Collins, D.J., Abbott, A. and Richards, H. (2011) *Performance Psychology: A practitioner's guide.* Churchill Livingstone.

Lewis, M. (2003) *Moneyball: The art of winning an unfair game.* WW Norton & Company.

Martindale, R.J., Collins, D. and Daubney, J., 2005. Talent development: A guide for practice and research within sport. *Quest*, *57*(4), pp.353-375.

Chapter Nine

Anders, G. (2011) *The rare find: spotting exceptional talent before everyone else.* London. Portfolio.

Lewis, M. (2003) *Moneyball: The art of winning an unfair game.* WW Norton & Company.

PART THREE

Chapter Ten

Boeckx, C. (2009) *Language in cognition: Uncovering mental structures and the rules behind them.* John Wiley & Sons.

Frydman, M. & Lynn, R. (1992) The general intelligence and spatial abilities of gifted young Belgian chess players. *British journal of psychology*, *83*(2), pp.233-235.

Goschke, T. (1997) Implicit learning and unconscious knowledge: Mental representation, computational mechanisms, and brain structures. In K. Lamberts & D.R. Shanks (Eds.) *Studies in cognition: Knowledge, concepts and categories.* The MIT Press.

Jackendoff, R. (1992) *Languages of the mind: Essays on mental representation.* The MIT Press.

Kagan, J. (2002) *Surprise, uncertainty, and mental structures.* Harvard University Press.

Reber, A.S. (1989) Implicit learning and tacit knowledge. *Journal of experimental psychology: General, 118*(3), p.219-235.

Rebuschat, P. (Ed.) (2015) *Implicit and explicit learning of languages* John Benjamins Publishing Company.

Shenk, D. (2010) *The Genius in All of Us: Why everything you've been told about genetics, talent and IQ is wrong.* Doubleday.

Smith, E.R. (1998) Mental representation and memory. In D.T. Gilbert, S.T. Fiske, & G. Lindzey (Eds.) *The handbook of social psychology*, pp.391-445.

Waters, A.J., Gobet, F. and Leyden, G. (2002) Visuospatial abilities of chess players. *British journal of psychology, 93*(4), pp.557-565.

Zatorre, R.J. (2003) Absolute pitch: a model for understanding the influence of genes and development on neural and cognitive function. *Nature neuroscience, 6*(7), pp.692-695.

Chapter Eleven

Azevedo, R., Faremo, S. and Lajoie, S.P. (2007) Expert-novice differences in mammogram interpretation. In *Proceedings of the annual meeting of the cognitive science society 29*(29).

Camerer, C.F. & Johnson, E.J. (1997) The process-performance paradox in expert judgment: How can experts know so much and predict so badly? *Research on judgment and decision making: Currents, connections, and controversies, 342.*

Chase, W.G. and Ericsson, K.A., 1981. Skilled memory. In J.R. Anderson (Ed.) *Cognitive skills and their acquisition*, Routledge.

Choudhry, N.K., Fletcher, R.H. & Soumerai, S.B. (2005) Systematic review: the relationship between clinical experience and quality of health care. *Annals of Internal medicine*, *142*(4), pp.260-273.

Chow, J.Y., Shuttleworth, R., Davids, K. & Araújo, D. (2019) Ecological dynamics and transfer from practice to performance in sport. In N.J. Hodges & A.M. Williams (Eds.) *Skill acquisition in sport: Research, theory and practice*. Routledge.

Collins, D.J., Abbott, A. & Richards, H. (2011) *Performance psychology: A practitioner's guide*. Churchill Livingstone.

Davids, K., Araújo, D., Shuttleworth, R. & Button, C. (2003) Acquiring skill in sport: A constraints-led perspective. *International journal of computer science in sport*, *2*(2), pp.31-39.

de Bot, K., Lowie, W. & Verspoor, M. (2007) A dynamic systems theory approach to second language acquisition. *Bilingualism: Language and cognition*, *10*(1), pp.7-21.

Ericsson, K.A. & Polson, P.G. (1988) A cognitive analysis of exceptional memory for restaurant orders. In M.T.H. Chi, R. Glaser & M.J.Farr (Eds.) *The nature of expertise*, Laurence Erlbaum Associates, Inc..

Grabner, R.H., Neubauer, A.C. & Stern, E. (2006) Superior performance and neural efficiency: The impact of intelligence and expertise. *Brain research bulletin*, *69*(4), pp.422-439.

Hambrick, D.Z., Oswald, F.L., Altmann, E.M., Meinz, E.J., Gobet, F. & Campitelli, G. (2014) Deliberate practice: Is that all it takes to become an expert? *Intelligence*, *45*, pp.34-45.

Hodges, N.J. & Williams, A.M. (2012) *Skill acquisition in sport: Research, theory and practice*. Routledge.

Kaufman, S.B. (2013) *The complexity of greatness: Beyond talent or practice*. Oxford University Press, USA.

Mann, D.L., Farrow, D., Shuttleworth, R. & Hopwood, M. (2009) The influence of viewing perspective on decision-making and visual search behaviour in an invasive sport. *International journal of sport psychology*, *40*(4), pp.546-564.

Miglioretti, D.L., Gard, C.C., Carney, P.A., Onega, T.L., Buist, D.S., Sickles, E.A., Kerlikowske, K., Rosenberg, R.D., Yankaskas, B.C., Geller, B.M. & Elmore, J.G. (2009) When radiologists perform best: the learning curve in screening mammogram interpretation. *Radiology*, *253*(3), pp.632-640.

Müller, S. & Abernethy, B. (2012) Expert anticipatory skill in striking sports: A review and a model. *Research quarterly for exercise and sport*, *83*(2), pp.175-187.

Renshaw, I., Davids, K.W., Shuttleworth, R. & Chow, J.Y. (2009) Insights from ecological psychology and dynamical systems theory can underpin a philosophy of coaching. *International journal of sport psychology*, *40*(4), pp.580-602.

Rodriguez-Paz, J., Kennedy, M., Salas, E., Wu, A.W., Sexton, J.B., Hunt, E.A. & Pronovost, P.J. (2009) Beyond "see one, do one, teach one": toward a different training paradigm. *BMJ quality & safety*, *18*(1), pp.63-68.

Sikes, P.L. (2013) The effects of specific practice strategy use on university string players' performance. *Journal of research in music education*, *61*(3), pp.318-333.

Spengler, P.M. & Pilipis, L.A. (2015) A comprehensive meta-reanalysis of the robustness of the experience-accuracy effect in clinical judgment. *Journal of counseling psychology*, *62*(3), pp.360-378.

Stone, J.A., Rothwell, M., Shuttleworth, R. & Davids, K. (2020) Exploring sports coaches' experiences of using a contemporary pedagogical approach to coaching: an international perspective. *Qualitative research in sport, exercise and health*, pp.1-19.

van de Wiel, M.W., Van den Bossche, P., Janssen, S. & Jossberger, H. (2011) Exploring deliberate practice in medicine: how do physicians learn in the workplace? *Advances in health sciences education*, *16*(1), pp.81-95.

Vickers, J.N. (2007) *Perception, cognition, and decision training: The quiet eye in action*. Human Kinetics.

Waters, A.J., Gobet, F. & Leyden, G. (2002) Visuospatial abilities of chess players. *British journal of psychology*, *93*(4), pp.557-565.

Woods, C.T., McKeown, I., Shuttleworth, R.J., Davids, K. & Robertson, S. (2019) Training programme designs in professional team sport: An ecological dynamics exemplar. *Human movement science*, *66*, pp.318-326.

Chapter Twelve

Araújo, D., Davids, K., Bennett, S.J., Button, C. & Chapman, G. (2004) Emergence of sport skills under constraints. In N.J. Hodges & A.M. Williams (Eds.) *Skill acquisition in sport: Research, theory and practice*, Routledge.

Baker, J. & Young, B. (2014) 20 years later: Deliberate practice and the development of expertise in sport. *International review of sport and exercise psychology*, *7*(1), pp.135-157.

Bond, W., Kuhn, G., Binstadt, E., Quirk, M., Wu, T., Tews, M., Dev, P. & Ericsson, K.A. (2008) The use of simulation in the development of individual cognitive expertise in emergency medicine. *Academic emergency medicine*, *15*(11), pp.1037-1045.

Clapper, T.C. & Kardong-Edgren, S. (2012) Using deliberate practice and simulation to improve nursing skills. *Clinical simulation in nursing*, *8*(3), pp.e109-e113.

Collins, D.J., Abbott, A. & Richards, H. (2011) *Performance psychology: A practitioner's guide*. Churchill Livingstone.

Davids, K.W., Button, C. & Bennett, S.J. (2007) *Dynamics of skill acquisition: A constraints-led approach*. Human Kinetics.

Duckworth, A.L., Kirby, T.A., Tsukayama, E., Berstein, H. & Ericsson, K.A. (2011) Deliberate practice spells success: Why grittier competitors triumph at the National Spelling Bee. *Social psychological and personality science*, *2*(2), pp.174-181.

Endsley, M.R. (2006) Expertise and situation awareness. In K.A. Ericsson, N. Charness, P.J. Feltovich & R.R. Hoffman (Eds.) *The Cambridge handbook of expertise and expert performance*, Cambridge University Press.

Ericsson, K.A. (2006) The influence of experience and deliberate practice on the development of superior expert performance. In K.A. Ericsson, N. Charness, P.J. Feltovich & R.R. Hoffman (Eds.) *The Cambridge handbook of expertise and expert performance*, Cambridge University Press.

Ericsson, K.A. (2008) Deliberate practice and acquisition of expert performance: a general overview. *Academic emergency medicine*, *15*(11), pp.988-994.

Hodges, N.J. & Williams, A.M. (2012) *Skill acquisition in sport: Research, theory and practice*. Routledge.

Krampe, R.T. & Ericsson, K.A. (1996) Maintaining excellence: Ddeliberate practice and elite performance in young and older pianists. *Journal of experimental psychology: general*, *125*(4), p.331-359.

Passos, P., Araújo, D., Davids, K. & Shuttleworth, R. (2008) Manipulating constraints to train decision making in rugby union. *International journal of sports science & coaching*, *3*(1), pp.125-140.

Pill, S. (2014) Informing game sense pedagogy with constraints led theory for coaching in Australian football. *Sports coaching review*, *3*(1), pp.46-62.

Ramos, A., Coutinho, P., Davids, K. & Mesquita, I. (2020) Developing players' tactical knowledge using combined constraints-led and step-game approaches—A longitudinal action-research study. *Research quarterly for exercise and sport*, pp.1-15.

Renshaw, I., Davids, K., Newcombe, D. & Roberts, W. (2019) *The constraints-led approach: Principles for sports coaching and practice design*. Routledge.

Sonnentag, S. & Kleine, B.M. (2000) Deliberate practice at work: A study with insurance agents. *Journal of occupational and organizational psychology*, *73*(1), pp.87-102.

Ward, P., Hodges, N.J. & Williams, A.M. (2004) Deliberate practice and expert performance: Defining the path to excellence. In Hodges, N.J. & Williams, A.M. (Eds.) *Skill acquisition in sport: Research, theory and practice*. Routledge.

Chapter Thirteen

Araújo, D., Davids, K., Bennett, S.J., Button, C. & Chapman, G. (2004) Emergence of sport skills under constraints. In N.J. Hodges & A.M. Williams (Eds.) *Skill acquisition in sport: Research, theory and practice*, Routledge.

Davids, K., Güllich, A., Shuttleworth, R. & Araújo, D. (2017) Understanding environmental and task constraints on talent development: Analysis of micro-structure of practice and macro-structure of development histories. In J. Baker, S. Cobley, J. Schorer & N. Wattie (Eds.) *Routledge handbook of talent identification and development in sport*. Routledge.

Davids, K.W., Button, C. & Bennett, S.J. (2008) *Dynamics of skill acquisition: A constraints-led approach*. Human Kinetics.

Gorman, A.D. (2010) Using constraints to enhance decision-making in team sports. *Motor learning in practice: A constraints-led approach*, p.144.

Hodges, N.J. & Williams, A.M. (2012) *Skill acquisition in sport: Research, theory and practice*. Routledge.

Pill, S. (2014) Informing game sense pedagogy with constraints led theory for coaching in Australian football. *Sports coaching review*, *3*(1), pp.46-62.

Chapter Fourteen

Collins, D.J., Abbott, A. & Richards, H. (2011) *Performance psychology: A practitioner's guide*. Churchill Livingstone.

Davids, K., Araújo, D., Shuttleworth, R. & Button, C. (2003) Acquiring skill in sport: A constraints-led perspective. *International journal of computer science in sport*, *2*(2), pp.31-39.

Davids, K.W., Button, C. & Bennett, S.J. (2007) *Dynamics of skill acquisition: A constraints-led approach*. Human Kinetics.

de Bot, K., Lowie, W. & Verspoor, M. (2007) A dynamic systems theory approach to second language acquisition. *Bilingualism: Language and cognition*, *10*(1), pp.7-21.

Ericsson, K.A. (2006) The influence of experience and deliberate practice on the development of superior expert performance. In K.A. Ericsson, N. Charness, P.J. Feltovich & R.R. Hoffman (Eds.) *The Cambridge handbook of expertise and expert performance*, Cambridge University Press.

Renshaw, I., Davids, K., Newcombe, D. & Roberts, W. (2019) *The constraints-led approach: Principles for sports coaching and practice design*. Routledge.

Renshaw, I., Davids, K.W., Shuttleworth, R. & Chow, J.Y. (2009) Insights from ecological psychology and dynamical systems theory can underpin a philosophy of coaching. *International journal of sport psychology*, *40*(4), pp.580-602.

Chapter Fifteen

Bandura, A. (1997). *Self-efficacy: The exercise of control.* New York: WH Freeman.

Burke, D. & Linley, P.A. (2007). Enhancing goal self-concordance through coaching. *International coaching psychology review, 2*(1), 62–69.

Butler, R.J., Smith, M. & Irwin, I. (1993) The performance profile in practice. *Journal of applied sport psychology, 5*(1), pp.48-63.

Corno, L. (1993) The best-laid plans: Modern conceptions of volition and educational research. *Educational researcher, 22*(2), pp.14-22.

Dale, G.A. & Wrisberg, C.A. (1996) The use of a performance profiling technique in a team setting: Getting the athletes and coach on the "same page". The sport psychologist, 10(3), pp.261-277.

Deci, E.L. & Ryan, R.M. (2000) The" what" and" why" of goal pursuits: Human needs and the self-determination of behavior. *Psychological inquiry, 11*(4), pp.227-268.

Doyle, J. & Parfitt, G. (1996) Performance profiling and predictive validity. *Journal of Applied Sport Psychology, 8*(2), pp.160-170.

Finnie, R., Poirier, W., Bozkurt, E., Peterson, J.B., Fricker, T. & Pratt, M. (2017) *Using future authoring to improve student outcomes.* Toronto: Higher Education Quality Council of Ontario.

Gagné, M., & Deci, E. L. (2005). Self-determination theory and work motivation. *Journal of organizational behavior*, 26, 331-362.

Jones, G. (1993) The role of performance profiling in cognitive behavioral interventions in sport. *The sport psychologist, 7*(2), pp.160-172.

Joseph, S. (2006). Person-centred coaching psychology: A meta-theoretical perspective. *International coaching psychology review, 1*, 47–54.

Kamenetz, A. (2015) The Writing Assignment That Changes Lives. *NPR ED* https://www.npr.org/sections/ed/2015/07/10/419202925/the-writing-assignment-that-changes-lives (Retrieved 18 November 2020).

Matthews, M.D. (2012) Cognitive and non-cognitive factors in soldier performance. *The Oxford handbook of military psychology*

Morisano, D., Hirsh, J.B., Peterson, J.B., Pihl, R.O. & Shore, B.M. (2010) Setting, elaborating, and reflecting on personal goals improves academic performance. *Journal of applied psychology, 95*(2), p.255-264.

Novak, E. (2014) Toward a mathematical model of motivation, volition, and performance. *Computers & education, 74*, pp.73-80.

Ryan, R. M. & Deci, E. L. (2000) Self-determination theory and the facilitation of intrinsic motivation, social development and well-being. *American psychologist, 55*(1), 68-78.

Skare, M., Hopkins, W.G. & Solberg, P.A. (2017) Determinants of vitality during a training cycle in a cohort of Special Forces operators, *Military psychology, 29*(1). pp.1-10.

Weston, N.J., Greenlees, I.A. & Thelwell, R.C. (2011a) Athlete perceptions of the impacts of performance profiling. *International journal of sport and exercise psychology. 9*(2). pp.173-188.

Weston, N.J., Greenlees, I.A. & Thelwell, R.C. (2011b. The impact of a performance profiling intervention on athletes' intrinsic motivation. *Research quarterly for exercise and sport, 82*(1), pp.151-155.

Weston, N.J.V. (2016) The application and impact of performance profiling in sport. In A. Lane (Ed.) *Sport and exercise psychology.* Routledge.

Chapter Sixteen

Ben-Shahar, T. (2009) *The pursuit of perfect: How to stop chasing perfection and start living a richer, happier life.* McGraw Hill Education.

Cannon, M.D. & Edmondson, A.C. (2005) Failing to learn and learning to fail (intelligently): How great organizations put failure to work to innovate and improve. *Long range planning, 38*(3), pp.299-319.

Carver, C.S. & Connor-Smith, J. (2010) Personality and coping. *Annual review of psychology, 61*, pp.679-704.

Dweck, C. (September 15, 2015) Carol Dweck revisits the growth mindset. *Education Week 35*(5) pp.20-24.

Dweck, C. (2012) *Mindset: Changing the way you think to fulfil your potential.* Little, Brown Book Group.

Dweck, C.S. (2002) Messages that motivate: How praise molds students' beliefs, motivation, and performance (in surprising ways). In J. Aronson (Ed.) *Improving academic achievement: Impact of psychological factors in education.* Academic Press.

Dweck, C.S. (2000) *Self-theories: Their role in motivation, personality, and development.* Psychology press.

Dweck, C.S. (1986) Motivational processes affecting learning. *American psychologist, 41*(10), pp.1040-1048.

Dweck, C.S., Chiu, C.Y. & Hong, Y.Y. (1995) Implicit theories and their role in judgments and reactions: A word from two perspectives. *Psychological inquiry, 6*(4), pp.267-285.

Dweck, C.S. & Leggett, E.L. (1988) A social-cognitive approach to motivation and personality. *Psychological review, 95*(2), pp.256-273.

Dweck, C.S. & Reppucci, N.D. (1973) Learned helplessness and reinforcement responsibility in children. *Journal of personality and social psychology, 25*(1), pp.109-116.

Elliott, E.S. & Dweck, C.S. (1988) Goals: An approach to motivation and achievement. *Journal of personality and social psychology*, *54*(1), pp.5-12.

Lazarus, R.S. & Folkman, S. (1984) *Stress, appraisal, and coping*. Springer publishing company.

Kamins, M.L. & Dweck, C.S. (1999) Person versus process praise and criticism: Implications for contingent self-worth and coping. *Developmental psychology*, *35*(3), pp.835-847.

Mruk, C.J. (2013) *Self-esteem and positive psychology: Research, theory, and practice, 4th edition*. Springer publishing company.

Seligman, M.E. (2006) *Learned optimism: How to change your mind and your life*. New York, Vintage books.

Seligman, M.E. (2002) Positive psychology, positive prevention, and positive therapy. In C.R. Snyder (Ed.) *Handbook of positive psychology*, Oxford University Press.

Wilson, T.D. & Gilbert, D.T. (2005) Affective forecasting: Knowing what to want. *Current directions in psychological science*, *14*(3), pp.131-134.

Yeager, D.S. & Dweck, C.S. (2012) Mindsets that promote resilience: When students believe that personal characteristics can be developed. *Educational psychologist*, *47*(4), pp.302-314.

Zeidner, M. & Saklofske, D. (1996) Adaptive and maladaptive coping. In M. Zeidner & N.S.Endler *Handbook of coping: Theory, research, applications*. John Wiley & Sons.

PART FOUR

Chapter Seventeen

Coon, D. & Mitterer, J.O. (2012) Introduction to psychology: Gateways to mind and behavior with concept maps and reviews. Cengage Learning.

LeDoux, J., (2003). The emotional brain, fear, and the amygdala. Cellular and molecular neurobiology, 23(4-5), pp.727-738.

Lindsay, P.H. & Norman, D.A. (1977) Human information processing: An introduction to psychology. New York. Academic press.

Mesagno, C., Marchant, D. and Morris, T., (2008) A pre-performance routine to alleviate choking in "choking-susceptible" athletes. The sport psychologist, 22(4), pp.439-457.

Peters, S. (2013) *The chimp paradox: The mind management program to help you achieve success, confidence, and happiness.* TarcherPerigee.

Toner, J., Montero, B.G. and Moran, A., (2015) Considering the role of cognitive control in expert performance. Phenomenology and the Cognitive Sciences, 14(4), pp.1127-1144.

Chapter Eighteen

Bakker, A.B. (2005) Flow among music teachers and their students: The crossover of peak experiences. *Journal of vocational behavior*, *66*(1), pp.26-44.

Bompa, T.O. & Buzzichelli, C. (2018) *Periodization-: theory and methodology of training, 6th Edition* Human kinetics.

Csikszentmihalyi, M. (1997) *Finding flow: The psychology of engagement with everyday life.* Basic books.

Csikszentmihalyi, M., Abuhamdeh, S. & Nakamura, J. (1990) Flow. In A.J. Elliot & C.S. Dweck (Eds.) *Handbook of competence and motivation.* Guildford Publications.

Groppel, J.L., Andelman, B. & Loehr, J. (1999) *The corporate athlete: How to achieve maximal performance in business and life*. John Wiley & Sons Inc.

Jackson, S.A. & Csikszentmihalyi, M. (1999) *Flow in sports: The keys to optimal experiences and performances*. Human Kinetics.

Kellmann, M. (2010) Preventing overtraining in athletes in high-intensity sports and stress/recovery monitoring. *Scandinavian journal of medicine & science in sports*, *20*(2), pp.95-102.

Loehr, J. & Schwartz, T. (2001) The making of a corporate athlete. *Harvard business review*, *79*(1), pp.120-129.

Loehr, J., & Schwartz, T. (2003) *The power of full engagement: Managing energy, not time, is the key to high performance and personal renewal.* New York. Simon and Schuster.

Lundberg, U. (2005) Stress hormones in health and illness: the roles of work and gender. *Psychoneuroendocrinology*, *30*(10), pp.1017-1021.

Lundberg, U. (2003) Psychological stress and musculoskeletal disorders: psychobiological mechanisms. Lack of rest and recovery greater problem than workload. *Lakartidningen*, *100*(21), pp.1892-1895.

Maslach, C. (2003) *Burnout: The cost of caring*. Cambridge, MA. Malor Books.

Maslach, C. & Goldberg, J. (1998) Prevention of burnout: New perspectives. *Applied and preventive psychology*, *7*(1), pp.63-74.

Maslach, C. & Leiter, M.P. (2006) Burnout. *Stress and quality of working life: Current perspectives in occupational health*, *37*, pp.42-49.

Matsui, T., Ishikawa, T., Ito, H., Okamoto, M., Inoue, K., Lee, M.C., Fujikawa, T., Ichitani, Y., Kawanaka, K. & Soya, H. (2012) Brain glycogen supercompensation following exhaustive exercise. *The journal of physiology*, *590*(3), pp.607-616.

Nakamura, J. & Csikszentmihalyi, M. (2014) The concept of flow. In M. Csikszentmihalyi (Ed.) *Flow and the foundations of positive psychology: The collected works of Mihaly Csikszentmihalyi*. Springer, Dordrecht.

Pines, A. & Aronson, E. (1988) *Career burnout: Causes and cures*. Free press.

Plutchik, R. (1997) The circumplex as a general model of the structure of emotions and personality. In R.E. Plutchik & H.R. Conte (Eds.). *Circumplex models of personality and emotions.* American Psychological Association.

Posner, J., Russell, J.A. & Peterson, B.S. (2005) The circumplex model of affect: An integrative approach to affective neuroscience, cognitive development, and psychopathology. *Development and psychopathology*, *17*(3), pp.715-734.

Russell, J.A. (1980) A circumplex model of affect. *Journal of personality and social psychology*, *39*(6), p.1161-1178.

Shirom, A. (2003) Job-related burnout: A review. In J.C. Quick & L.E. Tetrick (Eds.) *Handbook of occupational health psychology.* American Psychological Association.

Chapter Nineteen

Cohn, P.J. (1990) Pre-performance routines in sport: Theoretical support and practical applications. *The sport psychologist*, *4*(3), pp.301-312.

Chapter Twenty

Abma, C.L., Fry, M.D., Li, Y. & Relyea, G. (2002) Differences in imagery content and imagery ability between high and low confident track and field athletes. *Journal of applied sport psychology*, *14*(2), pp.67-75.

Adan, A. (2012) Cognitive performance and dehydration. *Journal of the American College of Nutrition*, *31*(2), pp.71-78.

Alford, B.A. & Beck, A.T. (1994) Cognitive therapy of delusional beliefs. *Behaviour research and therapy*, *32*(3), pp.369-380.

Armstrong, L.E., Ganio, M.S., Casa, D.J., Lee, E.C., McDermott, B.P., Klau, J.F., Jimenez, L., Le Bellego, L., Chevillotte, E. & Lieberman, H.R. (2012) Mild dehydration affects mood in healthy young women. *The journal of nutrition*, *142*(2), pp.382-388.

Arora, S. (2013) Surgeons in training may benefit from mental visualisation. *BMJ*, *346*.

Benton, D. (2002) Carbohydrate ingestion, blood glucose and mood. *Neuroscience & biobehavioral reviews*, *26*(3), pp.293-308.

Bloch, S. (1993) Alba Emoting: A psychophysiological technique to help actors create and control real emotions. *Theatre Topics*, *3*(2), pp.121-138.

Bloch, S., Lemeignan, M. & Aguilera-T, N. (1991) Specific respiratory patterns distinguish among human basic emotions. *International journal of psychophysiology*, *11*(2), pp.141-154.

Bodenhamer, B.G. & Hall, L.M. (1998) *The user's manual for the brain volume I: The complete manual for neuro-linguistic programming practitioner certification*. Crown House Publishing.

Bowers, L.A. (1996) An exploration of holistic and nontraditional healing methods including research in the use of neuro-linguistic programming in the adjunctive treatment of acute pain. *Dissertation Abstracts International: Sciences and Engineering*, *6379*.

Bradley, M.M., Moulder, B. & Lang, P.J. (2005) When good things go bad: the reflex physiology of defense. *Psychological science*, *16*(6), pp.468-473.

Brunyé, T.T., Mahoney, C.R., Giles, G.E., Rapp, D.N., Taylor, H.A. & Kanarek, R.B. (2013) Learning to relax: Evaluating four brief interventions for overcoming the negative emotions accompanying math anxiety. *Learning and individual differences*, *27*, pp.1-7.

Carney, D.R., Cuddy, A.J. & Yap, A.J. (2010) Power posing: Brief nonverbal displays affect neuroendocrine levels and risk tolerance. *Psychological science*, *21*(10), pp.1363-1368.

Chandla, S.S., Sood, S., Dogra, R., Das, S., Shukla, S.K. & Gupta, S. (2013) Effect of short-term practice of pranayamic breathing exercises on cognition, anxiety, general well being and heart rate variability. *Journal of the Indian Medical Association*, *111*(10), pp.662-665.

Chevalier, G. & Sinatra, S.T. (2011) Emotional stress, heart rate variability, grounding, and improved autonomic tone: clinical applications. *Integrative medicine*, *10*(3), pp.16-21.

Cockerton, T., Moore, S. & Norman, D. (1997) Cognitive test performance and background music. *Perceptual and motor skills*, *85*(3), pp.1435-1438.

Cuddy, A.J., Wilmuth, C.A. & Carney, D.R., 2012. The benefit of power posing before a high-stakes social evaluation. *Harvard Business School scholarly articles*.

Cuddy, A.J., Wilmuth, C.A., Yap, A.J. & Carney, D.R. (2015) Preparatory power posing affects nonverbal presence and job interview performance. *Journal of applied psychology*, *100*(4), pp.1286-1295.

de Tord, P. and Bräuninger, I. (2015) Grounding: Theoretical application and practice in dance movement therapy. *The arts in psychotherapy*, *43*, pp.16-22.

Dolbier, C.L. & Rush, T.E. (2012) Efficacy of abbreviated progressive muscle relaxation in a high-stress college sample. *International journal of stress management*, *19*(1), pp.48-68.

Eberth, J. & Sedlmeier, P. (2012) The effects of mindfulness meditation: a meta-analysis. *Mindfulness*, *3*, pp.174-189.

Feldman, G., Greeson, J. & Senville, J. (2010) Differential effects of mindful breathing, progressive muscle relaxation, and loving-kindness meditation on decentering and negative reactions to repetitive thoughts. *Behaviour research and therapy*, *48*(10), pp.1002-1011.

Froján-Parga, M.X., Calero-Elvira, A. & Montaño-Fidalgo, M. (2011) Study of the Socratic method during cognitive restructuring. *Clinical psychology & psychotherapy*, *18*(2), pp.110-123.

Ganio, M.S., Armstrong, L.E., Casa, D.J., McDermott, B.P., Lee, E.C., Yamamoto, L.M., Marzano, S., Lopez, R.M., Jimenez, L., Le Bellego, L., Chevillotte, E. & Lieberman, H. (2011) Mild dehydration impairs cognitive performance and mood of men. *British journal of nutrition*, *106*(10), pp.1535-1543.

Grandjean, A.C. & Grandjean, N.R. (2007) Dehydration and cognitive performance. *Journal of the American College of Nutrition*, *26*(5), pp.549S-554S.

Gregg, M., Hall, C. & Nederhof, E. (2005) The imagery ability, imagery use, and performance relationship. *The Sport Psychologist*, *19*(1), pp.93-99.

Gröpel, P. & Mesagno, C. (2019) Choking interventions in sports: A systematic review. *International review of sport and exercise psychology*, *12*(1), pp.176-201.

Grosu, V.T., Popovici, C., Dumitrescu, M. & Grosu, E.F. (2014) Expression of sensory submodalities by neurolinguistic programming methods in sport training. *Palestrica of the third millennium civilization & sport*, *15*(3).

Haldi, J. & Wynn, W. (1946) The effect of low and high carbohydrate meals on the blood sugar level and on work performance in strenuous exercise of short duration. *American journal of physiology*, *145*(3), pp.402-410.

Hardy, J. (2006) Speaking clearly: A critical review of the self-talk literature. *Psychology of sport and exercise*, *7*(1), pp.81-97.

Harmison, R.J. (2006) Peak performance in sport: Identifying ideal performance states and developing athletes' psychological skills. *Professional psychology: research and practice*, *37*(3), pp.233-243.

Hatzigeorgiadis, A., Galanis, E., Zourbanos, N. & Theodorakis, Y. (2014) A self-talk intervention for competitive sport performance. *Journal of applied sport psychology*, *26*(1), pp.82-95.

Hatzigeorgiadis, A., Theodorakis, Y. & Zourbanos, N. (2004) Self-talk in the swimming pool: The effects of self-talk on thought content and performance on water-polo tasks. *Journal of applied sport psychology*, *16*(2), pp.138-150.

Hatzigeorgiadis, A., Zourbanos, N., Galanis, E. & Theodorakis, Y. (2011) Self-talk and sports performance: A meta-analysis. *Perspectives on psychological science*, *6*(4), pp.348-356.

Hatzigeorgiadis, A., Zourbanos, N., Mpoumpaki, S. & Theodorakis, Y. (2009) Mechanisms underlying the self-talk–performance relationship: The effects of motivational self-talk on self-confidence and anxiety. *Psychology of sport and exercise*, *10*(1), pp.186-192.

Holmes, P.S. & Collins, D.J. (2001) The PETTLEP approach to motor imagery: A functional equivalence model for sport psychologists. *Journal of applied sport psychology*, *13*(1), pp.60-83.

Hölzel, B.K., Lazar, S.W., Gard, T., Schuman-Olivier, Z., Vago, D.R. & Ott, U., (2011) How does mindfulness meditation work? Proposing mechanisms of action from a conceptual and neural perspective. *Perspectives on psychological science*, *6*(6), pp.537-559.

Jerath, R., Crawford, M.W., Barnes, V.A. & Harden, K. (2015) Self-regulation of breathing as a primary treatment for anxiety. *Applied psychophysiology and biofeedback*, *40*(2), pp.107-115.

Jacobson, E. (1938) Progressive muscle relaxation. *Journal of abnormal psychology*, *75*(1), p.18.

Kalisch, R., Wiech, K., Critchley, H.D., Seymour, B., O'Doherty, J.P., Oakley, D.A., Allen, P. & Dolan, R.J. (2005) Anxiety reduction through detachment: subjective, physiological, and neural effects. *Journal of cognitive neuroscience*, *17*(6), pp.874-883.

Kalisch, R., Wiech, K., Herrmann, K. & Dolan, R.J. (2006) Neural correlates of self-distraction from anxiety and a process model of cognitive emotion regulation. *Journal of cognitive neuroscience*, *18*(8), pp.1266-1276.

Kim, S.H. & Hamann, S. (2007) Neural correlates of positive and negative emotion regulation. *Journal of cognitive neuroscience*, *19*(5), pp.776-798.

Kazantzis, N., Fairburn, C.G., Padesky, C.A., Reinecke, M. & Teesson, M. (2014) Unresolved issues regarding the research and practice of cognitive behavior therapy: The case of guided discovery using Socratic questioning. *Behaviour Change*, *31*(1), pp.1-17.

Kraft, R.G., Claiborn, C.D. & Dowd, E.T. (1985) Effects of positive reframing and paradoxical directives in counseling for negative emotions. *Journal of counseling psychology*, *32*(4), pp.617-621.

Lambert, N.M., Fincham, F.D. & Stillman, T.F. (2012) Gratitude and depressive symptoms: The role of positive reframing and positive emotion. *Cognition & emotion*, *26*(4), pp.615-633.

Langer, E.J. (1989) *Mindfulness*. Addison-Wesley/Addison Wesley Longman.

Lévesque, J., Eugene, F., Joanette, Y., Paquette, V., Mensour, B., Beaudoin, G., Leroux, J.M., Bourgouin, P. & Beauregard, M. (2003) Neural circuitry underlying voluntary suppression of sadness. *Biological psychiatry*, *53*(6), pp.502-510.

Lieberman, H.R. (2007) Hydration and cognition: a critical review and recommendations for future research. *Journal of the American College of Nutrition*, *26*(5), pp.555S-561S.

Löw, A., Lang, P.J., Smith, J.C. & Bradley, M.M. (2008) Both predator and prey: Emotional arousal in threat and reward. *Psychological science*, *19*(9), pp.865-873.

Löw, A., Weymar, M. & Hamm, A.O. (2015) When threat is near, get out of here: Dynamics of defensive behavior during freezing and active avoidance. *Psychological science*, *26*(11), pp.1706-1716.

MacIntyre, T. and Moran, A. (2010) Meta-imagery processes among elite sports performers. In A. Guillot & C. Collet (Eds.) *The neurophysiological foundations of mental and motor imagery*, Oxford University Press.

MacMorran, P.R. (1988) Brief treatment for disturbing memory: A neuro-linguistic programming submodality procedure.

MacPherson, A.C., Collins, D. & Obhi, S.S. (2009) The importance of temporal structure and rhythm for the optimum performance of motor skills: A new focus for practitioners of sport psychology. *Journal of applied sport psychology*, *21*(S1), pp.S48-S61.

McCallie, M.S., Blum, C.M. & Hood, C.J. (2006) Progressive muscle relaxation. *Journal of human behavior in the social environment*, *13*(3), pp.51-66.

McRae, K., Hughes, B., Chopra, S., Gabrieli, J.D., Gross, J.J. & Ochsner, K.N. (2010) The neural bases of distraction and reappraisal. *Journal of cognitive neuroscience*, *22*(2), pp.248-262.

Moritz, S.E., Hall, C.R., Martin, K.A. & Vadocz, E. (1996) What are confident athletes imaging?: An examination of image content. *The sport psychologist*, *10*(2), pp.171-179.

Ottley, C. (2000) Food and mood. *Nursing standard*, *15*(3) pp.46-52.

Páez, D., Martínez-Sánchez, F., Mendiburo, A., Bobowik, M. & Sevillano, V. (2013) Affect regulation strategies and perceived emotional adjustment for negative and positive affect: a study on anger, sadness and joy. *The Journal of Positive Psychology*, *8*(3), pp.249-262.

Parlamis, J.D. (2012) Venting as emotion regulation: The influence of venting responses and respondent identity on anger and emotional tone. *International journal of conflict management*, *23*(1), pp.77-96.

Randall, W.M., Rickard, N.S. & Vella-Brodrick, D.A. (2014) Emotional outcomes of regulation strategies used during personal music listening: A mobile experience sampling study. *Musicae scientiae*, *18*(3), pp.275-291.

Robb, S.L. (2000) Music assisted progressive muscle relaxation, progressive muscle relaxation, music listening, and silence: A comparison of relaxation techniques. *Journal of music therapy*, *37*(1), pp.2-21.

Saarikallio, S. (2011) Music as emotional self-regulation throughout adulthood. *Psychology of music*, *39*(3), pp.307-327.

Sanchez, X., Moss, S.L., Twist, C. & Karageorghis, C.I. (2014) On the role of lyrics in the music–exercise performance relationship. *Psychology of sport and exercise*, *15*(1), pp.132-138.

Shanteau, J. (1988) Psychological characteristics and strategies of expert decision makers. *Acta psychologica*, *68*(1-3), pp.203-215.

Shukla, A. (November 26, 2019) A 5-step mindfulness grounding technique to ease anxiety & why mindfulness works. *Cognition Today* (https://cognitiontoday.com/5-step-mindfulness-grounding-technique-to-ease-anxiety-why-it-works/) Retrieved 18 November 2020.

Stoeber, J. & Janssen, D.P. (2011) Perfectionism and coping with daily failures: Positive reframing helps achieve satisfaction at the end of the day. *Anxiety, stress & coping*, *24*(5), pp.477-497.

Stork, M.J., Kwan, M.Y., Gibala, M.J. & Martin Ginis, K.A. (2015) Music enhances performance and perceived enjoyment of sprint interval exercise. *Medicine and science in sports and exercise*, *47*(5), pp.1052-1060.

Tang, Y.Y., Hölzel, B.K. & Posner, M.I. (2015) The neuroscience of mindfulness meditation. *Nature Reviews Neuroscience*, *16*(4), pp.213-225.

Taylor, L.A. & Rachman, S.J. (1988) The effects of blood sugar level changes on cognitive function, affective state, and somatic symptoms. *Journal of behavioral medicine*, *11*(3), pp.279-291.

Teodor, G.V., Florina, G.E., Cornelia, S., Marin, D. & Gheorghe, F. (2014) The place of sensorial submodalities in ideomotor representations of neurolinguistic programming. *Global journal of arts education*, *4*(2).

Theodorakis, Y., Weinberg, R., Natsis, P., Douma, I. & Kazakas, P. (2000) The effects of motivational versus instructional self-talk on improving motor performance. *The sport psychologist*, *14*(3), pp.253-271.

Thoma, M.V., Scholz, U., Ehlert, U. & Nater, U.M. (2012) Listening to music and physiological and psychological functioning: The mediating role of emotion regulation and stress reactivity. *Psychology & health*, *27*(2), pp.227-241.

Tod, D., Hardy, J. & Oliver, E. (2011) Effects of self-talk: A systematic review. *Journal of sport and exercise psychology*, *33*(5), pp.666-687.

van Reekum, C.M., Johnstone, T., Urry, H.L., Thurow, M.E., Schaefer, H.S., Alexander, A.L. & Davidson, R.J. (2007) Gaze fixations predict brain activation during the voluntary regulation of picture-induced negative affect.

Neuroimage, *36*(3), pp.1041-1055.

Vadoa, E.A., Hall, C.R. & Moritz, S.E. (1997) The relationship between competitive anxiety and imagery use. *Journal of applied sport psychology*, *9*(2), pp.241-253.

Vogt, B.A. (2014) Submodalities of emotion in the context of cingulate subregions. *Cortex*, *59*, pp.197-202.

Vyskočilová, J. & Praško, J, (2012) Socratic dialogue and guided discovery in cognitive behavioral supervision. *Activitas nervosa superior rediviva*, *54*(1) pp.35-45.

Weineck, F., Messner, M., Hauke, G. & Pollatos, O. (2019) Improving interoceptive ability through the practice of power posing: A pilot study. *PloS one*, *14*(2), p.e0211453.

Williams, J.M. & Leffingwell, T.R. (2002) Cognitive strategies in sport and exercise psychology. In J.L van Raalte & B.W. Brewer (Eds.) *Exploring sport and exercise psychology*. American Psychological Association.

Zaccaro, A., Piarulli, A., Laurino, M., Garbella, E., Menicucci, D., Neri, B. & Gemignani, A. (2018) How breath-control can change your life: a systematic review on psycho-physiological correlates of slow breathing. *Frontiers in human neuroscience*, *12*, p.353.

Zeidan, F., Johnson, S.K., Diamond, B.J., David, Z. & Goolkasian, P. (2010) Mindfulness meditation improves cognition: Evidence of brief mental training. *Consciousness and cognition: An international journal*, *19*(2), pp.597-605.

PART FIVE

Chapter Twenty-Two

Besedovsky, L., Lange, T. & Born, J. (2012) Sleep and immune function. *Pflügers Archiv European journal of physiology*, *463*(1), pp.121-137.

Bryant, P.A., Trinder, J. & Curtis, N. (2004) Sick and tired: does sleep have a vital role in the immune system? *Nature reviews immunology*, *4*(6), pp.457-467.

Byrne, A. & Byrne, D.G. (1993) The effect of exercise on depression, anxiety and other mood states: a review. *Journal of psychosomatic research*, *37*(6), pp.565-574.

Cooney, G.M., Dwan, K., Greig, C.A., Lawlor, D.A., Rimer, J., Waugh, F.R., McMurdo, M. & Mead, G.E. (2013) Exercise for depression. *Cochrane database of systematic reviews*, *12*(9).

Dijk, D.J. & von Schantz, M. (2005) Timing and consolidation of human sleep, wakefulness, and performance by a symphony of oscillators. *Journal of biological rhythms*, *20*(4), pp.279-290.

Fitz, N., Kushlev, K., Jagannathan, R., Lewis, T., Paliwal, D. & Ariely, D. (2019) Batching smart phone notifications can improve well-being. *Computers in Human Behavior*, *101*, pp.84-94.

Goel, N., Basner, M., Rao, H. & Dinges, D.F. (2013) Circadian rhythms, sleep deprivation, and human performance. *Progress in molecular biology and translational science*. *119*, pp.155-190.

Irwin, M., McClintick, J., Costlow, C., Fortner, M., White, J. & Gillin, J.C., 1996. Partial night sleep deprivation reduces natural killer and celhdar immune responses in humans. *The FASEB journal*, *10*(5), pp.643-653.

Jena, L.K. & Basu, E. (2018) Deep Work: Rules for Focused Success in a Distracted World. *Vikalpa*, *43*(1), pp.58-60.

Lange, T., Dimitrov, S. & Born, J. (2010) Effects of sleep and circadian rhythm on the human immune system. *Annals of the New York Academy of Sciences*, *1193*(1), pp.48-59.

Leproult, R. & Van Cauter, E. (2011) Effect of 1 week of sleep restriction on testosterone levels in young healthy men. *Jama*, *305*(21), pp.2173-2174.

Loehr, J. &Schwartz, T. (2005) *The power of full engagement: Managing energy, not time, is the key to high performance and personal renewal.* Simon & Schuster.

Luboshitzky, R., Herer, P., Levi, M., Shen-Orr, Z. &Lavie, P. (1999) Relationship between rapid eye movement sleep and testosterone secretion in normal men. *Journal of andrology*, *20*(6), pp.731-737.

Mallis, M.M. & DeRoshia, C.W. (2005) Circadian rhythms, sleep, and performance in space. *Aviation, space, and environmental medicine*, *76*(6), pp.B94-B107.

Marcora, S.M., Staiano, W. & Manning, V. (2009) Mental fatigue impairs physical performance in humans. *Journal of applied physiology*, *106*(3), pp.857-864.

Marshall, L., Helgadóttir, H., Mölle, M. & Born, J. (2006) Boosting slow oscillations during sleep potentiates memory. *Nature*, *444*(7119), pp.610-613.

Newport, C. (2016) *Deep work: Rules for focused success in a distracted world.* Piatkus.

Rethorst, C.D., Wipfli, B.M. & Landers, D.M. (2009) The antidepressive effects of exercise: A meta-analysis of randomized trials. *Sports medicine*, *39*(6), pp.491-511.

Stickgold, R. (2005) Sleep-dependent memory consolidation. *Nature*, *437*, pp.1272-1278.

Walker, M.P. & Stickgold, R. (2004) Sleep-dependent learning and memory consolidation. *Neuron*, *44*(1), pp.121-133.

Weisner, T.S. (2010) Well-being, chaos, and culture: Sustaining a meaningful daily routine. In G.D. Evans & T.D. Wachs (Eds.) *Decade of behavior (Science conference). Chaos and its influence on children's development: An ecological perspective.* American Psychological Association.

Chapter Twenty-Three

Aarts, H., Paulussen, T. & Schaalma, H. (1997) Physical exercise habit: on the conceptualization and formation of habitual health behaviours. *Health education research*, *12*(3), pp.363-374.

Bryan, G., Karlan, D. & Nelson, S. (2010) Commitment devices. *Annual review of economics. 2*, pp.671-698.

Graybiel, A.M. (1998) The basal ganglia and chunking of action repertoires. *Neurobiology of learning and memory, 70*(1-2), pp.119-136.

Judah, G., Gardner, B. & Aunger, R. (2013) Forming a flossing habit: an exploratory study of the psychological determinants of habit formation. *British journal of health psychology, 18*(2), pp.338-353.

Harkin, B., Webb, T.L., Chang, B.P., Prestwich, A., Conner, M., Kellar, I., Benn, Y. & Sheeran, P. (2016) Does monitoring goal progress promote goal attainment? A meta-analysis of the experimental evidence. *Psychological bulletin, 142*(2), pp.198-229.

Lally, P. & Gardner, B. (2013) Promoting habit formation. *Health psychology review, 7*(1), pp.S137-S158.

Lally, P., Van Jaarsveld, C.H., Potts, H.W. & Wardle, J. (2010) How are habits formed: Modelling habit formation in the real world. *European journal of social psychology, 40*(6), pp.998-1009.

Richerson, P.J. & Boyd, R. (2005). *Not by genes alone: How culture transformed human evolution*. University of Chicago press.

Rogers, T., Milkman, K.L. & Volpp, K.G. (2014) Commitment devices: using initiatives to change behavior. *JaMa, 311*(20), pp.2065-2066.

Stawarz, K., Cox, A.L. & Blandford, A. (2015) Beyond self-tracking and reminders: designing smart phone apps that support habit formation. In *CHI 15: Proceedings of the 33rd annual ACM conference on human factors in computing systems* (pp. 2653-2662).

Windt, J. (2016) Rewire your life: sustaining behavioural change by habit tracking (Mobile App User Guide). *British journal of sports medicine, 50*(3), pp.193-194.

Wood, W., Tam, L. & Witt, M.G. (2005). Changing circumstances, disrupting habits. *Journal of personality and social psychology, 88*(6), pp.918-933.

Chapter Twenty-Four

Ariely, D. & Jones, S. (2008) *Predictably irrational.* New York, NY: Harper Audio.

Berger, A. (1997) Continuous improvement and *kaizen*: standardization and organizational designs. *Integrated manufacturing systems.8*(2). pp.110-117.

Gauch Jr, H.G. (2002) *Scientific method in practice.* Cambridge University Press.

Kahneman, D. (2011) *Thinking, fast and slow.* Farrar, Straus & Giroux.

Langer, E.J. (1975) The illusion of control *Journal of personality and social psychology 32*(2) pp. 311-328.

Leonard, T. C. (2008) Richard H. Thaler, Cass R. Sunstein, Nudge: Improving decisions about health, wealth, and happiness. *Constitutional political economy. 19*(4). pp.356-360.

Neuman, R.P. & Cavanagh, R. (2000) *The six sigma way: How GE, Motorola, and other top companies are honing their performance.* USA: McGraw Hill Education.

Pyzdek, T. (2003) *The six sigma handbook: A complete guide for green belts, black belts and managers at all levels* McGraw-Hill.

Rother, M. (2009) *Toyota Kata: Managing people for improvement, adaptiveness and superior results.* New York. McGraw-Hill education.

Masaaki Imai (2012) *Gemba Kaizen: A commonsense approach to a continuous improvement strategy, 2nd Edition.* McGraw-Hill Education.

Toivonen, T. (2015) Continuous innovation–combining Toyota Kata and TRIZ for sustained innovation. *Procedia engineering, 131*, pp.963-974.

Walsh, D. (2013) *Inside team sky.* London. Simon and Schuster.

INDEX

A

Academic experts 13
Academy Award 467
activation breath 363
Aldo, Jose 53, 54, 468
anandamide 47, 302
Antioco, John 443
Apple 59, 373, 374, 439
Atari 67, 374
Autonomy 237, 240
avatar 134, 135, 136, 140, 143, 149, 151, 154
Avoidance 265

B

Bale, Gareth 35, 36, 60, 61, 62, 467, 468
Barcelona 161, 184
BASIC 67
Batching 403, 510
Battle of Waterloo 329
Beckham, David 58
Bezos, Jeff 6, 336, 439, 475
Bias 7, 9, 129, 130, 374, 376
Blockbuster 373, 443
Boeing 737 286
Bolt, Usain 56, 66, 78, 101, 469, 470
Bowman, Bob 316, 319, 321, 356
Brady, Tom 119, 132
Brailsford, Sir Dave 14, 238, 443, 444, 448, 450, 451, 472, 478
Brand, Peter 134
Breathe 361
Britain xviii
Buffet, Warren 37, 40, 162, 163, 168, 169, 182, 183, 192, 193
Bussell, Darcy 61

C

Calibration 257, 259, 260
California 102
Cambridge University 56, 491, 493, 513
Carlsen, Magnus 161, 162, 169, 183, 215
Champions League 36, 372, 468
Chicago Bulls 159, 160, 471, 472
Circadian Rhythm 386
Coach 197, 227, 229, 233, 234
Cognitive test 61, 73, 502
Collins, Dave 14
Commodore VIC-20 67
Completeness 24
Concordance xv, 35, 38, 49, 51, 111, 113, 114, 115, 126, 279
Cost 25
Costa, Douglas 90, 470
Costner, Kevin 81, 83, 85, 86, 88, 114
Coutinho, Phillipe 214, 492
CrossFit 350, 405, 419
Csikszentmihalyi, Mihaly 301, 498, 499
Cues 346, 425, 435
Cultural Architects 237, 238
Cultural protocols 399
Cybertruck 261, 473

D

Dalio, Ray 101, 209, 392, 452
Deep Work 394, 510

Deutsche Bank 133
Diamandis, Peter 101
DiCaprio, Leonardo 3, 5, 467
Dimon, Jamie 56, 68, 70, 72, 73, 78, 103, 104, 113, 469, 471
DNA 37, 275, 281, 451
dopamine 47, 302, 404, 406

E

Ego 127, 266, 280
Elop, Stephen 443
Eminem 87, 470
Emotion 289, 481
Emotional Control Techniques 393
endorphins 47, 302, 397, 404
English Premier League 35, 176, 372
Exponential Breakthrough 19

F

F-35 189, 190, 212, 213, 214, 216, 472
Facebook 9, 19, 93, 119
Farah, Mo 61
Farrell, Owen 329, 330, 331, 332, 333, 335, 346, 351, 353, 356, 359, 361, 364, 474, 475
Federer, Roger 249, 251, 253, 254, 255, 256, 473
Feedback xv, 150, 223, 225, 227, 229, 230, 231, 233, 234, 235, 237, 239, 241, 242, 243, 405
Feedback loop 150
Ferguson, Sir Alex 238, 372, 380, 439, 476
Ferriss, Tim 64
Football Association 372, 372–524
Fraser, Mat 419
Friedman, Milton 68

G

Gates, Bill 371, 372, 373, 380, 439, 476
Glencore 118, 133, 141, 223, 224
Global Positioning Systems 236
Goldberg, Mike 53, 54, 499
Goldman Sachs 103, 104, 117, 120, 133, 136, 141, 375, 439
Google 120, 139, 442
Griezmann, Antoine 213
gymnast 24, 25, 26

H

Habit 421, 427, 429
Haldeman, Scott 92
Harvard 72, 103, 104, 139, 404, 487, 499, 502
HBO 275
heart rate variability 236, 502
Hedonic Adaptation 406
Heilman, Jeff 92
HIIT 405
Hill, Tyreek 286
Hollywood 3, 9, 89, 219, 238
Hunt-Davis, Ben 441, 447, 478
hypothalamus 78, 94

I

Independent Development Plan 241, 246, 247, 248, 249, 257, 258, 259, 377, 447
Individual Development Plan 241, 248, 328, 377
INEOS 14
Interests Appraisal 80
iPhone 443
IQ 6, 56, 143, 144, 163, 215, 487

J

James, Lebron 37, 119
Jobs 59, 392, 439
Jordan, Michael 101, 159, 160, 161, 166
JP Morgan Chase 56, 469
Juventus 90

K

Kansas City Chiefs 285, 473
Key Performance Indicators 236
Knowles-Carter, Beyoncé 351, 352, 353

L

LA Lakers 451
Las Vegas 53
Lyons, Dave 106, 483

M

Mahomes, Patrick 285, 286, 287, 290, 295, 302, 306, 309, 473
Malone, Karl 159, 160
Manchester City 14
Manchester United 124, 139, 372, 375, 439
Mandara Capital 117, 118, 119, 123, 124, 126, 133, 134, 137, 141, 142, 144, 145, 152, 215, 224, 225, 227, 231, 237
Marcario, Rose 102, 104, 105, 107, 110
Marshall Mathers 87
MBA 103
McGregor, Conor 53, 54, 55, 468
McKenzie, Joe 324, 329
McRaven, Admiral William 390, 477
mental structures 164, 165, 166, 167, 169, 170, 171, 172, 173, 176, 178, 180, 183, 185, 186, 187, 192, 195, 201, 202, 203, 211, 220, 225, 234, 237, 239, 241, 278, 290, 291, 292, 319, 345, 346, 405, 411, 486, 487
Messi, Lionel 161, 162, 163, 168, 169, 171, 182, 183, 184, 185, 192, 193, 197, 201, 202, 212, 213, 214, 216, 218
Methodology 29
MI5 136, 286, 437, 438, 477
Microsoft 371, 439
Minimum Effective Dose 64
MIT 19, 483, 487
Mixed Martial Arts 384, 409
Model excellence 135, 248, 259
Moneyball 129, 471, 486
Montgomery, James 384, 476
Morgan Stanley 133, 141
Musk, Elon 4, 67, 77, 78, 91, 92, 106, 113, 114, 261, 262, 263, 383, 439, 442, 456, 461, 469, 470, 471, 473
MVP 285, 286, 473

N

NASA 376
Navy SEAL 9, 101, 159, 301, 322
NBA 40, 159, 472
Netflix 409, 443, 456
Nevada 53
New York Times 69
New York Yankees 124
New Zealand 451
Nobel Prize 68
Nobu 117
Nokia 443
norepinephrine 47, 302, 404

O

Obama, Barack 9, 10, 376
Olympic Games xvii, 30
  Atlanta xvii
  Rio xvii

One-Dimensional training 177, 179
Opportunity 241
Outcome Bias 9
outlier 26, 27, 28, 32, 118, 135, 190, 273, 287, 295, 297, 301, 312, 390, 462
Overcompensation 267
oxytocin 47, 302, 406

P

panacea 49, 113
Panic Zone 199
Parasympathetic breathing 362
Pareto's Law 250
Parker, Andrew 437, 438, 439
Patagonia 102, 107, 471
Paypal 262
Performance 24
Personality strengths 61
Peterson, Jordan 101, 480, 483, 484, 494, 495, 500
Phelps, Michael 301, 315, 316, 317, 318, 319, 320, 321, 333, 335, 342, 346, 347, 349, 356, 361, 364, 390, 474
Physical exercise 404, 511
Pina, Hugo 95, 96
Potter, Harry 56, 88
PowerPoint 175
Power posing 364, 502
Progress 21, 29, 30, 372, 456, 457, 459, 510
Progressive Muscular Relaxation 335, 356, 357, 393, 408, 414
Psychological Firepower 42
Psychometrics 73
Pulitzer Prize 171

R

Ratey, John 404
Real Madrid 36, 451, 467
Reisman, Garrett 442, 478
Relaxation 335, 356, 357, 398
Retaining talent 151
Reverse engineering 135
Rogan, Joe 53, 54, 383, 384, 409, 456, 476, 478
Rolling Stone 384, 476
Ronaldo, Cristiano 90, 95, 96, 119, 132, 197, 337, 338, 461, 470
Rowling 56, 71, 78, 82, 83, 88, 89, 113, 120, 132, 461, 469, 470
Royal Air Force 56, 189, 190, 205, 472
Royal Ballet 61
Russell, Byron 160, 500

S

Salti, Muwaffaq 117, 118
Sanders, Bernie 383
Schwarzenegger, Arnold 9, 10
Self-Correction 197
serotonin 47, 302, 404, 406
Sheeran, Ed 37, 40, 87, 120, 132, 470, 512
Shell 133, 223, 224
Shults, Tammie Jo 287, 291, 295, 302, 306, 474
Silicon Valley 104, 105, 110, 238
Single discipline specialists 6, 7
Solar City 442
Southwest Airlines 286, 287, 291
SpaceX 4, 120, 262, 376, 442, 467, 473
Special Forces 12, 99, 100, 106, 137, 196, 219, 495
Speed 25
Sporting Lisbon 96
Spotify 153, 350, 383, 476
Stacking strengths 58
Strengths 39, 53, 57, 65, 74, 482, 483
Strengths Appraisal 65
Sunlight 389
Super Bowl 285, 286
Superficial screening 127

T

Talent confirmation 150
Team Sky 444
Technical strengths 60
Tesla 4
The four zones 299
Three-Dimensional training 182
Timson, Simon 14
Tipping Point 22
Tottenham 35
Trump, President Donald 103, 107, 376
Tufts University 70
Tyson, Mike 373, 374, 383

U

UEFA 372
UFC 53, 54, 476
University of Edinburgh xx
University of Oxford 175, 472, 484, 488, 497, 506
US 9, 19, 25, 102, 226, 317, 371, 477
US President 9

V

Values 39
Variability 203, 206
Vaynerchuk, Gary 88
Venting 339, 507
Victim mentality 266
Vitol 141, 223, 224
von Holzhausen, Franz 261, 262

W

Wall Street 103
Williams, Serena 4, 371, 372, 373, 380, 475, 488, 490, 491, 492, 493, 509
Win Agenda 278
Woods, Tiger 373, 374, 490
World Boxing Council 215
World Cup 4

Y

YouTube 5, 41, 88, 89, 177, 350, 443, 468, 469, 473, 475, 477, 478

Z

Zuckerberg, Mark 9, 10, 19, 120, 132, 392, 477

Printed in Great Britain
by Amazon

60907002R00312